5/05

KNIGHTFALL

Knightfall

Knight Ridder and How the Erosion of Newspaper Journalism Is Putting Democracy at Risk

DAVIS MERRITT

AMACOM AMERICAN MANAGEMENT ASSOCIATION

NEW YORK ▸ ATLANTA ▸ BRUSSELS ▸ CHICAGO ▸ MEXICO CITY
SAN FRANCISCO ▸ SHANGHAI ▸ TOKYO ▸ TORONTO ▸ WASHINGTON, D.C.

Special discounts on bulk quantities of AMACOM books are available to corporations, professional associations, and other organizations. For details, contact Special Sales Department, AMACOM, a division of American Management Association, 1601 Broadway, New York, NY 10019.
Tel.: 212-903-8316. Fax: 212-903-8083.
Web site: www. amacombooks.org

This publication is designed to provide accurate and authoritative information in regard to the subject matter covered. It is sold with the understanding that the publisher is not engaged in rendering legal, accounting, or other professional service. If legal advice or other expert assistance is required, the services of a competent professional person should be sought.

Library of Congress Cataloging-in-Publication Data

Merritt, Davis.
    Knightfall : Knight Ridder and how the erosion of newspaper journalism is putting democracy at risk / Davis Merritt.
        p.   cm.
    Includes bibliographical references and index.
    ISBN 0-8144-0854-0
    1. Press and politics—United States—History—20th century.   2. Knight-Ridder Newspapers, Inc.   3. American newspapers—Ownership.   I. Title.

PN4888.P6M38   2005
071'.3'0904—dc22
                                                                                    2004028598

Printing number

10   9   8   7   6   5   4   3   2   1

To Libby, without whom the journey would not have been possible.

and

To the hundreds of other people who helped make a life in journalism rewarding and at times, I hope, valuable. Many of them, including some good friends, will find things important to them missing from this effort, and much with which to disagree. I apologize for any such shortcomings, but each journey is necessarily different.

CONTENTS

AUTHOR'S NOTES

The concept of public judgment and its implications, as covered in Chapter 1, are based on the work of Daniel Yankelovich as expressed in his book *Coming to Public Judgment: Making Democracy Work in a Complex World* (Syracuse, NY: Syracuse University Press, 1991).

Portions of Chapter 4, Chapter 9, and Chapter 12 appeared previously in *Public Journalism and Public Life: Why Telling the News Is Not Enough*, second edition, by the author (Mahwah, N.J.: Lawrence Erlbaum Associates, 1998).

Interviews for the book were carried out from 2002 to 2004 in person, by telephone, and through e-mail. P. Anthony Ridder, chairman and chief executive officer of Knight Ridder, declined through a spokesperson to be interviewed or to provide other materials.

KNIGHTFALL

INTRODUCTION: CAN NEWSPAPER JOURNALISM SURVIVE?

The central idea of this book is that newspaper journalism is endangered, which puts American democracy in peril.

Given the inexorability and pace of technology, we may not need newspapers in our media mix at some point in the future—perhaps sooner than later. But we will need newspaper journalism, because democracy can thrive without newspapers, but it cannot thrive without the sort of journalism that newspapers uniquely provide.

The question is whether newspaper journalism can be successfully migrated to new technologies—the Internet or whatever might succeed it—before it becomes extinct, suffocated like the dinosaurs by the impact of the twenty-first century giant meteor labeled greed.

It is a race against time and circumstance.

What is newspaper journalism if not simply journalism that is in a newspaper?

It's much more, and these are the characteristics separating it from all other kinds of journalism and pseudojournalism:

- Its content is not shaped by a limiting technology, such as broadcast with its time strictures and, in television and online, bias toward the visual and against permanence.

- Its usefulness is based far more on completeness and clarity than immediacy.

▶ Its claim on credibility is based on its length and depth, which allow readers to judge the facts behind a story's headline and opening summary paragraph and then look for internal contradictions.

▶ It has intrinsic value and relevance to people rather than merely amusing or entertaining them.

▶ Opinions and analysis are labeled as such and are presented separately.

Those are, at least, the values newspaper journalism aspires to, if not always achieves.

It is a form of journalism that emerged from decades of evolving standards and practices and from newspapers' deliberate and layered process of collecting, sorting, writing, and editing information.

This book is an effort to explain what is happening to newspapers and therefore to newspaper journalism in the United States, why what is happening endangers democracy, and what steps might move both back from the abyss.

The 300 million people who constitute our nation are unable, each and on their own, to discover the facts necessary to make communal decisions. Instead, they rely upon specialized collectors, processors, and disseminators of information. For most of the nation's history, newspapers have been a constant and substantial, often dominant, supplier of the facts that we use to make decisions about public matters. Over those two-plus centuries, newspapers changed in form and substance just as the society around them changed. One attribute persisted through all the changes, however: A newspaper provided a set of facts common to all who read it; a tangible record of shared information on which citizens could base their deliberations and decisions about what to do. Most cities of any size had two or more newspapers, giving citizens more than a single source, and most American households, at least through the early years of the twentieth century, read more than one of them.

Newspapers built elaborate staffs and developed processes to collect, sort, prioritize, and interpret information. Reporters were assigned to seek out information, particularly about the activities of government, doing, as Walter Lippmann put it, "what the conscientious citizen would do given the time and resources." Editors were appointed to evaluate and critique this flow of facts from city halls and legislatures, police stations and battlefields, schools and businesses and ballparks. The physical structure of newspapers provided not only a repository for information but also a context for it. Editors' choices about the placement of stories within the pages and the size of headlines on the page provided a guide to relative significance, at least as evaluated by the editors. Newspapers represented a sophisticated and multilayered social transaction that was dependent for its success on the good intentions, professionalism, judgment, and experience of journalists and the willingness of readers to extend credibility to the process.

The people who owned newspapers discovered early in the nation's history that you could make good money publishing them. For some newspaper owners that was enough. Other, differently motivated owners believed that publishing newspapers was an important public service, and the fact that you could make good money doing it only made the process that much more rewarding. For them, the journalism that they did was the driving force; the purpose of the business part of newspapers—the advertisements and the revenue from circulation—was to make the journalism possible. Well into the twentieth century, newspapers of both sorts held a virtual monopoly on mass communication of information, but it was not to last.

Other methods of telling news were developed, and with each new method came fresh predictions that newspapers were doomed. First, radio would cause the demise, it was claimed, because newspapers, with their long production times and clumsy distribution systems, could never overcome the immediacy and intimacy of a radio broadcast. And seven decades ago when television was developed, paving the way for TV newscasts, there were similar, even more dire predictions, because now broadcasting included pictures. And two decades ago Ted Turner, the mogul who invented CNN and twenty-four-hour broadcast news, proclaimed that newspapers would be extinct by the end of the twentieth century. Now, we hear, the Internet will do the job.

Those predictions have not come about. Radio couldn't kill newspapers, nor could television, CNN and its copycats, nor, as yet, the Internet. But greed can kill newspapers—and thus newspaper journalism—and it is in the process of doing so. And if newspaper journalism becomes extinct because the people who own newspapers do not understand and appreciate its intrinsic and crucial strengths and its role in democracy, much more will be gone than simply one particular and traditional way of transmitting news and information.

With a handful of exceptions, American newspapers are being eroded, their traditional values subverted, their journalistic resources stripped away, their dedication to public service and local communities hollowed out, leaving a thin shell of public relations gimmicks that pretend to be public service and entertainment that pretends to be news.

What's going on is serial suicide on the part of the companies that own most of America's newspapers, not, as some apologists suggest, serial murder by evolving technology, changed societal circumstance, or altered public taste. If something doesn't change in newspaper corporate boardrooms, the source of the information that Americans need to govern themselves at all levels will be an unreliable and constantly shifting array of broadcast and Internet outlets that are often irresponsible, untrained, understaffed, and driven wholly by profit or ego. That information will be incomplete, unverified, and laced with the poison of partisan bias and narrow interests, if only because it has not been subjected to a rigorous editing process.

This period of decline did not arrive suddenly for America's newspapers, and its progress is gradual though, without major change, inexorable. How the decline began and how it is proceeding is one part of an immensely complex story, and saying with confidence and specificity what the decline implies for the future is a difficult proposition in a constantly shifting media environment. However, certain things are clear:

▸ American democracy cannot succeed in the long term if the information that fuels self-determination becomes unavailable or is so narrowly held that only a tiny minority of citizens possess the tools to make rational democratic choices. To answer democracy's "What shall we do?" question—that is, to arrive at public judgment—citizens need three things: shared, relevant information; an agora (i.e., a place or method of discussing the implications of that information); and shared values (at a minimum, a belief in the value of democracy itself). When citizens do not have access to shared, relevant information and do not have an active agora in which to act upon their values, democracy is left in the hands of insiders and special interests and at the mercy of their values.

Increasingly, American newspapers are failing to provide those essentials of democracy because they are being strangled by bottom-line concerns. For the last forty years, the consolidation of newspaper ownership into publicly held companies has increased. At the same time, accumulation of newspaper company stocks by institutional investors has exploded. Most institutional investors are not interested in the quality of journalism or the communities it affects; they are interested in short-term, ever-increasing profits. When newspaper profits fall, excessive concern about the next quarter leads to quick fixes on the cost side: hiring freezes, downsizing of space devoted to news, and cutbacks in travel, training, distant bureaus, and staff. Fewer reporters and copy editors and reduced news coverage reduce a newspaper's quality and erode its ability to provide relevant information.

▸ Newspaper journalists and the newspaper process, historically and to this day, are the primary first-gatherers and sorters of the shared information essential to democracy. The journalists, by instinct and training, and the newspaper process, by its deliberate and layered nature, are uniquely suited and positioned to provide meaningful information. While a majority of Americans tell pollsters that they "get their news from television" or, increasingly, the Internet, the fact is that most meaningful broadcast news and most "facts" bandied about the Internet, at all levels, national and local, originate with newspaper organizations. (This is easy to verify. Read *The New York Times*, *The Washington Post*, and *The Wall Street Journal* daily for a week and watch national television news and news-magazine shows daily for that week and the week following. Calculate the percentage of broadcast stories on substantive matters that are original, untouched by one or more of those newspapers. Try the same experiment with your local newspaper and television stations. The numbers will approach zero.) While the news organizations that underlie newspapers continue to erode, broadcast, cable, and the millions of individual Internet sites that trade in "news" simply cannot afford to take over that first-gatherer-and-sorter role because their economic models were built from the beginning on cannibalizing newspapers, not on maintaining full, freestanding, news-originating operations.

‣ Absent fundamental change by the people who run the corporations that own the great majority of America's newspapers, the nation will become dependent for democracy's plasma upon three or four newspapers in the largest cities, and those will maintain their missions only as long as they are in the right hands.

‣ The narrowing of informational channels is an enormous threat to personal and civic autonomy.

There is, however, hope. A slim chance exists that at least some newspaper companies will successfully transfer their news-gathering and sorting expertise onto emerging technologies before they fritter away their once-deep pool of reportorial and editing talent and thereby surrender their wondrous advantage and squander their primacy. While most newspapers already have Web sites, those sites also depend on the reporting and editing depth of their host newspapers' staffs, and their operators have not yet figured out how to make money in a medium where user expectations are to not pay for anything. Figuring out how to make money on the Internet will require substantial investment and experimentation, things that corporations focused on ever-increasing profits are unlikely to do.

Some major newspaper companies, most notably the Tribune Company and Media General, Inc., are experimenting with the concept of "convergence," which involves cooperative pooling of broadcast, newspaper, and Internet reporters and editors who are trying to develop "multiplatform" skills and understanding so that their work can be effective in any of those mediums. Whether convergence will be the savior of high-level journalism or just another step in its dilution is the subject of much debate within the profession.

Whatever the future holds, understanding in detail what happened and is happening to American newspaper journalism is important, if for no other reason than to provide markers along the way back from the abyss.

This book reflects the views of a journalist who spent forty-two years as a reporter and editor for Knight Newspapers and Knight Ridder, Inc. It is not *the history* of Knight Ridder, for no single point of view can reliably and objectively encompass all of the complex dynamics of a major corporation over nearly five decades. It is *a story* of Knight Ridder told by an informed participant/observer with a specific point of view.

The 1974 merger of Knight Newspapers and Ridder Publications, Inc. began a journey by people and institutions through the elastic labyrinth of the last third of the twentieth century and years of complex technological, cultural, and spiritual twists and turns. The journey transformed two mid-century family-owned newspaper companies with vastly different cultures into a prototypical twenty-first century American media corporation that is, like other companies in other fields, now forced to redefine its place in a constantly shifting financial and public service environment.

There are no pure heroes and no pure villains in this story. The players were doing what genetics, background, training, and the immediate, ever-changing environment urged them to do. But choices have consequences, and when those choices arise between competing foundational beliefs—that is, conflicting core cultural values—one value system is bound to suffer and the other prevail. When the prevailing value system sees journalistic quality as an expense to be mini-mized rather than an asset to be leveraged, the implications are profound for our society.

More important, journalistic performance and a viable democracy are fully interdependent, so a decline in journalistic quality caused by the erosion of foundational missions and dedication to public service has important and negative implications for public life, which is the way democracy is expressed and experienced.

This story is part reportage, part memoir, part analysis and argu-ment. The reportage involves dozens of interviews with the partici-pants, as well as extensive reading and research. The analysis and argument are capsulized in this introduction. The memoir portions are designed to show firsthand how the forces at work on newspaper journalists affected one life spent with one company, Knight Ridder, and to contribute a narrative thread to the larger fabric of what has happened to American newspapers.

My undeniable and inescapable bias will become clear soon enough, but let me state it concisely at the outset: Newspaper compa-nies have an obligation to public service and a special obligation to democracy that outweigh all other considerations, save actual sur-vival. When, as has happened, public service and democratic obliga-tions become secondary to profit considerations when actual survival is not at stake, vital aspects of American life are put in great peril. While such a retrospective bias comes easily and is comforting to hold, it does not, and cannot, provide the answers to the difficult underlying questions of how the current state of affairs could have been avoided and what now needs to happen. All along the route of this journey, choices were made by people who intended to make what were, by their inner compasses, right choices. The consequences of those choices were occasionally unpredictable, but in the main were foreseeable because the choices were based in competing under-lying philosophies that led only in one direction or the other.

This book is not intended as a paean to the past, a yearning for lost innocence or some supposed golden age of perfect public service journalism. Such a time never was. It is an attempt to sound, through one company's example, a cautionary note—perhaps even an alarm—

about the future. If, as seems likely, current journalistic and business trends continue, our democracy's need for the relevant information that is its plasma will be imperiled because the bulk of the nation's corporately owned daily press will not be able to meet that need while its leaders are motivated more urgently by the profit demands of Wall Street than by a desire to serve democracy,

The question—for citizens and for the nation's public life—is whether the environment that now molds the behavior and values of newspaper companies will provide enough oxygen to keep newspaper journalism alive long enough. The answer is crucial.

PART ONE: MORNING

1

Why This Matters

We . . . do not sacrifice either principles or quality on the altar of the countinghouse.
— John S. Knight

ON ONE OF those delightfully fresh South Florida fall mornings, Jim Batten is moved to get out of his office to start our conversation.

"Let's take a ride," he said to an old friend of a dozen years, so we left through the sixth-floor double doors freshly plated with a new name, Knight Ridder Newspapers, Inc., picked up his car in the parking garage, and turned onto Biscayne Boulevard, heading north away from *The Miami Herald* building.

We had much to discuss that morning in 1975 because each of our lives had just taken turns of their own. I was, at thirty-eight, only three months into the job of executive editor of two Knight Ridder–owned newspapers in Wichita, Kansas. He, at thirty-nine, had recently moved from the editorship of *The Charlotte Observer* to the post of vice president of news for the one-year-old corporation built by the 1974 merger of Ridder Publications, Inc. (RPI) and Knight Newspapers, Inc. (KNI). The merger had turned two regional newspaper companies into the nation's largest in terms of total circulation, and it had opened exciting possibilities for thousands of the companies' employees.

The two of us shared much history, including years together as reporters at the Knight-owned *Observer* and in Knight Newspapers' Washington bureau; a tennis rivalry battled out on courts in North Carolina, Virginia, and Maryland; southern upbringings; and wives who had known each other as students at Queens College in Charlotte. Most important, we shared a conviction that newspaper journalism was an exciting and worthy way to make both a difference and a living.

That conviction was matured and strengthened by our experiences with Knight Newspapers, Inc., which was much more a collection of newspapers than it was a corporation. Even after it went public in 1969, Knight Newspapers was almost wholly an expression of the values of John S. Knight (JSK), its founder, and Lee Hills, its president. Fierce independence from commercial concerns and local autonomy for editors were primary operating principles. The corporate staff was minimal and of little moment as far as the journalists were concerned, and many of the journalists' Holy Grail was to be the editor of a newspaper, for they believed, with JSK, that, "There is no better or higher title than editor."

So on that morning I needed the answer to a question.

"Jim, why in the world would you give up the editorship of a great newspaper for a corporate job?" I asked, giving the word *corporate* a disdainful roll off the tongue.

I anticipated a more measured James K. Batten answer, one typical of his Virginia Tidewater mannerliness and habit of careful reflection. This was not that.

"Somebody has to watch the bad guys."

Newspapers and Coat Hangers

Publishing newspapers is a good way to make money.

Publishing newspapers is an important undertaking, and you can make good money doing it.

Both statements are true but describe totally different concepts.

On the one hand, setting out to make money by producing newspapers expresses a specific objective, not unlike setting out to make money by producing coat hangers or carpets. You decide to do it based on a calculation of desired profit, what materials to use, how to use those materials most efficiently, and how to market the result. Eventually, you must decide what level of quality you want in the product, lowest to highest, with the decision driven by your assessment of the potential market. Decisions about how to react to market changes and competition invariably refer to and are controlled by the original objective: making coat hangers or carpets or newspapers in a way that produces a profit of a certain level. Over time, the efficiency of your operation determines your level of success. If your financial goal is not being achieved, you must find new efficiencies or adjust the quality of the product, upward or downward. (There is, after all, a need for lesser quality carpets or coat hangers.) Quality is a manageable variable in the calculation. Success is measured by whether the profit goal is met.

On the other hand, setting out to produce a newspaper that makes a difference in a community or a nation and to make money doing it is unlike any other business enterprise one can imagine. All other businesses begin, appropriately, with single-minded focus on the bottom-line objective. Newspapers have a built-in conflict, a natural and deep tension between the polar opposite, though not mutually exclusive, objectives of public service and making a profit. In the best newspaper operations, symbiosis exists, a comfortable, reinforcing coexistence between the journalistic and business aspects. But as with symbiotic relationships in nature, when one partner becomes dominant, the other dies and the partnership fails.

The driving force in newspapers that have public service at the core, in contrast to other businesses or newspapers published simply to make money, is a qualitative calculation: You want to act in ways that achieve certain nonmonetary goals, that reflect the conviction that journalism is a public trust, an institution that serves, advances, and protects the public welfare and supports a free democratic society. The ability to make some level of profit doing it is a necessary supporting factor in the qualitative calculation. The acceptable level of profit is a function of the owners' desires, needs, and values. Because the calculation began with a core decision about quality, profit becomes the variable in that calculation rather than quality; profit is an enabling force, not the driving one. Success is measured first by whether the nonmonetary, public goals are met. The obvious problem with this, of course, is that measuring profit is easy—it's simply a number—while measuring quality is complex and subject to facile rationalization.

Of course, if you cannot manage to make a profit at all given your qualitative goals, the newspaper will fail, but for most of the 220 years of American newspaper history, making a profit by producing newspapers was not particularly difficult for the people who owned them. In fact, for most of U.S. history, failing to make a profit with a newspaper required a high level of incompetence or inattention or truly wretched luck. After all, until the middle of the twentieth-century newspapers were by far the dominant news medium. Journalistically good newspapers made money; journalistically bad newspapers made even more money, at least in the short term until their failure to serve the public well caught up with them.

Compared to most business ventures, operating margins in newspapers have been incredibly high. Family dynasties lasting a century or more were built on operating returns as high as 50 percent. Profits of 20 percent to 30 percent were virtually automatic, leaving owners free to take the profits or, as many did, plow them back into the enterprise in the name of expansion or improvement in the newspaper's quality. Some people produced newspapers because they deliberately chose that over coat hangers or carpets. Some chose it motivated by the ideal of a public trust; some were motivated by the power and prestige it could bring; some by the sensational margins.

Journalism and Democracy: Fully Interdependent

The First Amendment to the U.S. Constitution does not require that the press be accurate or responsible or fair; only that it be free. It does not confer special status on a form of business; it confers on every citizen the opportunity to be heard without government interference. It was designed that way because the people who wrote the Constitution believed that truth, in a fair encounter with falsity, would always prevail; that the open clash of competing ideas produces better outcomes as a democracy seeks to answer the question, "What shall we do?"

A free press is essential to a functioning democracy. A functioning democracy is essential to a free press. The synergy of those two ideas is important because a free society cannot determine its course—that is, self-determination does not exist—without three things: shared, relevant information; an agora (that is, a place or mechanism where the implications of that information can be discussed); and shared values (at a minimum, a belief in personal liberty itself).

To understand the threat to democracy posed by a press that does not have public service as its driving force, it's useful to examine the synergy between journalism and democracy.

HOW A DEMOCRACY DECIDES

Throughout the middle decades of the twentieth century, newspapers, and to a lesser extent network television news, constituted the agora in which American public life, including political life, began its sorting-out process. The shared information they provided helped lead to public judgments about important matters. Not everyone read the same newspapers or watched the same newscasts, and not everyone gave them the same level of attention and interest, but virtually every citizen was exposed on a regular basis to the news of the day.

As a result, citizens were able to reach the public judgments that informed, instructed, and validated the actions of their government representatives, elected or otherwise. Absent public judgment, that is to say when no rough consensus can be reached, important issues remain unresolved.

Coming to Public Judgment is the title of a seminal book in which Daniel Yankelovich explains the phenomenon of public judgment and how it is formed. Published in 1991, it demonstrates that the democratic way of dealing with problems is to strive for a resolution that everyone can live with; that benefits more people than it harms; that recognizes and allows for differing opinions and values but nevertheless helps settle the issue so that the public's business can move on.

Public judgment, Yankelovich explains, is far more complex than mere opinion. In his three decades of research into public opinion preceding publication of the book, he developed ways to distinguish between off-the-cuff public opinion, as reflected in most statistical surveys, and true public judgment.

A public judgment is "the state of highly developed public opinion that exists once people have engaged an issue, considered it from all sides, understood the choices it leads to, and accepted the full consequences of the choices they make."[1]

Reaching public judgment about important and complex issues can take years or only hours. For instance, Americans reached public judgment about women's rights decades ago after more than a century of debate, but aligning that determination with life's realities is still a work in progress. On the other hand, surveys showed that public judgment on Operation Desert Storm in 1991 was almost instantaneous and supportive.

And, on some value-laden issues, even a solid public judgment does not settle them. Such is the case with abortion. For years, every reliable survey has shown that 12 percent to 15 percent of the people polled are opposed to abortion under any circumstances; 12 percent to 15 percent favor abortion at will; and 70 percent to 75 percent fall somewhere between those extremes, allowing it under some circumstances, which is the situation reflected in existing law. The surveys seem to indicate a strong majority have settled in the middle—a substantial public judgment has been reached—yet the loud struggle goes on in legislatures and the Congress every year, the initiative being taken and the issue framed by the groups at the margins as they attempt to alter existing law and practice. The lesson of the never-ending abortion debate may be that when opinions are deeply rooted in core values, even a substantial public judgment cannot be permanently implemented.

Yankelovich's definition of public judgment distinguishes between simply "opinion" based solely on instinct or information and "judgment" based on deliberation, which is "the thoughtful side of the public's outlook, the side that belongs with the world of values, ethics, politics, and life philosophies rather than the world of information and technical expertise."

In other words, public judgment contains a strong values component that need not be based on accurate or detailed information in order to express the public's point of view to its elected representatives. The lesson: It is unwise to overestimate the public's store of accurate information, but it is equally unwise to underestimate its grasp of the importance of self-determination.

True public judgment, once arrived at, reflects values at least as much as it reflects information because of the complex way in which the public arrives at the judgment, Yankelovich contends. The process involves three stages: consciousness raising, working through, and resolution. He describes them this way:

> *Consciousness raising* is "the stage in which the public learns about an issue and becomes aware of its existence and meaning. . . . When one's consciousness is raised, not only does awareness grow but so does concern and readiness for action." In other words, people decide: We must do something about this.
>
> But what? And how?

> *Working through* can be complex and time-consuming, for it involves individuals having second thoughts—that is, "resolving the conflict between impulse and prudence"; accepting new (and sometimes unsettling) realities; and resolving conflicts among the competing values that they hold. In other words, working through involves cognitive, emotional, and moral calculations.

> *Resolution* occurs only after successful consciousness raising and working through, and the accumulated mass of that effort then reflects a public judgment.

Consciousness raising—which journalists are good at and dearly love—does not alone lead to public judgment. The working-through phase is essential. So when newspapers, either deliberately or by lack of insight or public service orientation, limit their role to merely call-ing attention to things and flit, hummingbird-like, from one issue to the next, the process begins to break down; public judgments are not given time to mature; the working-through process is short-circuited.

Helping the working-through process is time-consuming, expen-sive, and full of risk. It is not the sort of thing that newspapers can do with one eye always on the bottom line.

JOURNALISM'S ROLE IN PUBLIC JUDGMENT

Although Yankelovich argues that arriving at public judgment is more an application of values than an application of factual information, the process is initiated by the presentation of information. This is where the traditional news media role is crucial to democratic proc-esses. In doing the job of discovering, reporting, and sorting facts, the news media aren't suggesting to people what to think, but they are suggesting what they should think about. This agenda-setting role of the media is well documented.

As Maxwell McCombs wrote:

Not only do people acquire factual information about public affairs from the news media, readers and viewers also learn how much importance to attach to a topic on the basis of emphasis placed on it in the news. Newspapers provide a host of clues about the salience of the topics in the daily news—lead story on Page 1, other front-page display, large headlines, and length, for example. Television news also offers numerous clues about salience including placement as the opening story on the news-cast, length of time devoted to the story, and promotional emphasis put on it. These cues, repeated day after day, commu-nicate the importance that journalists attach to a small group of issues.

Because of this unavoidable influence on the public mind, the values journalists apply in their decision-making process be-come critical. When the traditional news values are applied, one sort of influence occurs. When, however, other values in-tervene in the process, such as anxiety over ratings or confusing entertainment with substance, quite another sort of influence happens.[2]

Broadly shared information becomes a dubious proposition in today's media environment in which the audience in search of news is fragmented across a media landscape consisting not simply of evening network news shows and printed newspapers, but also twenty-four-hour cable newscasts, Internet Web sites, blogs and chat rooms, and online presentations of newspapers and broadcasters.

The twenty-first century's "on demand" culture and the infrastructure supporting it offer many advantages to individuals; for the democratic collective, however, those blessings are clearly mixed. Can shared relevance, the starting point for democracy, reach the critical mass necessary for public judgment to emerge in an "on demand" world? Can the agenda-setting role of the news media continue to work to the public's advantage when everyone with a personal computer and Internet access is both a potential source of "news" and a potential consumer of everyone else's "news"?

Opposites Attract

The 1974 merger of Knight Newspapers, Inc. and Ridder Publications, Inc. brought together two newspaper companies founded and operated on radically disparate ideas. By the standards of today's media mergers and conglomerates it was no big deal, involving only hundreds of millions of dollars rather than billions and only about three dozen newspapers and a handful of television stations. But in the context of 1974, it was major news within journalism and, as it turned out, a precursor.

Observers of the newspaper business were curious, and many insiders were anxious, about how this marriage of opposites would work. The deal certainly had some attractive aspects in addition to its size. There was a good geographic spread with no important overlaps. Each company had gone public in the 1960s and the stocks were solid. Each had grown substantially through acquisitions over the years, and each was run by family members who held controlling interests.

But under the sweet harmonies of the deal, two cultural dissonances could be clearly heard.

First, brothers John S. and James L. Knight had only two direct male heirs, while Bernard H. Ridder, chief of Ridder Publications, was surrounded by brothers, sons, nephews, and uncles, many of whom ran various Ridder operations. Second, Ridder Publications' newspapers were rated generally in the profession (and specifically by Bernie Ridder) as effective business operations but, at best, indifferent journalistic products, while the Knight-owned newspapers, even at that early date, were in many ways the gold standard for journalism, particularly in medium-size cities, but were not among the better financial performers.

"Merger" was the term of corporate art used by the companies in their official handouts, but the deal was in fact an acquisition by Knight Newspapers, a reality affirmed by the makeup of the original board of directors, with Knight appointing ten members and Ridder five. It was clear who was in charge, a point of some comfort to the journalistic employees of Knight Newspapers, who took great personal pride in their newspapers' dedication to journalism as the driving force of their enterprise.

How the dynamics of the Knight and Ridder merger played out over the next three decades is a story that reflects the trends that affected, often negatively, all of newspaper journalism in the last three decades of the twentieth century.

Ridder Publications and Knight Newspapers were hardly the only newspaper companies going public in the sixties. In fact, most of the seventeen largest newspaper chains had taken that step by 1975, and life changed drastically for many of them. Most of the ones going public, notably The New York Times Company, The Washington Post Company, Media General, and The McClatchy Company, structured their stock in two tiers—voting and nonvoting—so that operating control was tightly held by family members and trusted compatriots. Some, including Knight Newspapers and Ridder Publications, did not establish two tiers of stock and over time, as Jack Knight predicted, would "lose control of their destiny" as institutional stockholders, motivated solely by profit considerations, became the effective owners and Wall Street analysts the effective goal-setters.

In a cruel juxtaposition of trends, during the 1960s and 1970s, a majority of American newspapers were falling into the hands of public companies at the same time that the newspaper stranglehold on the delivery of news and advertising was being loosened. Television became much more of a player in news, the explosion of self-contained suburbs hollowed out cities and created traffic patterns that doomed afternoon newspapers, and shopping-mall sprawl and the accompanying development of huge retail chain stores changed the dynamics of shopping and thus of advertising. For the first time, newspapers faced truly serious competition for their core dollars, not just for peripheral dollars, and for the time of readers.

Privately held newspaper companies and those with two tiers of stock and devoted to quality and public service had choices: Accept less profit and put more money back into the news and business operations to match the new media competitors; accept less profit per newspaper and grow through acquisitions; or decide to simply adjust profit expectations to meet the changed environment. Publicly held companies with only one class of stock did not have the choice of accepting less profit. In fact, as the competitive pressures grew, so did the demand from Wall Street to not simply maintain profits but to increase them annually. The ironic effect of this was that newspapers owned by profit-driven corporations, which tended to be of lesser journalistic quality to begin with, were better able to meet the fiscal demands while newspapers owned by quality-driven corporations were drawn inexorably toward the standards of the profit-driven companies. The dedication of quality-driven companies and individual newspapers was harshly tested by the changing circumstances.

For Knight Ridder, those trends from the sixties and seventies were often magnified, even distorted, as the new company's leaders tried to establish a lasting culture out of the clashing philosophies of its parents. It was a struggle that would last for almost thirty years.

Concerns and Conceits

In 1975, it was still possible to meander around the streets of Miami in a car, and that's what Batten and I did that crisp fall morning, talking about our new assignments and new relationship. (I would report to Batten.) "Merritt," he said with a chuckle, "all you have to do for the first two years is what you already know how to do and you'll be a hero."

Easily said. The family-owned Wichita morning and afternoon papers had been purchased by Ridder Publications in 1973, the year before the merger. Just over a decade earlier, *Time* magazine had called the Wichita newspapers, then family-owned, "the bottom of the barrel of American journalism." Batten made clear he would be constantly available and supportive as I set about to escape that unfortunate heritage and establish new standards.

We discussed the concerns being voiced by our Knight Newspapers contemporaries about the just-accomplished merger, concerns fed by a certain arrogance. The conceit from the Knight journalists' side was that we had inherited a group of second- and third-rate, profit-driven newspapers that we'd have to whip into journalistic shape while managing to negate the money-grubbing instincts of the new partners. Confidence in our ability to do that was high because, after all, we were in charge, so journalistic purity would surely prevail over what we saw as pure materialism. Like most conceits and generalizations, that one would prove to be not wholly true.

But as it stood that day in 1975, the core cultural values of the new company were brightly outlined because they had been directly transferred from the Knight portion of the arrangement.

The idea of a high, thick wall between journalism and the countinghouse permeated the organization. Most Knight newspapers were operated by the equal partnership of an editor and a general manager. The editors ran the newsrooms and were responsible for the journalism; the general managers were in charge of the business side, including advertising, circulation, and production. The editor and the general manager reported separately to corporate officers who would resolve any conflicts that could not be resolved locally. Ideally, the editor and the general manager would be able to balance the natural tension between the newspaper's business aspirations and its journalistic responsibilities without involving corporate. The journalists were so sheltered from the business side that newsroom staffers below the

top editor rarely discussed or concerned themselves with such annoyances as budgets. Their focus, from the top corporate officers through
the editors to the freshest newsroom recruits, was on doing the best
possible journalism. Everything else in the organization existed to
support that effort.

A piece of the meandering conversation in Batten's car that morning in 1975 reflected that journalism-business tension as we remi-
nisced about some of our Charlotte adventures, including a punishing
advertising boycott by local car dealers over a syndicated column they
considered unflattering to car salesmen. Auto advertising is a heavy
percentage of a newspaper's annual revenue and the boycott would
cost *The Charlotte Observer* several hundred thousand in 1960 dollars.
But the word from the president, Lee Hills, had been, "You did the
right thing [journalistically], don't worry about the budget." That
1960s sanguine (if simplistic) view of journalistic independence from
fiscal pressure, cultivated over the first half of the twentieth century,
would not stand the tests of time and changing circumstances in its
last quarter. Twenty-five years later, when a similar boycott was aimed
at *The Wichita Eagle*, the corporate response would be quite different.
Even in 1975, currents that would erode the prevailing Knight Newspapers philosophy were already running beneath the surface. Viewed
from the perspective of 2005, the prevailing idea that journalism
could maintain its exemption from the worst pressures of the market-
place looks, at best, wildly naive.

At that moment, however, we were full believers in both the rectitude and importance of the principles upon which Knight Newspapers was founded and operated. In the words of Jack Knight:

> We endeavor to meet the highest standards of journalism.
>
> We try to present the news accurately with a high priority
> upon fairness and objectivity.
>
> We don't play politics, are not beholden to any political
> party, faction, or special interest. . . .
>
> Our chief executives and the policy makers studiously avoid
> conflicts of interest. We serve on no corporate boards or com-

mittees other than appropriate civic and cultural organizations, or in the fields of education and communications.

We believe in profitability but do not sacrifice either principles or quality on the altar of the countinghouse.

As responsible purveyors of information and opinion, our newspapers are committed to the philosophy that journalism is likewise a public trust, an institution which serves, advances, and protects the public welfare. . . .

The role of the press in a free democratic society demands total involvement in and dedication to the problems which beset that society.

We accept that role as vigorous defenders of our traditional liberties and as ardent advocates of purposeful progress for all men.[3]

But How to Define Quality?

It is both difficult and controversial to try to define, much less quantify, the journalistic excellence that Knight's creed described. You can get an argument in any newsroom or any bar frequented by newspaper people about whether a specific story or series of stories is "good journalism." Arguments about the relative journalistic merits of individual newspapers are as endless as they are unavoidable, because much depends on the subjective standards of the person doing the judging. Sometimes the true excellence of journalistic effort isn't seen or felt for years after the act; often the result of journalistic excellence is more cumulative than immediately specific.

However, some indicators are available, and the Pulitzer Prize is one. That premier recognition is bestowed by Columbia University, and the selections are made through a jurying process carried out, in the case of the newspaper awards, by panels of journalists backed by a board of trustees also composed of journalists. Any such process is, of course, subject to the politics of the profession, and over the ninety years of its history, the Pulitzer board's decisions have often been controversial.

The awards emphasize public service and extraordinary dedication to sound journalism. Whether, in a given year, the awards go to "the best" journalism is certainly subject to debate, but at a minimum, the prizes recognize substance and relevance rather than superficiality and exploitativeness. Thus, a look at the recent history of those awards is both instructive and alarming.

Pulitzers are given for specific examples of outstanding journalism, such as a series of investigative reports or coverage of a disaster, or for an individual's body of work over a given year. There is no Pulitzer for an individual newspaper's sustained good journalism over time, so the awards do not reflect that important dimension of a newspaper's mission. Occasionally a major news opportunity—a plane crash, a flood, social upheaval—will fall into a mediocre newspaper's lap and its coverage will earn it a Pulitzer. For the most part, though, newspapers that win Pulitzers consistently are also consistently good at their broader mission.

For this analysis, five major institutions have been grouped together: *The New York Times*, *The Washington Post*, the *Los Angeles Times*, *The Wall Street Journal*, and The Associated Press. Because of their size, two-tiered stock (in the case of three of them), and operating arrangements, these organizations are less susceptible to short-term financial pressures than most of the rest of the profession. We'll call them the Big Five. The number (and percentage) of Pulitzers won, by decade, are as follows:

	Total prizes	Big 5	Knight Ridder	All other newspapers
1980s:	136	35 (26%)	32 (23%)	69 (51%)
1990s:	141	52 (37%)	12 (8%)	77 (55%)
2000–2004:	70	42 (60%)	4 (6%)	23 (34%)

At least two observations leap from those figures: Domination by the Big Five has grown over twenty-five years—or, put another way, awards to non–Big Five organizations have dropped—and Knight Ridder's proportion of awards has dropped from significant to negligible.

Unavoidable questions suggested by those numbers include: What is driving the shift in awards toward those relatively sheltered Big Five institutions? Has that wide a performance gap opened between the Big Five and the rest of American newspaper journalism? Why is that? What is behind Knight Ridder's declining Pulitzer performance over twenty-five years? And what do those answers say about the status and course of newspaper journalism in the United States?

Another way of judging quality, arguably at least from the standpoint of public judgment and acceptance, is circulation. Weekday newspaper circulation in the United States has declined since 1990 by about 6 percent in absolute terms, but the situation is actually much bleaker. Prior to 1970, more daily newspapers were sold than there were U.S. households. About 1970, what is called the household penetration ratio reached 1:1. By 1990, household penetration had fallen to only 60 percent, and by 2004 it was at nearly 50 percent, meaning that only half of the nation's households read a newspaper daily. Using those numbers to buttress an argument about quality, or lack of it, is too simplistic however, because many newspapers and newspaper companies have deliberately excluded, or are indifferent about, portions of their potential audience because of bottom-line considerations.

Effect on Public Life

The implications of the decline in the public service orientation of many newspapers and newspaper companies are profound for our society. Journalistic performance and a viable democracy are fully interdependent. So the decline in journalistic quality, as exemplified by the erosion of foundational missions and dedication to public service, has been accompanied by a decline in the quality of public life, which is the way democracy is expressed and experienced. People ill served by dollar-driven, market-oriented journalism become alienated from public life, more inwardly focused, and cynical about the process of democracy. Today's journalism is clearly implicated in, and its freedom threatened by, that alienation.

Thus a detailed examination of the forces acting on journalism has meaning beyond one company and one set of newspapers, though this examination uses one company as a framework and exemplar.

2

The Heritages

"We are Catholics. We have many children and most of them turn out to be sons. We have to buy a newspaper for every son." — *Victor Ridder*

"If I don't like it, I can get out, and, number two, if I'm no good at it, I get kicked out." — *John S. Knight to his father*

IN 1890 in New York City, the son of a poor Westphalian immigrant borrowed money to buy a share of ownership in a fifty-four-year-old, German-language daily newspaper. Herman Ridder had made a good living selling insurance and had founded two weekly Catholic newspapers, but owning *Staats-Zeitung* seemed like a good way to ensure the future of his family, including his three sons.

In 1896 in North Carolina, the great-great grandson of an immigrant from England gave up an uninspiring Appalachia law practice to start a small newspaper, the *Journal*, in Winston-Salem. Charles Landon Knight, at thirty years of age, was scratching a lifelong itch to write, and owning a newspaper seemed like a good way to do that and invest in his future with wife, Clara, and the two boys they would produce.

While the instincts that urged the two men to try newspaper careers were different, each started down a path toward an unseen intersection.

The Ridder Path

Herman Ridder's father had left his native area near the Holland-German border in the 1830s for New York, bringing with him a surname that is the Dutch version of the German *ritter*, which, in an eerie linguistic twist, means "knight" in English. C. L. Knight traced his family back to St. John Knight, who arrived in Massachusetts from England in 1662 and whose great grandson, William, moved to Georgia where C. L. Knight was born. The similarity of surname origins and the first tentative steps into the newspaper business by Herman Ridder and C. L. Knight were only the beginnings of a series of coincidences and choices that would, a century later, mold the culture of one of the largest newspaper companies in the United States.

Herman Ridder's sons eventually joined him at the newspaper and in producing male heirs: Bernard H., the firstborn, had four sons, and his twin brothers, Victor and Joseph, each had two sons and a daughter. When Herman Ridder died in 1915, his sons were looking for additional opportunities to provide for their burgeoning families. Herman Ridder had attained complete ownership of *Staats-Zeitung* in 1906, and as the nation moved toward April 1917 and involvement in World War I, ownership of a German-language newspaper in America's largest city was not the most comfortable occupation. Herman had been active in New York and national Democratic political circles, including terms as treasurer of the Democratic National Committee and president of the American Newspaper Publishers Association. His civic and professional standing did not, however, totally insulate his sons and their newspaper from anti-German sentiment once war broke out, and they suffered advertiser and newsdealer boycotts and harassment from government intelligence agencies.

Like many German-Americans, the Ridders believed that a legally declared U.S. war must be supported, though they also favored relief for war victims in central Europe. Despite their support of the U.S. war effort, a German-language newspaper in New York City was too large and convenient a target for "Hun-haters" to ignore. The Ridder sons, aided by their connection to Democratic local politics and the church, managed to keep the newspaper afloat through the war years, but its future was clouded by strict postwar limitations on immigration from Europe. Faced with a changing business environment and growing families, the three brothers began to look for broader opportunities and in 1926 found one in *The Journal of Commerce*, a New York business newspaper specializing in shipping news. Their purchase of it was followed quickly, over three years, by the acquisition of all or controlling interest in the *St. Paul Pioneer Press* and *St. Paul Dispatch*, the *Aberdeen American News* in South Dakota, and the *Grand Forks Herald* in North Dakota. The acquisitions reflected what would become a dominating expansion philosophy for Ridder Publications, Inc. (RPI), buying small and medium-size newspapers in monopoly markets and avoiding the complexities of large-market newspapers, particularly their often-strained labor relations and draining competitiveness.

Years later, J. Montgomery Curtis of Columbia University asked Victor Ridder why the rush to acquire newspapers in that period. The response: "We are Catholics. We have many children and most of them turn out to be sons. We have to buy a newspaper for every son."[1]

As World War II approached, the spurt of diversification appeared even more prescient. In 1938, *Staats-Zeitung* was down to 80,000 circulation and the opening of America's second war with Germany in the century would drive it further against the wall. In 1956, Ridder Publications Inc., by then also owner of the *Duluth News Tribune and Herald*, the *San Jose Mercury and News*, and the *Long Beach Independent and Press-Telegram*, sold *Staats-Zeitung*, closing that seminal but sometimes difficult chapter in the company and family histories.

By World War II, the third generation of Ridders were heavily into producing both newspapers and male heirs. Of Bernard H. Ridder's four sons, Bernard Jr. (Bernie) was emerging as the family force. Though uncles and older cousins became established in RPI's various newspapers while he was still a history major at Princeton, Bernie Ridder would emerge as the family and corporate leader.

"In my senior year of college," he told an interviewer in 1974, "I decided that the newspaper business was what appealed to me the most. I was always fond of reading newspapers, and so by that time the whole field seemed to interest me. Of course living in a family that was already in the business, I heard an awful lot about it. But the only question I had at the time was whether to go into our business or into an outside newspaper operation."[2]

He chose the former, and upon graduation worked briefly at *The Journal of Commerce* and in Aberdeen in business department posts. After World War II service as a gunnery officer on the carrier *Bunker Hill* in the Pacific, he settled in Duluth at *The Herald and News Tribune*, working his way from ad director through various managerial chairs and, finally, to publisher. In 1959, he also became publisher of the *St. Paul Pioneer Press* and *St. Paul Dispatch*, giving him a major presence in the corporation's headquarters city.

Bernie Ridder Jr.'s choice of spending twenty-five years in Minnesota, while other family members scattered around the country, paved the way for his advancement within RPI. "I was the only Ridder in Duluth, and actually, I was so happy there that I wasn't looking for promotion elsewhere in the company. I really felt I was an executive of *The Herald and News Tribune* more strongly than a member of the Ridder family." [3] But by 1969, he was president and CEO in a company that had gone public with a secondary offering of common stock. Also by then, RPI had acquired *The Pasadena Star News*, the *Gary Post-Tribune* in Illinois, and controlling interest in *The Boulder Daily Camera* in Colorado. In 1973, RPI picked off *The Wichita Eagle & Beacon* in Kansas and was the fourth-largest newspaper company in the nation.

But even as such, RPI was very much a Ridder affair, as demonstrated by the family tree.

By contrast, the Knight family tree was limited.

The orderly march of the genealogical lines in the family tree doesn't reflect, however, the fiercely independent, sometimes raucous nature of the Ridder fiefdoms. Third-generation Ridders—Joe in San Jose, Bernard J. in Pasadena, Daniel in Long Beach, Eric at *The Journal of Commerce*, and Walter in the Washington bureau—jealously

Ridder Family Tree and Company Involvement as of 1975

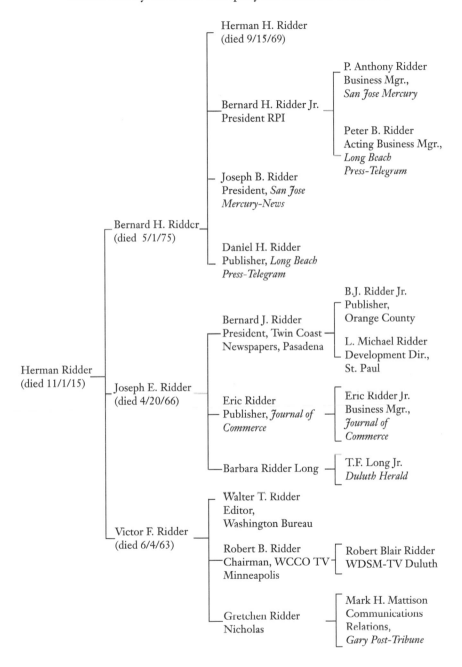

Knight Family Tree and Company Involvement as of 1976

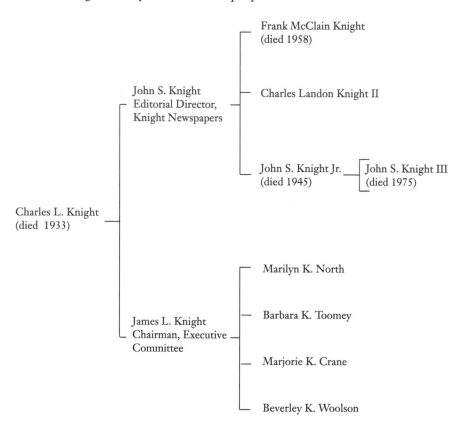

Frank McClain Knight
(died 1958)

John S. Knight
Editorial Director,
Knight Newspapers

Charles Landon Knight II

John S. Knight Jr.
(died 1945)

John S. Knight III
(died 1975)

Charles L. Knight
(died 1933)

Marilyn K. North

Barbara K. Toomey

James L. Knight
Chairman, Executive
Committee

Marjorie K. Crane

Beverley K. Woolson

guarded their operations in a manner that made RPI much less a confederation and much more a series of power outposts connected more by blood and profits than by any journalistic philosophy. By 1974, herding those corporate cats was an increasingly difficult job for Bernie Ridder. There were, after all, so many of them.

And the styles and personalities of the newspapers hardly reflected the conventional view of a "newspaper chain" as a cohesive group operating under one business and journalistic philosophy; rather, the newspapers were as varied as the personalities driving them. The single common corporate thread was purely economics, rather than business management or journalistic preferences.

Bernie Ridder expressed the Ridder philosophy in an interview in 1985: "The newspapers were a good investment. The family believed they would grow. Newspapers were the number one news media [*sic*]. Sheer power of the media meant that advertising revenue would continue to produce a profitable return."[4]

He also believed strongly that local autonomy in matters of journalism was the most appropriate way to operate. Local people knew best how to run local newspapers. "We're the parent company," he told another interviewer, "and what we're concerned with are the capital expenditures, newsprint, major personnel, aspects of that sort. There is no central line of news and editorial policy."[5]

The Ridder newspapers all operated under the publisher system, meaning that unquestioned authority in all matters rested with the man in that position. Since none of the Ridder publishers had any journalism training or background, the culture of the individual newspapers naturally reflected the corporate culture as Bernie Ridder expressed it: The bottom line is what matters.

The *laissez faire* approach to journalistic content may have been as much pragmatic as philosophical, because any effort to impose orderliness (or in today's vernacular, to "brand" the papers) would surely have been washed away in the family members' rambunctiousness and assertive individuality. "Autonomy" sometimes meant "anarchy." The newspapers' journalistic standards ranged from more-or-less traditional (if unspectacular) in St. Paul under Bernie to outrageously individualized in San Jose under Joe, where a TV dealer in town reported, "The free press in San Jose is exactly what Joe Ridder says it is and no more. He prints what he wants printed to serve his interests, and he will keep news out of the paper or distort news and editorial stuff which is not in his interest."

As 1974 opened, Bernie Ridder was concerned on at least two fronts. First, the public stock offering in 1969 had certainly changed the rules of the corporate game. The traditional Ridder notion that a newspaper's operations need please only the publisher first and, much less importantly, the family corporation was no longer sufficient. Now there were outside shareholders and directors and stock analysts to satisfy. Second, he worried about RPI's long-term future in terms of succession: How could an orderly transition of power emerge from the sprawling, sometimes warring Ridder clan? Would infighting over succession spoil the game for everyone in the family, or should the dynasty be broken up?

Recalling those concerns in 1985, Bernie Ridder told Knight biographer Charles Whited:

> Each family member ran his part of the operation like a duke in his private duchy. Each felt he was his own boss. Even in public ownership, some were unwilling to give that up. And yet we all suddenly had a responsibility to people who invested in Ridder stock. Some of the practices that had existed before would have to be corrected. We would have to brush up our act.[6]

Or, perhaps, find a merger partner who could help brush it up.

The Intersection

While Bernie Ridder fretted in St. Paul, some people in Knight Newspapers, Inc. (KNI) were also concerned. As 1974 opened, KNI owned sixteen newspapers, including operations in Detroit, Miami, and Philadelphia, each far larger than anything owned by RPI. The other Knight papers were in Charlotte, Akron, Boca Raton and Tallahassee in Florida, Columbus and Macon in Georgia, and Lexington, Kentucky. From the time Knight had gone public in 1969, the only consistency about its earnings had been their wild fluctuations, something neither Wall Street nor KNI management liked very much.

The roller coaster was driven by always-dicey labor relations in Detroit and the competitive struggles in all three of the major cities. Philadelphia was a particular problem as the morning *Philadelphia Inquirer* and the tabloid, afternoon *Daily News*, acquired only five years previously for $55 million, tried to compete with the city's journalistic grande dame, *The Philadelphia Bulletin*. The *Inquirer* and *Daily News* were burdened with hopelessly outdated production facilities, staffs stuffed with old retainers from years of paternalistic operation by the owning Annenberg family, and crushingly unfavorable labor contracts.

In contrast, the dependable bottom line of Ridder Publications was inviting, and its small-market, noncompetitive orientation was attractive, not only for the regular earnings it promised, but also as developmental grounds for young journalists. The geography also worked well, combining Knight's East-and-South distribution with Ridder's Midwest-West Coast spread. The geographic synergies represented more than the makings of a nice map; they made it possible for good economic times in one part of the nation to offset bad economic times in another.

But there were historic reasons for the stark differences that made a merger so attractive to both companies, and within those reasons lay both recognized and unrecognized incompatibilities that would complicate the next thirty years.

The Knight Path

C. L. Knight's nineteenth-century experiment with the North Carolina newspaper lasted less than a year before it failed, but it thickened the natural printer's blood in his veins and he found a job as an editorial writer with *The Philadelphia Times*, then moved with Clara and their young son, John Shively, to Ohio to become assistant editor of *The Woman's Home Companion*, published in Springfield. In Ohio, the journalistic roots of the Knight family business sank deep. In 1903, he and another of the *Companion*'s owners bought the *Akron Beacon Journal*. Four years later, Knight bought out his partner and became sole owner, editor, and publisher.

John Shively Knight's boyhood in Akron included the birth of a second son to C. L. and Clara, James Landon Knight, in 1909. John, by then known as "Jack," was fifteen at the time. Intent upon steering his sons into the family business, C. L. gave Jack odd jobs at the paper during his high school years and between semesters, while he was at Cornell. But progress toward journalism was slowed with the opening of World War I. Jack Knight enlisted for a tour of duty in France, emerging as a second lieutenant in what would later become the Army Air Force.

Though interested in seeking a law degree at Harvard University after his military service, Jack was prevailed upon by his father to join the *Beacon Journal* staff as a writer, beginning by covering sports and politics, then moving through various desks. He later said, "My father was very anxious to have me go into the newspaper business—and pursued this [plan] very avidly. I finally said, 'Well, I'll do it on two conditions.' He asked: 'What are they?' and I said, 'If I don't like it, I can get out, and, number two, if I'm no good at it, I get kicked out.' So we made a deal."[7]

C. L. Knight died in 1933, leaving the newspaper to his sons, Jack, thirty-nine years old, and Jim, twenty-four. The *Beacon Journal* was struggling against a strong Scripps-Howard competitor, the *Akron Times-Press*. It was the depths of the Great Depression, and both newspapers were breathing hard from the brutal competition in dire economic times. Jack Knight even had to borrow money to pay the taxes on his father's estate of $515,000, most of it in *Beacon Journal* stock. To get past the fiscally tough months after his father's death, he paid half of his employees' wages in script redeemable at businesses that owed the newspaper for advertising. The inheritance-tax burden provided a lesson that would, decades later, drive a crucial decision about his life and his company.

In those toughest of conditions, he exhibited two traits—aggressiveness and faith in the value of good journalism—that would become hallmarks of his life and his newspaper company's culture. While the rival *Times-Press* was retrenching, he expanded, spending more money on new features and a larger news staff. Deciding to forgo short-term profits for future gain, and using journalistic content to do it, was a strategic decision that would become a pattern over the next thirty years, usually with the same result as this one: destroying the competition. Within two years, the *Beacon Journal* was clearly winning the struggle for Akron's readers, and in 1938 Scripps-Howard stopped the hemorrhaging by selling out to Knight for 38 percent stock in the *Beacon Journal* company.

The philosophy and culture that would make Knight Newspapers, by mid-century, an acknowledged leader in U.S. journalism was taking shape in Akron. From his father, Jack Knight absorbed a belief in aggressive editorial positions and a conviction that the core job of a newspaper was simply to "find the truth and print it." But he also understood that in the depths of the Depression people needed diversions; that a full diet of news, particularly distressing news, needed to be supplemented. As managing editor while C. L. Knight was still alive and in charge, Jack had begun to buy entertainment features, additional comic strips, and other syndicated material. His father, who had sometimes simply left out the comic strips to create space for what he considered to be more substantial things, grumbled that feature content was "flotsam and jetsam which neither amuses nor instructs an understanding mind."[8] But his grousing diminished in direct ratio to the *Beacon Journal*'s circulation gains.

In 1937, *The Miami Herald*, one of three daily newspapers in that burgeoning city, became available from its founder, Colonel Frank B. Shutts. Though Jack Knight claimed to have no ambitions beyond Akron and expressed concerns about his desire or ability to run more than one newspaper, he paid $2.4 million for it and assigned younger brother Jim Knight to clean up its stodgy and stumbling business operations. JSK quickly bought one of his Miami competitors, *The Tribune*, from Moses Annenberg and began to zero in on the stiffest competition, *The Miami News*, owned by James Cox, the founder of present-day media giant Cox Communications.

The two Miami purchases were on favorable terms to Knight for reasons that later drove his own company's expansions: Knight's aggressiveness and journalistic convictions were attractive to aging owners concerned about inheritance taxes and anxious that their newspapers' reputations survive, and for decades their hopes were sustained.

The "leave it in good hands" issue arose again in 1940, when eighty-one-year-old Edward D. Stair, who had published the century-old *Detroit Free Press* for three decades, sought out Knight as a potential buyer. Stair accepted $100,000 in cash and $3.1 million in notes, far less than other buyers had been offering, because he wanted Jack Knight to be the new owner.

And the syndrome occurred again in 1944, when executors for Secretary of the Navy Frank Knox put his *Chicago Daily News* up for sale under a provision of his will instructing them to sell to the person best qualified to carry on the newspaper's traditions, not simply to the highest bidder. After quizzing by the executors, Knight was able to purchase the paper for $2.1 million. Fifteen years later, in 1959, it would sell for $24 million.

In each case—Miami, Detroit, Chicago—as in Akron, Knight would pour news and feature resources into the paper, hire like-minded editors, and create editorial policies fiercely independent of political parties and business pressures. "The Knight formula" was locking in.

So was Jack Knight's later-life persona: reserved, sometimes to the point of being stiff-necked; disciplined in thought and lifestyle so that, at least, he was wholly dependable. Knight possessed a physical presence and bearing that made him the focal point of any roomful of people without his doing or saying anything. His coolness under pressure, combined with his natural reserve, did not allow precipitous reactions or decisions; though, on the personal side, he exhibited a deep appreciation of champion racehorses, beautiful women, and shooting craps.

He could be a difficult man, particularly in his later years: sharp-tongued, judgmental, at times even a bully who was too aware of his vast power. Those who knew him best, however, respected him for that, just as they respected him for the intellectual honesty and courage they knew were underneath the blemishes. He made no apologies, even to family members who often found him cool and unresponsive; he had too much to do, too many places to go to be deflected by familial concerns. He was a consuming perfectionist totally focused on making great newspapers and making money doing so.

LEE HILLS AND THE SUPREMACY OF THE NEWSROOM

Knight's hires, like many of his important decisions, were instinctive, intensely personalized, and usually contained an element of risk, and so it had been with his hiring of Lee Hills. They met in 1942 when Louis B. Seltzer of Scripps-Howard told Knight about a restless young executive in his organization. Hills was then thirty-six, so not likely to be subject to the rapidly expanding military draft, and had been working in newspapers since he was fourteen years old, "doing whatever needed doing," in his words.

When he was fourteen, that meant sweeping up at the weekly *News Advocate* in Price, Utah. By eighteen, he was its editor, and the paper was recognized as the best weekly in that state. He attended Brigham Young and the University of Missouri, but had to leave before he could graduate because of lack of money. He found a reporting job at Scripps-Howard's *Oklahoma City Times* in 1932, where his incisive reporting and his completion of a law degree at Oklahoma City University caught the attention of Scripps-Howard executives. In 1935 they assigned him to *The Cleveland Press*, and by the end of 1936 he was its news editor.

For the next six years Hills "did whatever needed doing" at Scripps-Howard papers in Memphis, Indianapolis, and, for a second stint, Oklahoma City. In each case, he was a sort of clean up man, reorganizing news coverage or fixing a demoralized and tattered staff or advising corporate management about local personnel matters. He succeeded at every step, but by 1942 he wanted something more permanent, something he could build long term. So Seltzer put in the call to Jack Knight.

What Knight saw the morning they met at Knight's Akron home was a slender, immaculately dressed man whose relentless, crisp thought process flashed in his eyes but was launched upon the world in soft upper-Midwestern tones, rarely accompanied by smiles. He missed nothing that happened around him; every nuance of word and action was captured and cataloged by the powers of observation and analysis that made him a fine reporter. He was a few paces ahead of whatever was being said or done in any room that he occupied, but was never so rude or condescending as to let that be known. If he was rarely heard to laugh aloud, neither was he known to gratuitously injure or insult. Many of those who knew Hills slightly considered him a cold fish; those closer to him knew better. His power and effectiveness were 90 percent mental, 10 percent personality, creating a no-nonsense presence that inspired deep confidence and loyalty, if not immediate warm friendship.

At the end of that first conversation, Knight offered Hills the job of city editor at *The Miami Herald*, and he accepted. Both knew that the mid-level title belied the assignment. He was to take over the news operation and fix it. It was "what needed doing."

Miami quickly provided striking proof of the belief that solid journalism would ultimately pay off at the bottom line, despite short-term hardships. As World War II roared on, so did the competitive battle in Miami. *The Miami Herald* had a narrow circulation lead over *The Miami News* at the beginning of the war, but the battle was fierce and the stakes high as South Florida became a major staging area for the military. It was in some ways a newspaper publisher's dream: a booming economy creating a white-hot advertising climate; 150,000 new residents (and potential readers) courtesy of the U.S. government; and a major, continuing news story, the war raging around the world.

But there was a problem: newsprint. The stuff was tightly rationed, and as 1943 drew to a close, each paper had nearly exhausted its annual allotment. General Manager Jim Knight calculated that in order to get through December they would have to cut out a dozen pages a day and thirty-six pages on Sundays. That meant dropping substantial amounts of advertising or news, or at least meaningful amounts of each.

Though he had been at the newspaper for only a year, Hills came up with an audacious plan for stretching the newsprint supply. He proposed to Jim Knight that *The Miami Herald* stop running display advertising altogether and devote virtually all of its precious newsprint to telling news. Hills's plan did allow for one page on which its regular display advertisers could be listed for free, but all else in the paper was to be local and war news. He also recommended limiting circulation to the immediate Miami area. Jim Knight suggested calling his boss and older brother, who was then in London on a wartime assignment, but Hills said, "No, I think Jack would do the same."⁹ Jim Knight, with great apprehension, agreed to the plan.

Hills was right, confirming for the first time through a major decision the rapport with Jack Knight that would enable them, over the next twenty-five years, to build a major newspaper company based in trust, like-mindedness, and sound though aggressive journalistic practice.

Meanwhile, *The Miami News* took the opposite tack, stretching its newsprint supply by severely cutting back on news and jamming its pages with advertising. The *Herald* suffered heavy financial losses in December, traditionally any newspaper's best revenue month, surrendered some short-term advertising contracts, and saw scary circulation declines because of the geographic limitations Hills imposed. But when the newsprint-supply crisis passed, the Miami community, including most major advertisers, understood and deeply appreciated what the *Herald* had done. Both advertising and circulation bounded back so vigorously that *The Miami News* was never again a serious threat.

The cooperative relationship that allowed Hills and Jim Knight to resolve the newsprint crisis had been forged a year earlier, in Hills's first weeks at the paper. The afternoon *Miami News* had a Sunday morning edition that directly challenged the *Herald*, and on a Sunday morning in November 1942, Hills, then only months into his job, was jolted when he picked up the two papers. The *News'* front page featured major coverage of the disastrous Boston Coconut Grove nightclub fire in which almost 500 people perished. The *Herald* had not a word.

When Jack Knight hired Hills to go to Miami, he made it clear that while his brother had cleaned up a miserable business operation there, the newsroom still was far below acceptable standards. That Sunday's performance showed Hills how far it was from acceptable, and he summoned to the office the two editors he had left in charge when he had had gone home about 1:00 a.m. What he heard astonished and offended him: The editors had been aware of the story, but only the circulation manager and composing room manager had the authority to stop the presses once they were running. The two editors said they had tried to persuade the pressroom foreman to stop for the truly major fire story, but they were rebuffed.

To Hills, this meant that he, as an editor, was not fully in charge of the content of the paper, and he told Jim Knight the next morning, "If you're going to have the composing room and the circulation department make the editorial department's decisions on the *Herald*, you don't need an editor and I think your brother made a mistake hiring me. I think it's a hell of a way to run a newspaper."[10] It would never have occurred to Hills to inquire earlier about who had the authority to stop the presses; to him, it was clearly the editor's call. Jim Knight explained that he had instituted the rule as part of his turning around of the business operation after some poor and costly stop-press decisions by previous editors. Jim Knight immediately changed the rule, and their working relationship was clarified in a fashion that would become standard for Knight-owned newspapers: News decisions belong to the people running the newsroom and to no one else, even when large sums of money are involved.

LOSING AN HEIR

The war exacted a harsh personal penalty on the Knight family in an event that altered the course of Knight Newspapers. Only six weeks before Germany surrendered, Lieutenant John S. Knight Jr. was killed when his reconnaissance patrol was ambushed. The date was March 29, 1945; the place, near Munster, the capital of Westphalia, ironically the homeland of the Ridder clan. "Johnny," the first-born of Jack Knight's three sons, had married shortly before leaving for Europe, and his wife, Dorothy, was expecting their first child that April. Jack Knight arranged to delay the news of Johnny's death until after the child was safely delivered. They named him John Shively Knight III.

Young John Knight Jr. clearly had been the primary potential heir to his father's business. Not only was he the first-born, but each of his younger brothers, Frank and Landon, had limiting physical problems. Frank's were persistent throughout his life, but not well understood until, in 1958, thirty years old and in training in the advertising department of the *Akron Beacon Journal*, he fell dead with what was later discovered to be a brain tumor. Landon's physical problem was polio, contracted when he was nine years old, that forced him to move around by wheelchair and crutches and sapped his will and energy.

As World War II ended, Jack Knight's most valuable newspaper assets included papers in Detroit, Chicago, Miami, and Akron, and three key men—long-time Akron attorney and *Beacon Journal* shareholder Blake McDowell; the newspaper's financial officer, John Barry; and Hills. There was no formal corporate staff or office; Knight

Newspapers' headquarters, a magazine quipped, "is in John Knight's brown briefcase." For the next ten years, the focus would be on winning the battles of Detroit, Chicago, and Miami by upgrading news-editorial staffs and production facilities. Hills would be the quiet force that projected Jack Knight's newspaper philosophies.

By 1951, Hills, who was then executive editor in Miami, had led the paper to its first Pulitzer Prize Gold Medal for public service. *The Miami News* was in full retreat. And Jack Knight needed to ask a favor. Things were going badly in Detroit. Would Hills be willing to take over the *Free Press* while continuing to run the *Herald?* Few people are competent to run one newspaper well, much less two, but Hills accepted, despite protests from Jim Knight, by then the publisher of the *Herald,* that Hills's attention would be divided.

As was his habit, Hills had been thinking deeply about not only the *Herald* but also about Knight Newspapers. He understood better than most that newspapers are solely the reflection of the people who work there, meaning that great newspapers required great journalists doing the reporting and writing and decision making.

3

Building Toward Merger

"Jack, I think it will be fine—as long as you are alive." — Nelson Poynter to Jack Knight, 1969

WHILE LEE HILLS immersed himself in the two major newspaper operations in Miami and Detroit and also conferred with Jack Knight on corporate matters, the company expanded for the first time since 1944, this time buying *The Charlotte Observer* in 1955. It was a purchase that Jack Knight was cool about but Jim Knight and Hills favored, Jim Knight because of a friendship with the owning Johnson family, Hills because he was convinced the company needed medium-size papers as training and recruiting grounds. Jack Knight, who at sixty was more interested in the larger papers and concerned about overextending Hills and other executives, including himself, grumpily agreed to the Charlotte purchase. But, in a move that startled insiders, he named Jim Knight as president and publisher rather than himself. Thus Charlotte was "Jim's deal," and Jack rarely showed up there. So Hills and Jim Knight were once more teamed in the rebuilding of a newspaper.

Shaping Up Charlotte

In 1954, C. A. (Pete) McKnight, a native of Shelby, North Carolina and a Davidson College graduate, had taken a leave of absence from the editorship of the afternoon *Charlotte News* to head the Southern Education Reporting Service (SERS), a Ford Foundation agency that would monitor enforcement of the freshly minted Brown v. Board of Education U.S. Supreme Court school desegregation order. One of his reporting trips for SERS was to Detroit, where he met Hills and they talked not only about school desegregation, which both strongly favored, but also about *The Charlotte Observer*. Hills asked McKnight to put on paper his views about what needed to be done there. The bottom line for McKnight: Substantially raise the paper's level of journalism. That matched the views of Jim Knight and Hills and, in a move that shook both Charlotte newsrooms as well as the community, Pete McKnight became the new editor of the *Observer*.

After sizing up the *Observer* from inside, McKnight knew he needed better leadership and persuaded the highly respected and valued Tom Fesperman, managing editor of *The Charlotte News*, to become his number two man at the rival *Observer*. It was a stroke of genius that ensured a resurgence in the *Observer*'s quality while dealing a fatal blow to the *News*, which would surrender totally four years later and be purchased by Knight Newspapers.

Hills's other aspiration for *The Charlotte Observer*, making it a training ground for what he knew would be an expanding company, also was realized. Long-time staffer Jack Claiborne, in his 1986 history of the *Observer*, calculated that more than a dozen McKnight-Fesperman recruits from the 1950s and early 1960s became editors or publishers of Knight-owned, and later Knight Ridder–owned, newspapers. Dozens more went on to outstanding reporting, editing, and photography careers within the company and at *The New York Times*, *The Washington Post*, and *Time*, *Fortune*, and *Sports Illustrated* magazines, as well as dozens of smaller newspapers and magazines.[1]

One of those hires, a young reporter from McKnight's alma mater, Davidson College, was Jim Batten. McKnight tabbed Batten early as his possible successor at the *Observer*. Batten was the total package: He possessed a calm but determined demeanor wrapped in a natural, not contrived, Southern courtliness. He had high intellect; a deft touch with people; a crisp, authentic writing style; and an imposing physical presence. Most important for McKnight and Hills, he cared a great deal about the world around him and understood a newspaper's obligation to make that world better.

They constructed a personal development regimen that would take him to the Washington bureau, to Detroit for what had become known as *Free Press* boot camp, to the editorship of a newspaper, and ultimately, to the leadership of the company. While it was clear to many of his peers very early that Batten was on a corporate fast track, the negative aura of "The Chosen One" never attached to him because he never acted the part in any way.

Another of McKnight's early hires, Larry Jinks (later executive editor of *The Miami Herald* and editor, then publisher, of *The San Jose Mercury News*) also worked for a time as senior vice president for news for Knight Ridder. Rolfe Neill, hired as a business reporter in Charlotte, was editor of the *Philadelphia Daily News* and assistant to the publisher of the *New York Daily News* before returning to Charlotte as publisher. Charles Kuralt, who would became famous as the face and voice of CBS television, was one of their hires at *The Charlotte News* before McKnight and Fesperman wound up at *The Charlotte Observer*. Another hire was the fledging John S. Knight III as a reporter at *The Charlotte News*. It was a hire that caused *Charlotte News* management some pause and aroused great derision at the rival *Observer*, but it was a start for the grandson of the founder.

By the early 1970s, papers in Providence, Dallas, Winston-Salem, Fayetteville (North Carolina), Anderson (South Carolina), Akron, Portland (Oregon), Charleston (South Carolina), Bradenton (Florida), and Wichita were also headed by McKnight-Fesperman hires from that period of rejuvenating the *Observer*. The Charlotte operation had, indeed, become the company's most productive training ground.

The big papers in Detroit, Miami, and Chicago were talent sponges, and the rapid Knight-Hills improvements made them hunting grounds for the nation's larger newspapers. Hills began to put heavy, organized emphasis on maintaining a pipeline full of promising people. Full-time personnel people, armed with batteries of tests, were hired at most of the newspapers, and local editors were charged with seeing to their training by moving them through a series of newsroom assignments on almost a yearly basis. Clearly, the company's business was becoming too large for even Jack Knight's hefty brown briefcase. A corporation was beginning to take shape, and with its emergence came concerns: If the company grew too large, would local autonomy suffer? Could journalistic standards and the Knight mission be maintained? Were there enough truly dedicated and talented people around?

Practicing Journalists

Knight and Hills, despite the distractions of growth, set a tone that kept the company's priorities straight—they did journalism.

Knight continued to write his influential "Editor's Notebook" for the Sunday editions of his papers, a task he performed with only a handful of interruptions for thirty-nine years. In the last fifteen of those years, the column became widely influential beyond the Knight papers in which it appeared, and in 1968 Knight was awarded a Pulitzer Prize for "the whole volume" of his work.

Hills, even with several newspapers to oversee and growing corporate responsibilities, continued to think and act like a working reporter. In 1955, with the United Auto Workers Union, Ford Motor Company, and General Motors embroiled in high-stakes contract negotiations, Hills personally took on a delicate job of reporting and writing. The labor situation was threatening to both the city and the *Detroit Free Press*, and since the negotiations were behind closed doors, Hills had to call on his deep sources on both sides and staff reporters to produce a daily, unsigned column called "A Look Behind the UAW-Auto Curtain." The column kept rank-and-file people on both sides informed in ways the company and union bosses would not, squelched rumors, and finally predicted, correctly, that a settlement would be reached. "Behind the Curtain" was hailed as a major factor in keeping things cool and those most affected well informed, and it won for Hills and the *Detroit Free Press* his second Pulitzer Prize.

The decade from 1955 to 1965 was one of digestion. With a dozen newspapers and a sharply limited corporate structure, it was time to build upon the existing foundation rather than add more newspapers. In those ten years only two newspaper transactions occurred, both in the nature of the inevitable. In 1959, Jack Knight gave up on his Chicago dreams. The City of Big Shoulders was a hectic newspaper battleground. Knight's *Chicago Daily News*, an afternoon publication without a Sunday edition, was pitted against the all-powerful morning and Sunday editions of the *Chicago Tribune*, plus Marshall Field Jr.'s *Sun-Times* and Hearst Corporation's *Chicago American*. While Knight and his Chicago executive editor, Basil "Stuffy" Walters, had built the *Daily News* into a paper with more than 600,000 circulation and a reputation for tough journalism and smart content, its fiscal stability and future were threatened by its lack of a Sunday edition. All across the nation, cities large and small were losing second- and third-ranked newspapers, particularly afternoon ones. Television, urban traffic patterns changed by suburban growth, and the hollowing out of urban business districts contrived to make any afternoon newspaper's future questionable. Knight negotiated to buy *The Chicago American* for its Sunday position but was rebuffed. Then the *American* was sold to the *Chicago Tribune*, and the game was over for Knight. He sold the *Chicago Daily News* to Marshall Field for $24 million, fifteen years after he bought it for $2.1 million.

Meanwhile in Charlotte, the *Observer* juggernaut was rolling over the afternoon *Charlotte News*, whose owning family capitulated, selling to Knight Newspapers in yet another example of the dominant newspaper business trend of the decade—one-owner cities.

Except for those two financial events, however, the decade was one of quiet building of talent and improvement of the existing newspapers rather than the acquisition of more of them. When the *Chicago Daily News* was sold, Hills became executive editor of Knight Newspapers, a title that finally reflected the scope of his responsibilities. In Miami, the triumphant *Herald* was feeling the pinch of an outmoded building, and Jim Knight was planning a new one, on Biscayne Bay.

Turning Points

While the quiet journalistic development of the mid-1960s led to growing recognition for Knight Newspapers' aggressive reporting and courageous editorial stands, its business side was gaining a reputation as old-fashioned, disorganized, and falling short of its financial potential. This negative was tolerable as long as the Knight brothers, Hills, and a few others were the controlling shareholders; the company was making a handsome, if not maximized, profit. But, as Jack Knight approached his seventy-third birthday, other forces were building in addition to the weight of years on his shoulders.

A turning point for Knight and the company occurred suddenly in 1967. For several years, an old Akron friend from Goodyear Tire & Rubber Company, Eddie Thomas, had been urging Knight to start stepping back and to develop a succession plan for the company, something for which Knight had little appetite. In 1967, at Knight's insistence, Thomas became the company's first outside director. Charles Whited, in his 1988 biography of John S. Knight, tells of one meeting where JSK asked the new board member, "What have you got to say about us?" The exchange went as follows:

"If Goodyear operated its finances like you do, we'd have been out of business years ago. You're so out of date, I don't see how you get along at all. You need a full-time expert on financial affairs. . . . You've gotten away with things so far because nothing has been too pressing. You're not up to date, Jack."

"Are you finished?"

"No. You're also way behind in the way personnel is handled. . . . Your hiring is haphazard. I don't see a lot of training to speak of. . . . It's a new ball game, Jack. Get somebody in here who knows finance, who knows personnel, put them in charge, let them organize."

"Is that all?"

"No. You've got a deficiency in selling. . . . You seem to have the attitude that people have got to read your newspapers. Well, they don't have to read them. I think you can do a better selling job. . . ."

Knight smiled. "You certainly have been frank with us."[2]

Within a few months, Jack Knight announced to the board that he was stepping down as chairman and CEO, handing those jobs to brother Jim. Hills was elected president. Jack Knight remained as chairman of the executive committee and, of course, editorial chairman. A corner was turned and an operating structure and succession philosophy that would mark the next two decades was established. Key to both was the pairing of people with journalism backgrounds and business backgrounds in the top positions, each being a check on the other. JSK, still the primary shareholder, was succeeded as chairman and CEO by brother Jim, a business-side person. Hills, with a strong journalism background, was president. The design was to ensure that neither of the necessary ingredients of good journalism dominated the mix for too long and without strong advocates for each.

FINDING ALVAH CHAPMAN

Despite Thomas's criticism, some progress was already under way on a more up-to-date management operation. Byron Harless, a Tampa psychologist, had been hired as a consultant for personnel planning and development, and Knight and Hills had talked about a succession plan. One person emerging on the succession horizon in 1967 was Alvah H. Chapman Jr., who had been hired in 1960 by Jim Knight as assistant general manager in Miami.

Chapman had been a spectacular organizational success, doubling *The Miami Herald*'s business and introducing both rigor and technology to its processes. He was able to move quickly, he said in a 2002 interview, because, "as [Jim Knight's] assistant, I could do anything, go anywhere. Nobody knew what my job description was, and I didn't care to write it down. So . . . [I could] talk to anybody, get any figures I wanted to about any of the operations, and just kind of meddle around all I wanted to. . . . It was a great way to learn the business."

His hiring was another of those spontaneous events characteristic of Knight Newspapers' operations during the period. It was not willy-nilly or frivolous, but neither was there any particular grand design at work. Jim Knight decided he needed an assistant to manage day-to-day affairs of the newspaper while he focused on the design and construction of a huge new *Herald* building. Chapman, whom Knight knew through Southern Newspaper Publishers Association activities, happened to be at loose ends, having just sold his ownership share in the Savannah, Georgia, newspapers.

Chapman was of a newspaper family, his grandfather and father having been publishers of *The Columbus Ledger-Enquirer* in Georgia. He graduated from The Citadel at the top of his cadet class in 1942 and led his bomber squadron on thirty-seven combat missions over Europe. He returned to his Columbus roots after the war, but quickly outgrew that and moved up to become general manager of the *St. Petersburg Times* before buying a piece of the Savannah company with an Atlanta banker. After three years, he and the banker decided that banking and newspapers were a poor mix and both sold their interests, freeing Chapman for Jim Knight's overtures.

What Knight got in Chapman, at thirty-nine, was a highly organized mind with a great affinity for details, a strong moral commitment, and, through his military education and high-risk combat experience, iron discipline. Those traits made him a high-potential manager. His early years as grandson and son of local newspaper publishers made him appreciative of a newspaper's role in a community, though virtually all of his work experience was other than in a newsroom.

Dependence and Independence

As the end of the sixties neared, the larger family-owned newspaper companies were warding off punishing inheritance taxes and finding money for expansion by going public: Dow Jones in 1963; Richmond Newspapers, which was to become Media General, in 1966; Gannett and The New York Times Company in 1967; and Lee Enterprises in 1969. Faced with the same set of problems, Knight Newspapers' directors were watching closely. But Jack Knight was skeptical.

"When you go public," he grumbled to his editors gathered outside of Philadelphia in 1969 for one of their annual get-togethers, "you lose control of your destiny."

For JSK, independence, the ability to make editorial judgments free of any outside influences, was an absolute necessity. "I know what I know, I know what I think. I'm not afraid of anybody. I have my own code, how to live, and I live up to it," he once wrote in his "Editor's Notebook" column. He not only liked that attitude on the part of his editors, but he also insisted upon it, and their independence in thought and action extended even to independence from him, despite the fact that he owned the company and all its newspapers.

People not understanding, or not believing, how deeply he lived independence for himself and his editors would have considered surreal an exchange that happened at that 1969 editors' meeting. During the presidential campaign of 1968 that pitted Richard Nixon against Hubert Humphrey, Knight, a moderate Republican by nature and philosophy, had been impressed by Nixon. In an "Editor's Notebook" he praised Nixon's New Economic Policy, essentially a first iteration of his "trickle down" economic theory. All of Knight's newspapers printed Knight's weekly column, though often, and never with penalty, expressing strong editorial exception to his political stances. The editors' independence and local autonomy extended even to the endorsement of presidential candidates, but in the weeks preceding the 1968 election, JSK did something unprecedented. Editors received a brief telegram from him beginning with, "I suggest you may want to . . ." take a close look at Nixon's economic policies. No firmer than that. Yet during the question-and-answer session following his after-dinner speech at the Philadelphia meeting, he was confronted by a red-faced and outraged John McMullan, newly appointed editor of *The Philadelphia Inquirer* and a *Miami Herald* veteran, who began with, "Jack, how dare you send such a telegram!" He followed with a sharply disapproving mini-lecture about the dangers of corporate-think. After McMullan sat down, Knight, who had stood unblinking during his editor's tirade, said he had thought long and hard about it and felt it was important that the editors at least understand Nixon's policy. But he then conceded that he probably should not have sent the telegram. In fact, about half of his newspapers endorsed Nixon and about half endorsed Humphrey.

While Jack Knight grumbled about "losing control of your destiny" and endangering independence by going public, he understood the realities of inheritance laws and the need for money for growth, so he did not actually oppose the move to offer stock to the public; after all, he held the vast majority of it.

And as the company's Wall Street debut neared, he was at times enthusiastic.

Nelson Poynter owned the *St. Petersburg Times* in the 1960s and willed it to the Poynter Foundation, assuring, he felt, the Florida paper's independence from the rigors of the stock market, which he felt was crucial. His editor, Eugene Patterson, greatly appreciated the legacy and the latitude it provided compared with his profit-nagged peers, so he told this story often and with great relish:

> Jack [Knight] saw Nelson at a Gridiron dinner in Washington. They were in the men's room, standing at the urinals beside each other. And Jack leaned down to Nelson, who was a diminutive guy, and he said, "I've got an announcement coming up next week and I wonder what you think of it." Nelson said, "Well, what is that?" And Jack said, "I'm taking Knight Newspapers public. Whaddya think about that, Nelson?" And quick as a shot Nelson replied, "Jack, I think it'll be just fine—as long as you're alive." Nelson loved to quote that conversation. He was vastly amused by it. Knight was not amused.[3]

At that time, 1969, the merger of Knight Newspapers and Ridder Publications was not on the horizon. JSK and other insiders owned most of the stock of Knight Newspapers, and Wall Street was years away from fundamental changes in the investing environment that would make Poynter's riposte prophetic.

As Chapman recalled years later, "Jack wasn't opposed to going public. He was opposed to talking with the analysts." In fact, in his first—and, it turned out, only—meeting with analysts after the 1969 public stock offering, a time when most owners try to impress the Wall Street specialists with their grasp of the realities of public ownership, Knight declared, "You are not going to tell me how to run this company." In Chapman's words, "He told them to go to hell."

Knight's confidence in his ability to control the company and maintain independence carried into the seventies. In 1972, his grandson, John S. Knight III, then an editorial writer at the *Detroit Free Press*, expressed concern about the future of publicly held newspapers. Jack Knight wrote to him, "I do not share your apprehension that the company may someday fall under control of market investors, bankers, or business people having no real interest in good newspapering. . . . Professional management now realizes how imperative it is to have a great 'product'—a term I detest—to sell. There will always be editors, managers, and good production people to work together for the institution which is greater than any of them."[4]

But a strategic decision early in the going-public process would ultimately undermine those brave words and intentions. Many family-owned companies going public in the 1960s did so by establishing two classes of stock, one with voting shares and power retained by the family members, the other public shares without voting rights. Knight Newspapers did not do that.

"There was no serious discussion about two classes of stock," Chapman would explain. "We were advised by Goldman Sachs, our financial adviser, that the marketability of the stock would be better if we had only one class. The Knights were going to retain most of the stock anyway, even after going public. It did not seem a pertinent question at the time."

The Deal Is Done

The Ridder board had made the same calculation backed by the same lack of concern about the immediate future because the vast majority of stock was in the hands of family members. By 1973, however, Bernie Ridder was actively concerned about succession at Ridder Publication, Inc. (RPI). Alvah Chapman, who would in 1974 help negotiate Knight's acquisition of Ridder Publications, told an interviewer years later, "We found out later that the main reason they wanted to merge was that they could not figure it out internally who was going to succeed Bernie. Bernie was capable of running it—they had all confidence in him, but they didn't have confidence in Joe Ridder, who was the next brother in line, and Dan, who was the next brother to him. They just didn't think either one of them could run it, or maybe they didn't want to get into other family."

Knight Newspapers was also in a mood to merge and, Chapman said, "explored several merger opportunities" during 1973 and early 1974, "but not seriously . . . just kind of fleeting conversations." That is until March 1974, just before the American Newspaper Publishers Association convention, when Chapman called Bernie Ridder and asked directly if he would be interested in a merger of Knight and Ridder. His answer was yes, he'd like to talk about it.

Hills and Chapman negotiated with Bernie Ridder and Ben Schneider, RPI's chief financial officer. According to Chapman, "Bernie told us that when it came time to settling the matter of . . . how many directors you're going to have, he said he needed five directors, one for each of the three branches of the family" plus Washington insider and presidential adviser Clark Clifford and Schneider. It was also agreed that Bernie Ridder's only role would be as chairman of the executive committee. Knight would have ten board members and Hills and Chapman would continue as CEO/chairman and president, respectively.

All this suited the Knight brothers, despite the fact that Jack Knight had often said he never wanted to own more newspapers than he could read in a day. Said Chapman: "They [the Knights] were not at all reluctant. They saw it as a good fit economically, and they could see that the Ridder papers were not particularly strong journalistically, and they saw the prospect of helping strengthen their papers journalistically, which would enhance their own prestige and their own sense of accomplishment."

But there was a devil in the details of the merger that, again, would significantly affect the new company's future. The merger was done on a "pooling of interests" basis, meaning that there would be only one class of stock, as each of the two predecessor companies had done five years earlier when they went public. Under the then-existing law, later changed, a pooling of interests had enormous tax advantages over its opposite, a direct purchase of one company's stock or assets by the other. The pooling of interests method required that the companies be treated as fully equal and the burdens and benefits equally distributed among the shareholders, thus only one kind of stock was permitted. In addition, at that time the New York Stock Exchange did not allow two tiers of common stock for its listed companies.

As the majority of shares in the new company were held by Knight and Ridder family members and trustees, this arrangement did not seem to be a problem. It would, however, within a few years make Knight Ridder more vulnerable to outside fiscal pressures than most other newspaper companies with their two classes of stock.

By November 1974, the deal was done: ten shares of Ridder stock for six shares of Knight Newspapers. Despite their five years as public companies, Knight and Ridder were still closely held: Almost half of the ten million shares of Knight Newspapers was controlled by officers and directors, 46 percent of them by the Knight brothers; Ridder family members also controlled about 50 percent of RPI shares.

Predictably, at least two members of the Ridder family were not happy with the deal. Eric and Joe Ridder announced that they would vote against it. As they owned only 9.6 percent of the company's shares, their opposition was futile. On November 30, 1974 the new company was born. According to *Editor & Publisher* magazine, the merged company had:

‣ Thirty-five daily newspapers in twenty-five cities from coast to coast

‣ Weekday circulation of 3.8 million; Sundays 4.1 million

‣ A nationwide news and feature service

‣ Full-time employees numbering 14,500; physical assets of $240 million; total assets of $468 million

‣ Operating revenue of $506 million and net income of $36 million[5]

At the start of 1975, job number one was "strengthening the papers journalistically," something the people settling in at Knight Ridder Newspapers Inc. headquarters on the sixth floor of *The Miami Herald* building were confident they knew how to do. It was, for them, a matter of moving some people out of former Ridder newspapers and moving Knight people in. As it turned out, by design or happenstance, the first such exchange would involve me. I shared the corporate confidence, but quickly discovered that doing what our experiences of the 1950s and 1960s taught us wouldn't meet all the coming tests, for the 1970s were turning out to be radically different from any preceding decade—in values, in the business environment, and in the way people looked at themselves and their institutions. Change would be the only constant.

Wichita: A Marriage Made In . . . ?

"For the first two years, just do what you know how to do and you'll be a hero." —
Jim Batten to the author, 1975

BYRON R. HARLESS grabbed your attention. Tall, rangy, shock of white hair atop a head always thrust energetically forward, falcon eyes. As Knight Newspapers' headhunter, psychologist, and trusted friend of Lee Hills and Alvah Chapman, his sign-off was mandatory for any meaningful jobs in the newly formed Knight Ridder Newspapers, Inc.

So when he looked me in the eye and said with only the thinnest hint of a smile, "You summbitch, you better make this work," my response was, "Yes, sir, I will."

"This" was the editorship of two newspapers in Wichita, Kansas: the morning *Wichita Eagle* (122,000 daily circulation) and the afternoon *Wichita Beacon* (48,000 circulation)—a challenging enough proposition. But that wasn't the primary thrust behind Harless's admonition. It was the summer of 1975 and Wichita would be the first place that a Knight editor and a Ridder publisher would work together; the first consummation of the odd-couple marriage that, in 1974, had made Knight Ridder the largest newspaper company in the country in terms of weekly circulation.

Following the merger, like most young, ambitious Knight News-papers editors, I looked at the map of the new company and devel-oped a list of targets. Wichita was not among them. In the summer of 1975, after four years as news editor of the Washington bureau, I was anxious to run a newspaper again. Bureau life, particularly in Washington, can be exciting, but Watergate was behind us and the capital had returned to the routine and unappetizing business of making legislative sausage. Bureau life, particularly in Washington, can also be frustrating: You lob journalistic shells out across the country but have no control over who, if anyone, prints them and how they are displayed. So, with dozens of other would-be newspa-per editors, I held up my hand; I wanted once again to make the decisions about what a newspaper looked and felt and smelled like.

In July, our family had fled sultry Washington for a cooling week in the mountains of North Carolina, taking advantage of the hospi-tality of Libby's parents in their log house atop Little Mountain near Valle Crucis. The unexpected phone call came from Derick Daniels, then vice president for news at Knight Ridder. "How would you like to be executive editor of two newspapers in Wichita, Kansas?"

"Sure like to talk about it," I said, and we made plans to meet back in Washington in a week. Meanwhile, I had Wichita to think about; but how, isolated up there on the mountaintop? In the Littles' bookshelf was a 1942 Compton's Encyclopedia. I grabbed the K vol-ume and was alphabetically guided to a picture of a grain elevator. The article began: "While Kansas has produced no notable people. . . ." Then it went on to talk of wheat and cattle and a little about airplanes. It didn't mention newspapers.

But there were two newspapers in Wichita, the state's largest city, and they had distinctive histories, as later research revealed. In 1959, *Time* magazine had, in fact, commented on them, calling Wichita "the bottom of the barrel of American journalism." The assessment was based on a tawdry background of fierce rivalry between *The Wich-ita Eagle*, owned by the Murdock family (not to be confused with the current media mogul Rupert Murdoch), and *The Wichita Beacon*, owned by the Levand family, whose newspaper operatives learned their craft at the feet of the notorious Bonfils of Denver.

Time reported: "Trying to outdo each other in sensationalism, they reach desperately for banner headlines, inflate insignificant news, and spend most of their time shrieking at each other, e.g., TOP EXECUTIVES OF EAGLE BRANDED AS LEADERS OF ABORTIVE POLITICAL PLOT." The magazine went on: "When a girl (sic) staffer at the *Beacon* shot herself, the *Eagle* tried to associate a Levand with the case. A rumor that a Murdock relative was homosexual caused a *Beacon* campaign for an ordinance to require the registration and fingerprinting of every pervert in town." That was in 1959, not 1859.

Those gutter struggles ended in 1960, when the Murdock family finally bought out the exhausted Levands. But, by 1972, the Murdock heirs were equally weary of their own endless, internal struggles over the newspapers. The leading stockholder, with a third of the shares, was Britt Brown, great-grandson of Marshall Murdock, who had founded the *Eagle* a hundred years before. Other Murdock family members owned portions ranging from one-sixth downward, so Brown was in control. He and his attorney, Paul Kitch, dominated the board of directors.

"Scorched Earth" Policy

It was an expansive time in the U.S. newspaper business, with companies such as Knight, Gannett, Ridder, Thomson, and Harte-Hanks constantly on the prowl for acquisitions, and the bidding wars were fierce and high-stakes. Brown assigned Kitch to hang out the "For Sale" sign and negotiate a deal. To make the newspapers' bottom line more attractive, Brown launched what long-time staffers recall as "the scorched earth policy," a yearlong, determined slashing of staffing levels, pay scales, newshole—shorthand for the space devoted to news—and coverage. In a front-page editorial, he declared an end to investigative reporting; new coverage rules were written to make sure that local advertisers were not offended by stories; the most talented and highest-paid staffers were discouraged into resignations.

It worked. In 1973, Ridder Publications outbid Thomson and Harte-Hanks and paid more than $42 million for the company, which at the time was more than twice the highest cash price ever paid for a single newspaper operation, according to analyst Lee Dirks. Testifying in a lawsuit over the proceeds from the sale, Dirks opined that the enormous premium probably justified the $1.2 million finder's fee paid to Kitch and the ten-year, $65,000 annual employment contract extended to Brown. Family minority shareholders and a local bank executor for the Murdock estate did not agree, however, since both Brown and Kitch had been on the board of directors and had not bothered to disclose their side deals with Ridder Publications to other board members or shareholders. After five years of litigation, including numerous appeals, Brown settled out of court and, in 1982, when the U.S. Supreme Court refused to hear his appeal, Kitch was forced to distribute most of his finder's fee to minority shareholders.

So Ridder Publications acquired a newspaper company rich in profit but journalistically and ethically bankrupt. With Brown relegated to publisher in title only, Ridder appointed Clarence Darrow "Duke" Tully as general manager to run the Wichita operation. Tully had been a rising star in the Ridder management firmament since coming on board in 1955. He had never worked in a newsroom, but had dealt effectively with tough labor situations in Ridder newspapers in Duluth and Gary. He was fond of saying, "I play hardball," and he was clearly on the Ridder corporate escalator.

But, in 1974, the merger gave everyone, including Tully, new bosses—the people who had been running Knight Newspapers. And Chapman, Hills, Daniels, and Harless were anxious to begin putting the Knight journalism stamp on the newly acquired papers. Thus, the call to the North Carolina mountains in mid-1975 that, by the end of July, had me, a Knight Newspapers editor, sitting across the desk from Tully for a get-acquainted conversation. Both of us knew that it was not a job interview; the people in Miami had decided I would be the editor. The session was more in the nature of a preflight check of each other, a reconnoiter, and I assumed that Tully had also heard some version of the Harless admonition, "You summbitch, you better make this work."

What he had also heard, if he listened, was the résumé of his new acquaintance, covering eighteen years as a journalist for Knight Newspapers. It told of a senior year at the University of North Carolina covering Atlantic Coast Conference sports for *The Charlotte Observer*; three years of sports writing for that newspaper after graduation; three years as a city government reporter; five years as an assistant city editor, city editor, and national editor; a year in the Washington bureau, then two years as editor of *The Boca Raton News* in Florida, before returning to Washington for four years as news editor of the bureau. What the résumé didn't tell, but what was surely implied by my assignment to Wichita, was how deeply those years had imprinted in me the notions of editorial independence and journalistic rigor as the entire reason for existence of newspapers. Imbued was the idea that a huge and impenetrable wall existed between the news operation and the business operation; that the newspaper business by its nature existed in an alternate universe from all other businesses. Editors, the philosophy dictated, answered to no one save higher-ranked editors.

Tully was undeniably formidable: He was of average stature but exuded an aura and personality that rendered him large in presence: in his early forties, with broad shoulders, light, almost-blond hair, and startlingly blue aviator's eyes—icy and beginning to show the creases that go with staring long hours into high skies. He seemed open, even garrulous, and that first conversation, which he dominated while I mostly listened, became significant to me only years later and in retrospect. Just minutes into our meeting, he was talking about flying airplanes, using his large, thick hands to weave attitudes and angles in the air.

"... [A]nd so I put that bird down in the rice paddy and was totally surrounded and had to take off into the bush." He was talking about the Vietnam War, which explained a couple of the photos on his office wall of Tully, in full-dress Air Force formal, rows of ribbons on his chest, standing next to Secretary of Defense Robert S. McNamara, in one, and next to a couple of senators in another. So, add war hero to his résumé. And add loving husband of Patricia, the strikingly beautiful brunette in the full-length portrait on another wall. They had married in October 1974, five months after Sylvia, his first wife, died. "Sylvia had a brain tumor and was terribly depressed," Tully said in that first conversation, "and one day I went home to lunch and she had shot herself."

Patricia and Duke were married in Acapulco; he had flown there, he explained, in the personal jet of Olive Ann Beech, matriarch of Beech Aircraft Co., one of Wichita's largest employers. Harless's words still echoed in my brain, so I did not raise the obvious question about the propriety of the newspaper's general manager roaring off for his wedding in a primary news source and advertiser's private airplane, but I filed it away.

We talked no journalism and, in fact, discussed nothing of substance. For him, the conversation was a negotiator's ploy, geared toward establishing his dominance. He asked no questions of me, which was perfect as far as I was concerned. I was playing the role of inquiring reporter, and, at any rate, the deal was done. We agreed that I would come back in a week or two, with Libby, for a deeper look at the city and the newspapers. I had already decided I very much wanted the job; the allure of having two newspapers to turn around was irresistible. But there were four other people to consider: Libby, a son who was a rising senior in high school, a son in junior high, and a daughter in elementary school.

A Ride Around Town

The return visit almost quashed the deal. Three wind-blasted days of hundred-plus-degree temperature included a daylong tour of the area in Tully's huge Cadillac, viewing flat, treeless subdivisions sprouting amid grain elevators and hearing how Wichita city schools were deteriorating (translation, turning black rapidly), which dictated living in a suburb, most likely one in the cheaper western areas of town where the featureless plains stretched to the shimmering horizon. Not many good restaurants or much entertainment, our tour guide told his guests from Washington, D.C.; you mostly need private clubs to have a good meal. He drove by two of them that "you won't be able to join" and several comfortable residential areas that actually had some trees where "you can't afford to live."

As Libby and I, wrung out from the heat and tension, collapsed in our hotel room that evening, she was near tears. "That man is evil," she declared, uncharacteristically judgmental. "He's a phony and he doesn't want you here, and I don't see how this can work." While unhappy with the day and Tully's performance, I didn't fully understand what her intuition was picking up, and the trip back to D.C. and the days after were tense. I ached to put the final okay to the deal and, after much discussion, we agreed that the move was worth the risks. We had, after all, moved three times in five years into new and strange circumstances, and the family was, if anything, stronger for it.

I headed west buoyed by some welcomed advice. Lee Hills: "Sit down and write some goals for the next couple of years. Keep them to yourself in a drawer and pull them out every once in the while to see how you're doing." He didn't say what the goals should be, just that they should be privately mine. Jim Batten: "All you have to do the first couple of years is what you already know how to do, and you'll be a hero." And, importantly, "Don't hesitate to call anytime, about anything. I'm here to help you succeed."

Important in our thinking was that I would be reporting not to Tully but to Batten in Miami, under the Knight philosophy of separation between the news and business operations with separate reporting lines to corporate. Batten made it clear that it was only necessary to coexist with Tully or any other Ridder person, who had their own reporting lines to Miami. So the Merritt family became Kansans, at least "for three to five years," we thought privately, then it would likely be off to somewhere larger and more accommodating. Meanwhile, a huge journalism task lay ahead.

A Modest Start and a Modest Goal

How large a task I began to discover immediately, when the story announcing the new executive editor's arrival amounted to six inches—on the business page.

Following Hills's advice, I wrote down some goals. The first one, for the first year, was to get to the point of not being embarrassed by my newspapers twice a day. The desk drawer I put those goals into revealed just how formidable that task would be. In it, a folder marked "newsroom policies" contained a series of memos outlining some of the rules invoked during the "scorched earth days" of preparing the newspapers for sale to Ridder. One, noting that the *Eagle* had reported the rape of a woman in the downtown Macy's department store parking garage, declared that henceforth, the address and location of crimes related to businesses would not be reported. Another established that "favorable movie reviews will always appear on the page containing the movie advertisement; unfavorable reviews will always appear on some other page." Another rule: Wichita's economy is heavily dependent on four aviation plants—Boeing, Beech, Cessna, and Learjet—and in the event of an airplane crash, the paper would not report the make of plane, unless it was a Piper or some other brand built elsewhere. Another was a list of (presumably, to a newcomer) prominent people whose names would not appear in a negative light in the newspaper without clearance from "the second floor." The newsroom was on the third floor; the business office was on the second. And there were instructions to make sure that some "good news" was on the front page of the newspapers every day, adorned with the round, yellow smiley-face icon then popping up everywhere. Pointedly, the definition of "good news" included store openings and important new building permits. I assumed the smiley face was in case some feckless reader didn't understand he was reading good news.

It took only a week for the first cultural skirmish. The *Eagle*'s "ears," the space on each side of the Page One masthead, were, to my eye, typographically cluttered and not sufficiently useful to readers. Among the clutter was a reference to a Weatherline telephone number that seemed superfluous, since the weather was reported just above it. That seemed like a place to make a small but reader-friendly start on change. Early in the morning after the first revamped "weather ear" appeared, Tully, under a full head of self-righteous steam, was in my office and in my face.

"That space is the publisher's prerogative," he declared, "and that space is under contract." He did not explain to whom or for what reason, and I didn't ask, immediately realizing that I should have inquired about the arrangement before changing it. It simply had not occurred to me that space anywhere on the front page of a newspaper would be for sale in any fashion. I found something else to do with the weather ear for the time being. And the time being wasn't very long, for within a few months Tully was gone, hired away to San Francisco to manage the joint operating agreement involving the *San Francisco Chronicle* and *San Francisco Examiner*. For Wichitans, just getting their first taste of corporate journalism's gypsy tendencies, his move was a jolt, particularly since he had talked widely and fervently around town about his desire to remain forever in his newly adopted city, to retire there someday and teach journalism at Wichita State University, then be buried next to Sylvia. It was the last we'd hear of Tully for several years until, through a bizarre set of circumstances, everybody in journalism would hear of him again.

Tully's sudden departure was a relief, for our ambitions and personalities and vastly different backgrounds inevitably would have led to more substantive confrontations. But the succession plan for Wichita became immediately clear when Eugene L. Lambert, publisher of the Duluth newspaper and a long-time Ridder labor negotiator, was assigned to Wichita as general manager. He was also named president of *The Wichita Eagle & Beacon Publishing Co.*, a title addition that signaled coming changes.

My days and nights and weekends were filled with trying to meet my first modest goal, so Lambert's arrival did not seem particularly significant to me; after all, I didn't work for him; I worked for Knight Ridder. Ed Lahey, the crusty Chicago newsman and later Washington bureau chief for Knight Newspapers, had been fond of saying, "The only thing I require of my publisher is that he remain solvent." That made sense to me. As long as Lambert, or any other general manager or publisher, got the ads sold, the papers printed and distributed on time, and poured money into the newsroom budget, he was doing his job. Mine was to tell news.

I had grown up in newspapers in which the business-side people, from the top down, were not only never seen in the newsroom, they were in fact unwelcome in that precinct of fierce independence and assumed rectitude. I could go about my journalistic tasks without reference to or regard for anyone else in the building. If Jim Batten was happy, I was happy. If Gene Lambert was not happy, that was corporate's problem, not mine.

Gene Lambert wasn't happy. He had operated in newspapers in which the publisher dominated not only the total operation but often the community as well. He had been mayor of Duluth, a prominent social figure there, a power in labor relations, active in civic affairs. He had never been a journalist. The editor, he made clear in our first conversation, was in his view simply another department head, no different from the advertising and production and circulation managers. Well, okay, I thought, he's working for the Knight people now, so I should mind my business and he his.

It would not be quite so clear-cut, however. Lambert brought with him a Ridder tradition of executive perks, such as company cars and private club memberships. Suddenly I was the beneficiary of a corporate *quid pro quo*, with the velvet inducement of a new automobile and memberships in an exclusive, old-line downtown club and a very nice country club within five minutes of my house. I did not know quite what such perks had to do with making a good newspaper, but if they were offered and there were no strings attached, why not?

No Place at the Table

A standard operating procedure at many newspapers, including Wichita's, was a weekly meeting of department heads chaired by the general manager or publisher. As I walked into my first such Wednesday meeting, I found a long table seating ten, with nine places filled and the tenth, at the head of the table, awaiting Tully's arrival. There were chairs around the periphery of the room and I took one. At the table were the managers or assistant managers of production, circulation, retail advertising, classified advertising, personnel, community relations, and the chief financial officer. All of them reported to Tully.

I was in shirt sleeves, tie pulled down, cuffs rolled up, as was my working habit. The others, all male, were in two- and three-piece dark suits. Tully swept into the room, pulling on a suit jacket. Those around the table did not actually leap to their feet, but they visibly snapped to attention. Reports were made, conversations had, and it was over.

There was no talk of journalism, which both bothered and pleased me. It bothered me because I thought journalism was what the enterprise was about. It pleased me because I did not want to have to begin teaching journalism to people with no background in it, particularly against the sort of odds the room presented.

The Wednesday sessions continued under Lambert, and I listened from my accustomed chair against the wall, near the door, and rarely participated, since none of the discussions were about anything journalistic.

Within a few weeks, Batten came for a "how ya doin'?' visit. As I pulled into the *Eagle*'s parking lot from picking him up at the airport, I searched for and finally found a parking space a few hundred feet from the building. Next to the door were four parking spaces covered by an awning, all taken.

"Who parks there?" Batten asked.

I told him that Britt Brown (who at that time still had a ceremonial office in the building), the general manager, the chief financial officer, and the production manager used the covered area.

"Hmm," he said, nothing else.

It was a Wednesday and Batten sat in on the weekly session, one of the regulars having given up his seat at the table.

Afterward, he said, "Why aren't you sitting at the table? Why are you over by the wall?"

"The seats were all filled and I just haven't made an issue of it," I said. "Doesn't seem important."

"Hmm."

A few days later, an unsmiling Lambert told me to park henceforth under the awning (the production manager having been evicted) and, on Wednesday, I was at the table next to Lambert (one of the advertising people having been moved to the periphery). Neither Batten nor I were personally inclined to worry about or value such things, but he properly invoked the symbolism to make an important point to Lambert and the others that the editor mattered.

Batten's standing on ceremony about the small things took on importance late in 1976, when Lambert's title was changed to president and publisher. "Vice president" was added to my executive editor tag. Not to worry, Batten said, it's part of the long-term plan under Chapman, the KR chairman, to install publishers at every newspaper, but the reporting relationships would not be changed by the titles.

Straightening out such things as seating and parking was the easy part. Much else was agonizing for a couple of years—agony that was relieved only by the knowledge that the newspapers were getting better, thanks to hard work, some good early hires on key desks, and continuing interventions by Batten and the other people at Knight Ridder in Miami.

Job one was to recruit better staffers to fill some of the spots scoured out during the presale cutbacks. The problem: no budget for recruiting staff. Lambert's view of recruiting journalists, who were in his mind simply fungible assets, was: "Use your contacts and call people on the phone. Why do you need to bring them here? You can check them out and interview and hire them by phone."

And there was no budget for relocating people once hired. "If they want to work here badly enough, they'll get themselves here." As this was *The Wichita Eagle* and south-central Kansas, not *The New York Times* and the East Coast, that clearly wouldn't result in impressive hires. Batten intervened with budget help.

Job two was dealing with the past in other ways. The family shareholders' lawsuit against former owner Brown and lawyer Kitch was coming to trial. One of the issues was Brown's role in the continuing operations of the newspaper. He had none—a fact made very clear to me at the outset by Knight Ridder—but he had a ten-year employment contract and the suing family members needed to demonstrate that the contract was a sham, that he did nothing to earn the money and thus the contract payments should properly be part of the sale proceeds and should be split with them.

Said Lambert: "When that comes to trial, you may be called to testify about Britt. If you are, you need to say that he is very involved in the operation of the newspaper." I certainly did not want to perpetuate that idea around the community, and more important, testifying that way sounded a lot like perjury to me, so I appealed to Lambert's corporate boss, William Ott, who sighed and said, "I'll take care of it." He presumably did, because Brown settled out of court and, soon thereafter, Knight Ridder bought out the rest of his contract, and another covered parking space opened. Within days, however, Lambert announced that henceforth, any communications with Miami corporate would go through him. I told him, diplomatically I felt but firmly, that was not my understanding of how it was supposed to work; that talking with Batten and other people in Miami was crucial to doing the job that had been described to me. I heard no more about it, but then it was difficult to hear much of anything through the frosty air between us.

Hang in there, Batten kept saying. Lambert will retire soon and we'll get you a publisher you can work with. "I promise you it'll be someone with a news background and good journalistic values. Things will get better."

It was not a good four years by many measures, and I was hardly blameless. In my narrow, naive view, the job of the editor was to produce one copy of one really great newspaper. How it was supported, how many were sold, and how they were distributed was somebody else's responsibility. I was to do my job, separate from all that, and they were to do theirs. Separation, protecting the independence of the news operation from both inside and outside pressures, trumped all other cards. The advertising director kept complaining about "purist" newsroom people so inflexible in their journalistic virtue that they were of no help to him; the production manager fumed aloud about the newsroom's "arrogance"; the personnel director roared about "elitism." They were right about at least some of that, but I was fighting out of a defensive crouch.

Another One?

I eagerly anticipated Batten's phone call following Lambert's 1979 retirement.

"Want to tell you about your new guy," he said, "but first I have to tell you that he's from the Ridder side." I went coldly silent. "I know what I promised, but don't make any assumptions about him. You have to meet him before you make any judgment."

Did he have a news background? "Well, ah, no, but you gotta meet him. Don't leap to any conclusions. Why don't you come to Miami and get acquainted?"

Norman J. Christiansen was a bundle of fissile energy. Even at rest he seemed to be exploding. For our meeting in his office at Knight Ridder headquarters, he had arranged two straight chairs only three feet apart in the middle of the room. He was a large man full of tics and flailing hands and, at the end of a long right leg crossed over his left, a constantly bobbing foot. I was wary. Here was the new publisher-to-be, another Ridder old retainer, a former FBI agent whose only direct journalism experience was as a reporter on his college newspaper. On his lap was a yellow legal pad with carefully prepared notes that he referred to constantly.

He told me about his background, his ideals, how he had spent the previous five years as a vice president of operations for KR in Miami learning about the Knight philosophy of newspapers (being "knight-ized" was the shorthand Knight Newspapers veterans used for that process). We could work well together. He would not try to run the newsroom. He liked what he saw in the Wichita newspapers.

His was a well-thought-out, sensitive introduction that ignored the fact that there were no decisions to be made, the deal had already been done. But I was impressed, which apparently mattered both to him and to the corporate people. And it did work out. With Christiansen as the publisher, what had been a four-year war between the second floor and the third reached a comfortable détente. I could do journalism with a partner who encouraged and appreciated journalism, who understood and valued the natural tension between the business role and the journalism role, and who was willing to work to balance that tension.

He was tested on that point after only a few months in Wichita, when a couple of news judgments inflamed local car dealers who were already upset with the newspapers because of aggressive advertising price increases. All but one of them joined in a boycott that lasted almost nine months and put heavy pressure on the papers' bottom line. The boycott finally ended when a car dealer told me, "We have punished the *Eagle* as much as we can afford to." Translation: They weren't selling many cars. Unlike the Charlotte experience, however, and even with Christiansen's unflagging support, there was no budgetary forgiveness this time. In an ominous signal of the new rules of corporate journalism, the hangover from the auto dealer boycott turned out to be even worse for the newsroom than the reality of it. Constant bottom-line improvement year-over-year had become mandatory, so making up for 1980's boycott-cratered results meant cutbacks for 1981, including the loss of four newsroom positions.

The uniting of a Knight editor with a Ridder business person that Harless had rumbled about and Batten had encouraged me about had turned out to be at least as much continuing horror story as honeymoon for me. But, as the 1980s opened, I had a publisher who was indeed a partner, and the company was beginning to gain some balance and trajectory as the next generation of leadership figured out how to manage three dozen newspapers in an environment in which thousands of anonymous shareholders were allowed a seat at the table.

Good Journalism with Good Journalists

By 1980 and Christiansen's arrival, the afternoon *Wichita Beacon* was moribund, as were most afternoon newspapers. The demise of downtowns, the dominance of evening newscasts, and changes in family lifestyles and working patterns had steadily eroded afternoon newspaper readership. In Wichita, our newsroom staff of 155 was stretched to produce seven morning and six afternoon editions. No editor likes to see a newspaper die, but the *Beacon* was clearly doing that, having dropped from a 1972 circulation of 55,000 to barely 30,000, with some editions carrying as few as a dozen display advertisements. At one point, I asked the president of a local bank, clearly not strapped for cash, why he had dropped the *Beacon*. "The guy came to collect," he said, "and I just decided I didn't need to spend the money anymore." The subscription price was about $1.80 a week. We decided to pull the plug.

If we killed the *Beacon* with journalism and public service as the goal, the result could be a much-improved morning *Eagle*. If we did it with maximization of profit as the goal, the result would simply be the disappearance of a newspaper and the layoff of about fifty journalists. With the support of Batten and Hills, we did it right. *The Wichita Beacon*'s best features, including all of its comics and columnists, were incorporated into the *Eagle*; no newsroom staff were laid off, although we gave up a dozen positions to natural attrition over two years; we beefed up the Sunday *Eagle* and added daily op ed pages.

But it was the retention of most of the newsroom staff that provided, virtually overnight, a margin for excellence that allowed the *Eagle*'s journalism of the eighties to erase the agonies of the seventies.

Good journalism attracts good journalists, and now we had access to both. With the margin, we were able to pursue the important stories that do not present themselves either in the routine of coverage or in short-term disasters. We devoted two reporters for three months chasing down all of the area's National Merit Scholarship semifinalists from ten years before to discover why most of them were no longer in Kansas. The series, "Kansas' Brain Drain," was revelatory. We reported in depth on a private-government scheme to build a coal gasification plant in Wichita, though that process had long been proven not viable. It wasn't built. We spent six months developing an extensive project on the state's water problems ("We're Running Out") that led to important changes of both attitude and approach. We were on a roll that, by 1984, had *Time* magazine—which years before had declared Wichita "the bottom of the barrel" of American journalism—recognizing us as one of five smaller papers that by virtue of our size could never make its list of the nation's top-ten newspapers but did that level of work.

But critical changes were under way both inside and outside Knight Ridder that would greatly alter the landscape.

A Coda

The final grace note of the early Wichita years would sound in 1985. Darrow "Duke" Tully, by then publisher of *The Phoenix Gazette* and *The Arizona Republic*, somehow offended a Maricopa County attorney who bothered to check with the Pentagon about Tully's much-flaunted military service. There was none. The man who "put that bird down in the rice paddy," posed with a secretary of defense in full military plumage, and claimed 105 combat missions had never been in any branch of the armed forces. Unmasked, he resigned and faded into obscurity.

PART TWO: MIDDAY

5
Introducing Change

"Change is inevitable . . . adapting to change is unavoidable, it's how you do it that sets you together or apart." — William Ngwako Maphoto

AS THE KNIGHT and Ridder marriage bumped along in Wichita, new challenges were rushing at the newspaper business from all angles. By 1975, newspapers' decades-long and luxurious domination of mass-distribution news and advertising had already been eroded by television, but that competition was visible, direct, and bearable once relatively minor adjustments were made in sales philosophy and the approach to news. By the end of the 1980s, however, other changes, many beyond the control of the industry, would begin to chip away at newspapers' core comfort zone, their ubiquitousness.

Newspapers had prospered using a simple formula: Produce one daily package of news and advertising, the larger the better, and distribute it to as many people as possible at as low a price as possible. The pure numbers would do the rest. It was the task of the advertising department to convince business owners that they needed mass distribution in order to reach all potential customers. It was the task of the journalists in the newsrooms to evaluate the day's events and pass along to readers those that seemed most important and/or interesting. But American society was fragmenting in unpredictable ways and business practices were changing. The newspaper industry's one-size-fits-all structure and habits of mind would make it slow to respond to the fragmentation and change.

Tied to massive, expensive, stationary presses and with hours-long production and distribution patterns based on trucks, cars, bicycles, and fourteen-year-old kids, the industry was a 300-pound heavyweight wrestling champion accustomed to dominating the ring, suddenly being attacked from all sides by flyweights wielding knitting needles and pinking shears: a jab here, a snip there, demanding attention and response in many directions at once, sapping energy, and occasionally drawing real blood.

Great social earthquakes were under way: the civil rights and feminist movements, the divisiveness of the Vietnam War, the Watergate scandal, the sexual revolution, urban riots, a series of political assassinations. More subtly, but at least partly in reaction to those thunderous, threatening events, people became increasingly self-referential, altering the nature of civic life as Harvard's Robert Putnam documented so persuasively in his book *Bowling Alone*. The business environment also began to change as the increasing sophistication of data processing allowed new marketing approaches that altered the prevailing concept of a mass consumer market into discrete, identifiable target markets.

Data processing also helped speed an unforeseen transformation in the investing environment. New financial instruments such as IRAs, new investing mechanisms such as the 401(k), a huge spurt in the number and size of mutual funds, the development of indexed funds, and overall, a burgeoning economy would turn the stock market, once the province of a relatively few wealthy individuals, into a brawling, jet-assisted, minute-by-minute mass bazaar. By the late nineties, about half of all adults in the country owned stock, and they wanted to get rich.

Most important in terms of newspapers not being ready for the new environment was the fact that they were, more often than not, directed and produced by people whose almost exclusive focus and passion was the uninhibited gathering, sorting, and presenting of news—the feeding of the broad stream of relevant information essential to a democracy. It was the conceit of those of us in newspaper journalism that reasonable stewardship of our calling—and that is what we considered it—would, by itself, ensure our continued acceptance by the public. We were, after all, doing important—even, to us at least, indispensable—work.

A complicating factor was that newspapers have historically operated out of a defensive crouch. American freedom of the press as embodied in the First Amendment was hard won over centuries, despite efforts by the powerful, including governments, to suppress it. Significantly, the First Amendment itself is expressed as an affirmative negative: "Congress shall make no law . . . abridging . . . the freedom of the press." That was a license to self-define unique among American institutions. Neither clergy nor bar nor medicine nor academe can claim, and have validated in the courts, more latitude of action and deed.

For newspaper companies, the devotion to fundamental origins, the near-absolute freedom to perform—and those deceptively comfortable profit margins—deadened the roar of the tidal waves of change bearing down on them. Thus, newspaper people and newspaper companies entered the last two decades of the last century ill-prepared to respond quickly and effectively when that sound did reach their ears. With little institutional memory about bad times and the natural suspicion of and concern about outside influences, they were interested in extending and perfecting their role in the synergistic relationship with democracy that had evolved over the centuries. They were not interested in matters that interfered with that mission. So the waves washed over them.

The industry's potential responses to the new circumstances were limited by its own altered nature. The sixties and early seventies had been years of concentration as publicly held chains scoured the market for the few remaining independent newspapers. Recall that Jack Knight said he didn't want to own more newspapers than he could read in a day. Behind that plaint was the conviction that in order to manage newspapers properly, one needed to know what they were saying and how they were saying it. For Knight, the top person was supposed to worry about journalistic performance. Corporate managers with dozens of newspapers to oversee can't possibly read them all, but they can read reports of the numbers the newspapers are generating, and when managing newspapers means making numbers move around, reading financial reports is how one manages.

From "Editorial Autonomy" to the "Publisher System"

Knight's former company now owned thirty-seven newspapers strewn from coast to coast. Good managers of far-flung operations know that the way to exercise control and enforce standards is to identify like-minded people and put them in place with the expectation that they will do things close to the way you would do them. That's how corporate cultures are seeded. The former Knight Newspapers people who were in control of the new company wanted their newspapers run by people who believed with Knight that newspapers were "a public trust . . . which serves, advances, and protects public welfare." The people they put in place took seriously JSK's admonition that "we do not sacrifice either principle or quality on the altar of the countinghouse."

But publicly held companies must also worry about the numbers, and the people in charge in Miami in 1975 quickly set about creating a corporate structure to reflect the dual concerns of making quality newspapers while returning reasonable and steady profits in a public market environment.

The core of the organizational plan recognized the natural tension between journalistic concerns and business concerns. Vice presidents for news and for operations were appointed, with separate reporting lines to corporate for the newspapers' editors and general managers. At the highest corporate levels—president and chairman-CEO—the succession plan contemplated alternating people with news and business backgrounds in the top jobs. All of this was aimed at balancing the natural tension. As 1975 drew to a close, the balance existed, with

Lee Hills, with his deep news background, acting as chairman and CEO, and Alvah Chapman, the businessman, serving as president. The duality was replicated down the corporate structure, with vice presidents of news and of operations for groups of newspapers first arranged geographically, and later by size.

At the newspaper level, the general manager and editor slots were rapidly being filled, primarily with editors from the Knight side of the merger and general managers from the Ridder side.

In 1976, however, Jack Knight, at eighty-one, decided it was finally time to retire. As planned, Hills became chairman of the board, Chapman president and CEO. Knight's absence from the executive offices marked the first time in fifty-six years that the journalism he so profoundly valued would not directly hear his voice and feel his presence. He would die in June 1981, at eighty-six years old.

The timing of the 1976 successions was probably just right for him. Debilitating changes were going on all around him. In 1973, his grandson and only potential heir, John S. Knight III, moved from an editorial writing position at the *Detroit Free Press* to *The Daily News* in Philadelphia as an assistant managing editor. "Johnny" had shown an affinity for both the newspaper business and the life of a wealthy young bachelor, and he worked equally hard at both. Educated at Harvard and Oxford and financially secure, he was moving on a typical high-achiever track within the company. But in the early morning hours of December 7, 1975, the thirty-year-old was stabbed to death in his Philadelphia apartment by one of three drugged-out intruders, and the Knight family newspaper legacy was near its end. JSK was also struggling with heart problems, and with changes in the company that gave him concerns he could do nothing about.

One change that Knight constantly grumbled about was the erosion of the "separation of powers" operating principle of keeping news and business on separate sides of a high, thick wall. But once Knight was gone, Chapman, the new CEO and president, felt that the size of the new company dictated a more streamlined structure. He quickly appointed publishers, rather than general managers, in five former Knight papers, including Akron and Charlotte. The "publisher system" resulted in the editor—the person in charge of the newsroom—being clearly subordinate to the publisher—now the person in charge of both the business and editorial functions.

According to Chapman, the change was necessary for two reasons. First, he believed that the number of people officially reporting to corporate was too high; the publisher system would chop that in half. Second, he felt that the dual system at the newspaper level resulted in a lack of effective decision making on truly crucial issues. Too often, he contended, when a general manager and an editor could not agree on an issue—for example, adding a suburban edition—rather than taking the matter to corporate for resolution they would simply not make a decision, not act. By the end of 1976, all of the former Ridder papers had publishers and, by 1979, the publisher system existed in all Knight Ridder newspaper operating companies except Philadelphia. In a few cases, general managers were replaced by newly named publishers who had at least some news background, and it was Chapman's eventual goal to put into all publisher spots people with solid news backgrounds. In many cases, however, the change to the new structure was effected simply by changing the incumbent general manager's title to publisher, which meant, as it did in San Jose and Wichita, that the new top people had no meaningful news experience.

The appointments in San Jose brought together two men who would figure prominently in the company's future. P. Anthony (Tony) Ridder, son of Bernie Ridder, was picked to head the business operation. He had no significant newsroom experience, so the balance at that key newspaper was accomplished by naming Larry Jinks as editor. Jinks was the former executive editor of *The Miami Herald*, a lifelong Knight journalist.

In a bow to the deep tradition of separation, however, some organizational ambiguity was built into the new publisher system. On news and editorial matters, individual editors still had a dotted line connecting them to corporate vice presidents for news, despite the fact that on the organizational chart the editors technically reported to the publishers. Publishers reported to corporate vice presidents of operations on business matters and, when necessary, to vice presidents for news on news/editorial matters. Ambiguity often is the grease in the wheels of progress, and that was true, and necessary, in the case of the merger of the contradictory Knight and Ridder cultures. At newspapers, where the relationship between the publisher and the editor was difficult, the dotted reporting line provided an alternative route around confrontations. If an editor could not persuade a publisher on a point of major journalistic principle, the vice presidents for news understood it was their role to educate the publisher or, failing that, instruct the publisher to do the right thing journalistically. The organizational ambiguity faded over time as editors left the company or retired and were replaced by people not raised in the separation tradition, but the process was often painful and took until the end of the century.

The structure put in place for the 1980s and beyond would be quickly and sternly tested. As that decade opened, internal and external forces began to breach the wall of separation not by main force, but through a series of tiny fractures. Each in itself would not cause a structural catastrophe, but compounded over time they would turn newsrooms into marketing divisions and editors into accountants.

The following four chapters examine some of those forces.

6

External Change: Boomers, Wall Street, and Technology

"Hell, the paint can tells you how to paint the damn kitchen!" — A frustrated newspaper editor

Change One: Boomers or Bust

In 1972, the first battalions of the post–World War II baby boom were reaching maturity, and they weren't reading newspapers. Not to worry, some smart demographers told nevertheless worried newspaper executives, when that huge population bulge reaches middle age, you'll reap the benefits in circulation because the newspaper habit is established in early adulthood; when the boomers get spouses and houses with mortgages and are raising kids, they will be more like their parents. This would have been a good thing, because the average household in the 1940s read *more than one* newspaper every day. The demographers' assurances went against conventional newspaper wisdom—and the traditional rationale for comics pages—that the newspaper habit needs to be formed early in life.

But the boomers had television; they were the first generation that would have TV cradle-to-grave. By the time they reached maturity, the average boomer had watched television for more than 20,000 hours—that's more than two years of round-the-clock viewing. The predicted newspaper readership boom not only didn't happen, the drainage worsened as more boomers matured. By 1998, when the earliest boomers were in their fifties, newspaper readership in the United States had fallen by 57 percent, despite enormous gains in education, population, and number of households. They and their later cohorts—people born between 1946 and 1970—didn't pick up the habit and, for the most part, still have not. The boomers are unlike any previous generation, and they are one-third of the adult population. They will maintain their numerical supremacy well into this century. Dealing with them was a major challenge facing newspapers as the 1970s drew to a close.

In *Bowling Alone*, Robert Putnam identified many of the differences in that generation that was so affected by the social and political traumas of mid-century: They were less interested in politics than previous generations, less likely to vote, far less involved in civic life, more internalized, less trusting of institutions of all sorts, less involved in religious matters, spent far more time by themselves than with other people, though they were more tolerant of people not like themselves.[1] They married later, began families later, and in a huge majority of their households, both adults held full-time jobs.

If one tried to write a description of people not likely to read newspapers, it would include most of those traits. Unfortunately (it turns out), newspapers were being produced by people who were like the boomers' parents—who in fact *were* the boomers' parents—brought up with the newspaper habit, engaged in political and civic affairs, relatively more trusting of institutions, and more extroverted. Could such people produce newspapers that would attract their polar-opposite progeny?

No, the answer kept coming back, though it wasn't for a lack of trying on the part of newspapers. Individually, boomers defied easy compartmentalization; they were determinedly singular. As a demographic cohort, they could be measured and described, but newspapers aren't sold to and read by demographic groups and cohorts; they are sold to and read by individuals who are infinitely more complex than they can be rendered in statistical portraits. The shotgun methods of traditional mass media such as newspapers and general magazines couldn't hit them as they retreated into their personal niches of interests. Yet could those traditional mediums learn to fire BBs at individual targets?

Like newspapers, a handful of broad-interest magazines had dominated their publishing arena for decades, most notably *Life, The Saturday Evening Post,* and *Look,* but they were swept out of business by the first wave of baby boomers. Those and other general magazines made what has been called "a crucial strategic mistake" in the early days of television's explosion on the media scene. Journalist Joe Cappo wrote: "The mass magazines saw television as the enemy, so they erected defensive campaigns in order to keep advertising on their pages. What magazines should have done was to view television as another way to expand their brands. They could have become providers of programming for television. As a result of this attitude, there have been virtually no television programs based on magazine editorial content. Ironically, there are more magazines based on television than television programs based on magazines."[2] They didn't adapt, and they died.

As one result of their miscalculation, suddenly in the mid-seventies bookstalls and newsstands were cluttered with special-interest publications firing BBs. Fascinated by chess? There were periodicals dedicated to it. Kitchen makeovers? Bodybuilding? Quilting? Running? All were nourished by niche advertisers who couldn't care less if *Life* or *Time* had millions of readers; they had discovered demographic analysis and were willing to buy only that fraction of the population intensely interested in some activity or subject that fit with what they had to sell. And they knew that the niche publications could provide just the right targets for their BBs. Newspapers and general magazines could not, and the result was slumping advertising and circulation figures for that genre.

An old journalistic conundrum was demanding to be rethought. It went like this: There are things people want to know and things people ought to know, and they often aren't the same things. Newspapers need to provide both, but if forced to choose, "good" and "responsible" newspapers must make sure people know first what they ought to know, then provide as much as they can of what they want to know. (In today's market-driven journalism, this situation is derisively called "Eat-your-spinach journalism.") The admittedly self-serving definition allowed journalists to focus their efforts on what *they* felt people needed to know, and those things tended to revolve around government and politics—the First Amendment/Thomas Jefferson public service core of the news business. It had worked for decades. With the boomers it didn't seem to work. They were ignoring newspapers at a terrifying rate.

Newspaper companies hired researchers, conducted surveys, founded institutes, convened panel discussions, and mostly fretted about how to attract the boomers. A considerable specialized industry emerged of self-styled experts and consultants with sometimes spooky theories about how to run down the boomers in the multiple and complex niches into which they retreated. The newspaper industry, often subsidized by the companies that made newsprint, spent enormous sums of money trying to discover what people said they wanted to know and to meet those perceived needs. The extensive surveying sometimes was less than helpful or encouraging.

Two problem areas, in particular, frustrated editors.

First, according to the research, a lot of people wanted to know minute details about a lot of different things, thus the rise of the niche publications and the exposure of the weakness of general-interest newspapers and magazines.

Second, people who were surveyed consistently expressed high levels of interest in "local" news, although that term was not defined in most surveys. One interpretation is that "local news is something that happened here," which could lead editors into putting emphasis on the micro-news in a community (e.g., Who's the next high school band director? Where can I sign up for a softball league?). Another interpretation in that "local news is something that has an impact here," and that can lead to quite another set of content decisions in which emphasis is put on stories that might have an impact locally no matter where they happen. When an editor is forced to choose, for instance, between devoting time and space to a story about a strictly local event and a story about a medical breakthrough at Harvard University that affects people everywhere, including the local community, which one is truly "local"?

Spurred on by the hordes of consultants and researchers they hired, newspapers began to scurry about chasing the ever-elusive boomers. They redefined their features and women's sections into "lifestyle" sections that attempted to emulate the edgy new magazine competitors, but most newspapers' efforts in that direction were like a circus elephant doing a rumba: grotesque, superficial, and, finally, unmemorable. Daily newspapers with their generalized staffs and persistent daily deadlines could not compete in style or substance with weekly or monthly periodicals, their knowledgeable specialists, and most important, their practice of viewing their audiences through the small end of the telescope. They redefined front-page news, substituting celebrity and entertainment news for more substantial fare, and dropped traditional concerns about their competition with television and became avid promoters of it.

All of that chasing around behind the boomers expended considerable psychic as well as real capital. In a particularly symbolic moment during a national editors' convention, an exasperated, mid-fifties participant sat still as long as he could while an expensive consultant rhapsodized about newspapers needing to help boomers with their personal lives by running stories about such things as how to paint the kitchen. That was too much, and the editor in the audience exploded: "Hell, the *paint can* tells you how to paint the damn kitchen!"

His rant resonated with many of his fellow editors. The chasing of the boomers was deflecting resources and attention from newspapers' traditional core concerns, those First Amendment/Thomas Jefferson concerns. Targeting the boomers involved creating pages and sometimes whole sections of the newspaper aimed at their specialized interests, including persuading advertisers to support those sections and devoting staff resources to them. This was pleasing to advertisers because the sections were more efficient than general news sections: Their dollars had a better chance of attracting the eyeballs of their potential customers. Stories and pages and sections were created devoted to pets, home electronics, first-home buyers, personal finance, and, yes, repainting the kitchen.

Looked at in a vacuum, those efforts were harmless enough, and probably useful. As long as adequate resources were available, newspapers could do those things and also fulfill their traditional public service role. Editors who were focused on substance could tolerate the additional presence of almost any superficiality as long as the core was supported. But when the inevitable, cyclical resource crunches arrived, it was the democratic core that suffered first. The fluffy, market-driven content was heroin to newspapers. Giving up the pet page that was supported by advertising in order to continue to cover the state legislature properly, but without direct advertising support, was not an option if the corporation insisted on ever-rising profits. Boomers not interested in what's happening in state politics? Then let's cut back there and do more stories about pets and painting the kitchen. If somebody runs off with the statehouse, too bad.

Of course, that didn't work either insofar as attracting boomers went. The boomers were just as likely to read the paint can as the newspaper. Unfortunately for newspaper companies, the next named generation, the Gen Xers, while different from their predecessor generation in many ways, shared the boomers' lack of affinity for newspapers. There was television, of course, but the Xers had an even more troubling way to spend time not reading newspapers: the Internet, where they could not only get news, but also almost instant access to any other information on demand and, most important, access to each other.

Change Two: The Wall Street Syndrome

The fiscal pressures that would ultimately force newspapers to choose between fluff and substance built slowly, an insidious undercurrent in the flood of change. The Dow Jones Industrial Average, which had bumped along in three digits for decades and finally passed 1,000 in 1972, was near 3,000 in 1989, even with an early eighties recession, and in the nineties it burst through 5,000 en route to nearly 12,000 by the decade's end. If you owned a company or were in an industry that was not aboard that rocket, things were difficult.

Fundamental changes in the nature of financial markets fueled the rocket. New investing instruments such as IRAs and 401(k)s hugely expanded the universe of individual investors. The markets became the domain of everyman and everywoman, rather than the playgrounds of the wealthy. Mutual funds, once a device for specialty investors, became a major force. In 1970, there were fewer than 300 mutual funds involving about $48 billion; today, there are more than 10,000 funds controlling $7 trillion on behalf of more than 80 million investors. Conventional wisdom for small investors has always dictated balanced portfolios with reasonable investment horizons, but the drivers of today's market are funds operated by managers for whom churn is money. The resulting market volatility makes short-term thinking inevitable. Mature industries such as newspapers are devalued in a short-term environment unless the companies that own them make the numbers dance the right tune.

CYCLICAL, TOP TO BOTTOM

The Wall Street dynamic creates a dilemma, for the newspaper business is relentlessly and unavoidably cyclical across both time and circumstance. About 80 percent of most newspapers' revenue is from advertising, and the flow of advertising varies day-by-day through any given week. It is light on Mondays and Tuesdays, bulked up by food advertising on Wednesdays and Thursdays, and Sundays are huge. It varies through the year: The holiday-jammed fourth quarter produces more than half of the annual advertising revenue for many newspapers. It varies with short- and mid-term economic trends: Classified advertising, typically 40 percent of all advertising revenue, suffers quickly as the economy slacks off because employment advertising drops, as does auto advertising. The inevitable periodic, brief slumps that any economy incurs are quickly and directly reflected in newspaper revenues. True recessions are absolutely murderous for advertising revenue.

All of this was historically well understood by investors in newspaper companies whose owners and shareholders were in it with the expectation of mid- to long-term profits, which they eventually would receive when the economy bounced back. The hyperactive investing mood of the 1990s, however, brought new and different pressures. All companies, newspapers not exempted, are expected to deal with business cycles in ways that will keep profits steadily rising. When revenues are in a flat or down cycle, the only way to produce ever-rising short-term returns is by cutting costs. The top two costs—by far—for newspapers are people and newsprint. Cutting costs in either place immediately and visibly diminishes the size and quality of the product.

Newspapers are by nature a long-term investment now caught up in a short-term investing culture. In the book *Taking Stock*, researchers from the University of Iowa School of Journalism explain the situation as follows: "When newsprint prices rise or an economic downturn cuts into advertising revenue, excessive concern about the 'next quarter' can lead to quick fixes on the cost side in the form of hiring freezes, downsizing and cutbacks in newshole, [and reductions in] travel and training. Fewer reporters and fewer copy editors and reduced news coverage almost always detract from a newspaper's quality. How much weight analysts and the investors they service give to short-term factors, therefore, can have a direct bearing on what happens in newsrooms across the country."[3]

As with advertising, the flow of news also varies from day to day, month to month, though in a perversely irregular way. Newsroom staffing levels cannot be finely tuned in reaction to short-term events, unlike, say, the aircraft or auto industries where furloughs and layoffs, hiring freezes, and temporary help can adjust basic costs when no one is ordering airplanes or cars, or take temporary advantage when they are. Newsroom staffing inflexibility is real because:

> ▸ Major news has no predictable rhythm. It happens. The big storm, the plant closing, the 9/11 attacks—such events can come singly or in clusters. When major events happen, it's too late to recall furloughed reporters and editors to work; there's no time to run out to hire temporary help while the fire engines howl down the street. Newsrooms must maintain a reasonable, steady level of staffing for such contingencies, even when news is slow.

‣ Routine news doesn't go away just because a plane crashes or a tornado strikes. Even when there are no major, breaking stories, a newspaper committed to its community or state or nation has obligations to the routine business of readers' lives and fortunes. There are lifestyle sections to be filled, city halls and statehouses to cover, sports events and business developments and television listings to be handled.

‣ Even more important, some of the most meaningful and helpful news does not make itself evident either suddenly or as part of the routine. It must be discovered, teased out from the complex organisms of governments, institutions, and businesses. A newspaper operating in the public interest must be more than a crisis-response team and a stenographer of routine events. Investigative reporting, computer-assisted reporting, and fulfilling the press' watchdog role require constant patrolling of the institutions that comprise public life. An unasked question here, a failure to probe there can allow important institutions to be captured by special interests or fall into decay or fail to fulfill their missions.

When short-term fiscal pressures lead to reductions in newsroom staffs, it is obvious that some of those things must be left undone. But what? Good reporters, editors, photographers, and graphic artists are not fungible assets that can be harmlessly exchanged. An effective news operation needs people of varied backgrounds and talent levels to ensure that it can reach all the areas it needs to cover. The distressing reality for a newspaper's public service responsibility is that cutbacks affect most sharply the third and arguably most important category of news: that which does not present itself but must be sought out by smart, experienced reporters. Newspaper owners cannot have it both ways. They cannot cut back news staffs and continue to fulfill what—in terms of sustaining democracy, at least—is their most important responsibility: protecting the public interest.

Such an argument for maintaining quality through bad economic times works fine when investors and the analysts who serve them have a long view. Newspaper companies are historically solid investments for the long haul because of their hefty underlying profit margins, so they can offer a safe haven for investors even during soft times in the general stock market. Beginning in the 1980s, however, long-term thinking became scarce around Wall Street. So-called "mature" industries—that is, those with established profit yields and patterns—lost their luster. "Long term" came to mean next month; "mid-term" the end of the trading day; "short term" five minutes from now. Before the bubble burst, everybody wanted to be part of the dot.com, IPO world where paper millionaires were created daily and no end seemed in sight. Staid, mature industries were largely ignored by both individual and institutional investors except for the small minority of "value" funds.

The investment resources available to support newspaper stocks shrunk, meaning that within the newspaper category itself, the competition among the companies for share of available resources sharpened. Knight Ridder, whose margins historically and for the right reason (i.e., because it insisted on quality newspapers) were among the industry's lowest, came under particular stress. During his time in the early eighties as president and CEO, Jim Batten had relentlessly stressed journalistic quality both inside and outside the company. That's where the business started; that's what it was about. Like his predecessors and mentors Jack Knight and Lee Hills, Batten viewed a reasonable level of profit not as an end in itself but as the fuel for the real enterprise: newspapers as an essential service in support of people and democracy.

ON DEAF EARS

As articulate and persuasive as he could be, however, Batten had a difficult time convincing gimlet-eyed stock analysts and institutional investors to buy that idea. While some analysts linked newspaper quality to long-term financial success, the great majority were not impressed when Batten, in the semi-annual conferences with them, talked about the Pulitzers his papers were winning, the services they were performing for communities all across the nation, the investigative reports that helped keep governments honest, the editorial freedom his newspapers enjoyed. The analysts wanted to get at the numbers, and they saw Knight Ridder's numbers as underperforming in relation to much of the rest of the industry.

If there is a connection between journalistic quality and financial success in most analysts' minds, it goes like this: Quality newspapers should be able to attract more readers and therefore more advertising, which translates into financial well-being. Batten and his journalistic brethren could not disprove, nor disapprove of, that formulation, of course, but missing from it was an important—at least for journalists—element: readers can be attracted and money made in many different ways. Certainly grocery-store tabloids attract readers in hordes and make a great deal of money. But how do they serve the public interest?

Such questions simply don't compute in most of the financial community. "I'm not sure I'd go too far in saying newspapers have a special role in society," Morgan Stanley analyst Douglas Arthur told *Columbia Journalism Review* in 2001.[4] The CJR article went on to say, "Others in the investment community are less diplomatic. 'I think that's a joke,' says one money manager who spoke on the condition that his name not be used. 'The media is manipulated by whoever wants to manipulate it. To say they are high and mighty is an outdated notion.'"

For most analysts and fund managers, publicly owned newspapers are not at all distinguishable from coat hanger manufacturers and cannot be treated any differently. "The second they became a public company, they became like any other business," Lauren Fine of Merrill Lynch told researcher Gilbert Cranberg.[5] But that is not all bad. According to Arthur, of Morgan Stanley, quality "can be a strategic advantage," particularly following the bursting of a speculative bubble, such as in early 2004. "Newspapers become a safe haven."

Along with Gannett and the Tribune Company, Knight Ridder does not have the luxury, in a volatile market atmosphere, of telling the analysts, as Jack Knight did in 1969, "You're not going to tell me how to run my company." Neither do they have the undergirding of family ownership of voting stock to say, as did CEO Donald Graham of the two-tiered Washington Post Company, "If people need more than a 15 percent return they can put their money somewhere else." For a company such as Knight Ridder, consistently underperforming in the eyes of analysts can make money for expansion or acquisitions hard to come by and, because of the single class of stock, render it vulnerable to unfriendly takeover. When the breakup value of a company is higher than its stock value, it becomes a tempting target for raiders.

According to Cranberg and his fellow researchers at the University of Iowa, institutional investors own more than two-thirds of the shares in publicly traded newspaper companies, most of it in mutual funds and other such instruments. Mutual funds are, by nature, short-horizon investments, as the array of stocks in a fund means some will be rising, some falling at any time. If, as happened in early 2000, the newspaper increment of those portfolios is downgraded by analysts, those shares will be in play quickly.

When Jack Knight moaned to his editors in 1969 that "You lose control of your destiny," he was reflecting a legitimate concern about the well-understood contemporary danger of stock analysts' influence on company philosophies. He could not have imagined at that point how bad it would get. When the investment climate changed radically in the last decade of the century, newspapers—and therefore newspaper readers—paid a huge price. By the year 2000, some newspaper companies, including Knight Ridder, had already cut back substantially on their news operations. But it wasn't enough. When newspaper stocks swooned after an across-the-board downgrade by most analysts in 2000, even more severe cuts were made. In 2001, Knight Ridder imposed a 10 percent reduction in personnel to be carried out mostly with buyouts and attrition. Those jobs, chairman Tony Ridder said, would not come back even if the economy improved; they were gone forever. Staff reduction through buyouts hits newsrooms particularly hard because the amount of the buyout is based on years of service and thus is more attractive to the most veteran employees who will then be replaced, if at all, by less experienced people. A newspaper's institutional memory and its news staffers' community knowledge make important contributions to its news coverage every day.

When those assets are removed, it shows line by line, story by story, and news judgment by news judgment.

In 1968, at the nadir of the Vietnam War, U.S. forces were desperately trying to stop the Vietcong surprise Tet Offensive by denying them shelter in friendly villages. This often involved fierce firefights, the burning of huts, and the "neutralizing" of villagers. An ironic and perhaps apocryphal quote attributed variously to a commander, a briefing officer, and an artillery captain entered the language of war: "We had to destroy the village in order to save it." As yet, no serious takeover has been mounted against major newspaper companies, including Knight Ridder, in part because they responded to the downturn by slashing costs. But the question for the future is, at what assessment against quality and public service?

Change Three: Technology

In 1980, Knight Ridder began to experiment with something it called Viewtron. Partnering with AT&T, the company put together a database from resources already available at *The Miami Herald*: information on restaurants, television shows, movie theaters, airlines, cruise lines, and the like, and, of course, news. Viewtron used a specially designed terminal and keyboard to call up, via telephone lines to the *Herald*'s database, information on a television screen. The idea was to see if families would use such a database to find out what was playing at the movies, to make restaurant reservations, to keep up with the news and weather, and to order airline tickets or goods from stores. There was also a bulletin board where people could post notices of their own. It was a test too far ahead of its time, and the effort was shut down after more than five years of national trials. KR's investment was more than $50 million.

THE INTERNET

The Viewtron experiment was a decade before public access to the Internet and before the explosion in personal computers. People were not yet umbilically connected to computers, the videotext Sceptre terminal was unhandy and expensive (AT&T could never get the cost below $400 and the target was $200), and the thing tied up the family

TV set and a phone line. The experiment did produce one precursor of the Internet explosion, however. While the ordering of goods and the making of reservations drew minimal activity, by far the busiest part of the database was the bulletin board. People quickly discovered it was a nifty way to talk to each other, and that's mostly what they did.

Philip Meyer, now Knight Professor at the University of North Carolina, worked on Viewtron for three years. During a 2003 virtual roundtable sponsored by The Poynter Institute, Meyer said: "We made the mistake of thinking in newspaper analogies. Thus the central computer was like a printing press in our minds, and telephone wires were the delivery trucks. We never foresaw anything as free and open as the Internet, or grasped that there would be no central computer. As newspaper people, we were looking for a community-based natural monopoly, like a newspaper, but without the variable costs of paper, ink, and transportation."

Reid Ashe, chairman of Viewtron for seventeen months near its end (and, later, the KR publisher in Wichita and now president and COO of Media General), said to the roundtable: "I believe that at the end [of the experiment], we were finding our way toward a viable service, but we were burdened with too much cost and with a technical design that was optimized for an already-obsolete delivery mode."

Viewtron and Gateway, a similar experiment by the Los Angeles Times Co. in the 1980s, were the first efforts by U.S. newspaper companies to migrate their information advantages to a new technology. Had their trials with the limited technology then available met with more success, they nevertheless would have been overwhelmed in the 1990s by the development of the open architecture Internet and World Wide Web.

Yet Viewtron got some things right. Said Meyer: "It saw that value could be added to newspaper information by adding speed—tomorrow's headlines tonight—archiving, and narrowcasting, (such as) selling last-minute travel bargains. It provided e-mail. It recognized the potential for classified advertising."

Those insights, however, were simply too far ahead of their time.

With the development of the Internet and World Wide Web,

newspapers quickly found a piece of their business franchise seriously endangered. It wasn't news. It wasn't weather. It was classified advertising, which was among the first commercial applications by competitors—job searches, auto sales, help wanted—all searchable with the click of a mouse. That imminent threat, as much as anything, pushed newspaper companies into developing Web presences, and today virtually every newspaper has a Web site that offers not only the newspaper's database but also links to news and advertising sites anywhere. Newspaper companies, including Knight Ridder, participate in online advertising cooperatives tied to their print operations.

Creating such gateways is one thing; figuring out how to attract money through them is quite another. Internet users are willing enough to pay a reasonable monthly fee for access to it, but the notion of paying additional money to other gatekeepers is foreign to them. Newspapers can hardly afford to give away their expensively gathered news content online, but they meet stiff resistance to the idea of requiring people to pay for access to it. Meanwhile, they are having a difficult time persuading major advertisers to move online while staying in the newspaper.

While the Web's first threat to newspapers was financial, by the year 2000, its exponential growth generated another sort of challenge—to the news-and-opinion franchise. Web logs, familiarly called blogs, started in the early nineties with a handful of Web-savvy people with strong opinions they were driven to share with the world. The first blogs were simply electronic diaries posted on individual Web sites, usually with an invitation for browsers to add their own comments. It was yet another proof of the phenomenon the Viewtron experimenters discovered: People are garrulous by nature and crave good conversation. By the end of the decade, software tools for constructing such sites were readily available and hundreds of thousands of blogs actively involved perhaps millions of people. In effect, any person with Internet access became a potential journalist able to post information and opinion to the entire world. Or to post nonsense. Or libel. Or falsehoods.

Traditional news organizations employ a verification and editing process designed to conform their news output to their standards and format. The premise is that "everybody needs an editor"—that is, every piece of writing designed for consumption by others needs at least a second set of eyes on it before publication, to raise questions, challenge assumptions, verify facts, and enforce standards. Most blogs reverse the process: An individual's words are published and the questions, challenges, and verifications (or lack of them) come afterward, if they come at all. The blog world may be journalism's first true meritocracy, as some of its enthusiasts claim, but it also is a ready platform for fools and knaves operating unencumbered by such niceties as accuracy, fairness, and accountability.

That said, a reality of the early part of this century is that traditional news organizations must pay at least some level of attention to the most prominent blogs for several reasons: They can on occasion come up with important information. They can be a way to listen to at least a portion of the public. They constitute a deep fact-checking mechanism, as shown by the rapid exposure of CBS's Bush-Guard records during the 2004 presidential campaign. They are part of a public conversation that often has immediacy and authenticity. They reflect better than any other medium the rich diversity of humankind.

MARKET FRAGMENTATION

The ability to collect and process huge amounts of information that enabled development of the Internet and the transformation of financial markets also gave businesses the ability to more closely control their marketing and make it more efficient. With access to increasingly sophisticated information about their customers, retailers began to challenge the traditional newspaper concept of mass marketing. Why, they asked, should I pay your full rate to put my advertising in front of people unlikely or unable to buy what I am selling? Your newspaper may reach 60 percent or 75 percent of the households in this county, but my customer base resides in only a fraction of those households, and I now know which ones they are. Newspapers initially did not have a persuasive answer to that challenge, but plenty of entrepreneurs did have answers: direct mail; geographically targeted fliers; packages of advertisements bundled together and delivered to discrete areas, including parts of specific

ZIP codes; pseudo-newspapers that combined advertising with warm stories about the merchants, providing a welcomed, "friendly" environment. Such devices and variations on them took small but painful bites out of newspaper revenues.

Newspapers eventually began to offer their own versions of the new devices, including "neighbors" sections aimed at geographic areas, and they tried to persuade advertisers (who were delighted to be saving so much money) that their ads benefited from the credibility that attached to general newspapers. Unfortunately, in the last decades of the twentieth century, newspaper credibility as measured by national surveys was tumbling.

For many merchants, the ability to fragment mass markets meant efficiency. For newspapers, it meant trouble. Geographic fragmentation soon gave way to demographic fragmentation, in which the public was sorted not by location but by characteristics such as income, race, gender, and education. Then came psychographics, in which people were sorted into affinity groups by ideology, values, beliefs, and attitudes, and the groups were given names like "early adopters" or "I am me's." There was no longer any such thing as "the public." Done in ever more complex ways—in part simply because the machines could do it—the slicing and dicing convinced more and more advertisers that mass media was yesterday and that money spent in general-circulation newspapers was spent inefficiently.

And, indeed, general-circulation newspapers couldn't deliver the targeted bits and pieces, but neither could they ignore the demand from advertisers for more efficiency—that is, delivering the most promising customers for less money. One way to do that was for newspapers to become more efficient themselves, trimming their costs to avoid upward pressure on their advertising rates while maintaining or improving their bottom lines. For many, this meant trimming circulation in areas where it was, in effect, subsidized, such as in lower economic areas where maintaining circulation was costly because of turnover (called churn) and poor collection rates on subscriptions, and distant areas where, because of transportation costs, delivering a newspaper was a losing proposition.

This strategy had more than fiscal ramifications; it had social ones as well. When a newspaper views its obligation solely through the prism of profit, it sees only a part of its world, the part susceptible to advertising reach and efficiency. But in doing so, it eliminates from its world certain kinds of people and certain styles of life. It is an ominous sign, because the people most often affected by what amounts to circulation redlining—rural people, poor people, under-educated people—are the very ones most in need of a newspaper's public service efforts. If they don't exist in the newspaper's world, their problems don't exist, either.

7

Internal Change:
Creeping Corporatism
and Catastrophe

"The first step [in the McNamara Fallacy] is to measure what can easily be measured. . . . The second step is to disregard that which can't be measured. This is artificial and misleading. The third step is to presume that what can't be measured easily isn't very important. This is blindness. The fourth step is to say that what can't be easily measured doesn't exist. This is suicide." — Daniel Yankelovich

THE EXTERNAL FORCES working on Knight Ridder and all other newspaper companies affected each in a slightly different way but affected all deeply. All of the companies had to be concerned about the baby boomers and the niche marketing they demanded, and about getting aboard the technology rocket. Private companies and those public companies with two tiers of stock worried less and slightly less, respectively, about the growing muscularity of Wall Street analysts. For a single-stock public company such as Knight Ridder, however, all three trends began to eat away at the philosophical foundations that had made it successful: local autonomy, single-minded editors, and journalistic purpose.

In each case, the damage would be rationalized as necessary for the sort of economic efficiency that the real world—that is to say, the market—demanded, but that facile rationalization did not lessen the impact on the company's journalists and the communities they served.

Change Four: Leave Autonomy Alone

When merger conversations began between Ridder Publications, Inc. and Knight Newspapers, Inc., the companies shared at least one important trait: local autonomy among the newspapers they owned. In both cases, if for radically different reasons, the people in charge of RPI and KNI as separate companies felt that local autonomy was the best way to operate. In both news/editorial and business matters, the people on the scene were best positioned to make all but the most far-reaching decisions, it was felt. They could always be removed if they made too many bad choices.

Within Ridder, autonomy sprang from the nature of the organization. Various family members were the publishers of highly individualized newspapers. It was, in Bernie Ridder's words, a collection of fiefdoms. There was no corporate take on news or editorial policy and little in the way of corporate affairs or staff. It was a family operation. After the company went public in 1969, certain business practices had to be standardized for SEC reporting purposes, but other than that, no one directed the individual papers on details of either business or news judgments.

Within Knight, the autonomy was not familial, but it was certainly by design. Corporate headquarters were bare-bones, an extension of Jack Knight's big brown briefcase. Most of the newspapers were run by a partnership of equals: an editor responsible for the news and editorial operations and a general manager responsible for production, advertising, and circulation. Each reported separately to a corporate officer when it was necessary to report at all. Weeks passed in which there was no contact between corporate people and the local editors and general managers. When the editor and general manager couldn't agree, corporate would decide. There was no detailed corporate policy about news and editorial decisions; the mandate was to produce the best possible newspapers. As with Ridder, when Knight

Newspapers went public, some business practices had to be standardized.

A publicly held company with thirty-five daily newspapers in twenty-five cities, as the merged company became, is a different animal. Even a deep corporate staff would have trouble with seventy different people reporting to it. The Ridder side of the merger presented no problems for the new corporate entity, for those newspapers were run by publishers who were clearly the number one people for that location; the editors reported to and were subordinate to the publishers. The Knight side, however, presented huge problems that went to the core of the separation of newspapers' news interests from their business interests.

In today's profit-driven, highly centralized publishing atmosphere, it is difficult to understand how deeply that separation was ingrained in the editors who ran Knight's newsrooms. In the 1960s and 1970s, those editors were people at middle age and beyond. They had apprenticed in a journalistic atmosphere very different from the one they now occupied. They began their careers in the late 1930s and early 1940s when newspapers were, for the first time in American history, becoming truly professionalized. They and their compatriots were the first escapees from the Bad Old Days of yellow journalism, of William Randolph Hearst promoting a war, of major advertisers who could keep stories out of the paper or arrange for stories to be printed, of the whiskey bottle in the bottom drawer and money sliding under the table. They were serious about serious news, and they were determined that concerns about offending advertisers or other interest groups would not enter into their calculations about news. In many newsrooms, business-side people were simply not welcomed, even general managers. Should the advertising manager show up in the newsroom, the anxiety level would go up several notches. Surely, the journalists believed—often based on painful experience—the advertising person wanted something the journalists were unwilling to provide: a favor for an advertiser or protection from an unfavorable news story. It was tough enough, they felt, doing their job of telling news without such interference from insiders with a different agenda.

The defensiveness, justifiably or not, extended to the journalists' relations with the corporate structures that were buying up all the newspapers in sight. It strikes most businesspeople as both silly and not useful to have to tolerate within any enterprise a segment that considers itself immune from the people who own and run the business and that does not share their single-mindedness about profits. "Just leave us alone," the journalists improbably demanded. "Let us do our jobs without 'external' concerns." While it was an attitude properly based on bad experiences and good journalistic principles, it also was an attitude that most businesspeople neither appreciated nor were willing to indulge for long.

The schism was bearable, if sometimes uncomfortably so, when business was going well, as it did in the decades following World War II. But when newspaper companies' bottom-line performance came under extreme pressure beginning in the 1980s, the journalists' notions about autonomy and immunity would be severely challenged.

Two internal changes—perhaps "drifts" would be a better characterization—began to undermine local autonomy. Both had their roots in financial considerations, but each also crossed the line to affect local news judgments and the Knight Ridder newspapers' relationships with their communities.

CREEPING CORPORATISM

Local newspapers—meaning all of the Knight Ridder papers—are dependent on the local business community for their advertising lifeblood. By the last quarter of the twentieth century, television and magazines had largely absorbed what relatively little national advertising local newspapers enjoyed. An airline or a major food brand could reach more people more efficiently, more quickly, and with more control over quality of presentation through those mediums than through an array of general-interest newspapers with varying rules, print quality, and even page widths. The loss of lucrative national advertising made local advertising even more important, and business managers worked hard to maintain relationships with local businesses. Typically, for instance, a newspaper in a medium-size community would use several banks, giving its payroll account to one, its idle-funds account to another, other bits of business to a third, keeping them all relatively happy and willing to spend their advertising money with the newspaper. The newspapers and local businesses would jointly sponsor events; the executives of the companies would serve together on civic and charitable boards. Working together for the community's overall benefit was a glue that held things together; the not-unreasonable expectation of local businesses was that the newspaper, which coveted their advertising dollars, would reciprocate in the way it spent its own dollars.

That traditional and comfortable coexistence between local newspapers and their advertising partners would begin to crumble as bottom-line pressures grew and the corporation looked for ways to cut costs. The local people in charge of the company's newspapers in the 1980s would dub the search for savings "creeping corporatism." The corporate people called it efficiency and economies of scale.

The template for corporate cost savings was already in place: the purchase of newsprint, one of a newspaper's two largest and most volatile expenses. Negotiating the contract price of such a major item on behalf of all Knight Ridder newspapers made sense because it led to lower prices than each newspaper could get on its own. It was one of the major advantages of group ownership.

Why not, the corporate thinking became, leverage that size and clout advantage by applying it to other purchases? But it was not so simple a matter. When applied to other goods and services, the principle of economies of scale put pressure on local newspapers' relationships with their advertising customers and their communities.

When, for instance, Knight Ridder recognized it could get a slightly better interest rate by consolidating all its newspapers' idle funds in one New York bank, it made sense from the corporation's point of view. But that money was extracted from local communities, and the extraction disrupted well-established relationships with local banks. The incremental interest earned by the consolidation was measurable on the corporation's books; the relationship—and monetary—damage at the local level was not. When *The Wichita Eagle*'s idle funds were spirited away to Manhattan, the head of a local bank called to warn that he would have to rethink all of his bank's involvement with the newspaper. "If you aren't going to support the local community," he said, "we have to take that into account." In another Knight Ridder city, the newspaper and a bank had been longtime cosponsors of a golf tournament, an event that was jeopardized by the move.

As the corporate staff discovered other "savings" such as purchasing supplies—photographic film, for instance—in bulk from a central source, the disruptions to local newspaper-merchant relationships were multiplied. In some cases, irked merchants reduced their advertising or stopped altogether, meaning that while the local newspapers saved pennies on a corporately purchased carton of film, they lost dollars in advertising revenue.

Air travel was a particularly sore point. Knight Ridder mandated that all travel be booked through a national agency that had been instructed to provide only the cheapest possible tickets. Employees, including reporters on assignment, suddenly found themselves flying in nonjet aircraft on circuitous routes that wasted both time and energy. In most Knight Ridder cities, the people booking travel held long associations with local travel agencies, who were, of course, also regular advertisers on the newspapers' travel pages. Those relationships were fractured. The advent of Internet travel booking eased the hassle for individual newspapers, but did not heal the wounds.

A MATTER OF TONE

When editor John McMullan openly scolded Jack Knight in front of all Knight's editors about his Nixon-endorsement telegram, no one in the room—least of all Jack Knight—was shocked. That's how things worked. The periodic gatherings of Knight Newspapers editors were hardly pinstriped affairs; they were occasions to get things off your chest, demand answers and accountability from the hierarchy, then have a few drinks together.

Gene Roberts, editor of *The Philadelphia Inquirer*, recalled:

> Jack Knight, the greatest thing he had goin' for him is he liked an organization in which everybody spoke their minds and even finger-pointed at one department or another. Jack told me one time that he felt most comfortable as a manager when produc-

tion was yellin' at the newsroom for slowin' copy, and the newsroom was yellin' at circulation for not delivering the papers on time and truck drivers were screamin' at the mailers. He said that automatically built in checks and balances, and that if people felt free to say, 'I'm holdin' up my end and you're not holdin' up yours,' it was easier for people like him to manage because problems got out on the table instead of being buried. And that's true. . . . But that changed. People said less and less, and it got to be so that what is wanted is [that] they tell you what the plan is and you to say 'yes sir' and anything less than that is seditious."

The tonal transition evolved gradually. When John S. Knight retired and Alvah Chapman brought his tough business mind-set and military background to the post of chairman, he nevertheless expected to have a staff that would argue with him and his corporate aides, and they did. It was the Knight school of management, and even its leading guru, psychologist Byron Harless, was a player. Harless—who used friendly expletives the way most psychologists use "How did that make you feel?"—contributed to the company lore at a meeting of publishers in which representatives of smaller papers were complaining about the paperwork burden from personnel matters such as workers compensation and insurance. One publisher howled that he did not have the staff to handle such things and that corporate should do it. He raved on and on until Harless, finally insulted, leaped to his feet and said, "You little shit-ass, when I think of every goddamn thing I've ever done for you and you're standing here pissin' and moanin' that we don't do enough!" Most of the publishers, including the complainer, were laughing. That's the way they liked it, and it was effective. As a result of the openness, a workaround was developed instead of having the problem fester in silent resentment.

Batten, for all his rapport with his editors and publishers, brought his Southern mannerliness and sense of decorum to his office of president. One could say anything to him in private, but his serious demeanor in public forums dampened, perhaps by design, the argumentativeness. But it did not dispose of it.

When Chapman was retiring in 1989, he carefully prepared a valedictory for the editors' meeting in Long Beach. Economic pressures were tightening, and the editors were in a surly mood that Chapman did not ease with his after-dinner speech. He talked about dealing with hard times, choosing the metaphor of packing a trunk for a long, hard trip: You first put in bowling balls, then cannonballs, then softballs, baseballs, tennis balls, golf balls, and just when you think the trunk is as full as possible, you realize there's room for BBs, and you pack tight and hard with BBs. The editors listened restlessly, if not resentfully, to what was clearly a call to go beyond the painfully tight operations they already oversaw. The next night, the closing dinner was interrupted by a procession of black-robed editors winding through the tables carrying on their shoulders an object that looked suspiciously like a coffin, murmuring incantations about "cannonballs, softballs, BBs." It was a funny, if edgy, piece of business, and Batten sat through it on the dais, white-faced and unsmiling. When the procession wound its way back out of the hall, Larry Jinks, then senior vice president and the emcee for the evening, salvaged the situation. "I can see we've broken their spirits," he cracked.

But the culture of the editors' meetings—which reflected the culture and attitude of the editors and their corporate superiors—had irrevocably changed. By the early 1990s, the give-and-take atmosphere was gone; the meetings of editors and publishers were instructive and more about controlling costs than doing journalism. The final meeting I attended was only months after Batten's 1995 death. At the primary dinner, a huge picture of a smiling Batten was briefly, and for the editors heartrendingly, projected on the wall behind the dais. Tony Ridder, the new chairman and CEO, had the difficult task of addressing a roomful of Batten protégés who, he knew, were at best wary of him. After a speech with brief and seemingly obligatory bows to the need for good newspaper content, he opened the floor to questions.

The first one was, "Tony, what keeps you up at night; what do you most worry about?"

He thought for a minute. "Electronic classified," he said.

The air went out of the room. He explained the serious financial threat presented by the vigorous new competitors for classified advertising and the need to find ways to compete in the online arena. He could have, but did not, talk to that roomful of his editors about the danger to democracy of failing newspapers, nor did he seek their support to make Knight Ridder newspapers the best anywhere. He was not wrong; electronic classified is a substantial threat. But he described the threat as one to the bottom line, rather than a threat to the company's tradition of public service journalism. He may have had those concerns as a subtext, but they were not expressed; he and his editors were speaking different languages.

ONE SIZE FITS ALL

One of the touted advantages of the merger of Knight and Ridder was the geographical distribution of the companies' newspapers: Ridder papers were predominantly Midwest and West, Knight papers, East and South. The theory was that when one part of the country was suffering an economic slump, other parts might not be. Nationwide holdings allowed for balancing of good and bad times, at least as far as the corporation was concerned. Implicit in that arrangement was that if, for instance, San Jose's economy was exploding, as it did in the 1970s and 1980s, and Detroit's was suffering, the company could rely on San Jose to make up for Detroit's deficits.

This worked only as long as the corporate financial goal was steady, long-term profits. The bad periods would, over time, balance out and all papers could maintain their quality levels in bad times and raise them when the good times rolled around. When the goal became constantly increasing profits rather than solid, steady ones, however, the system broke down; the synergy didn't work. Setting a corporate goal such as increasing operating return from 18 percent to 22 percent and requiring each newspaper to contribute equally meant that bad periods could not be tolerated anywhere. For instance, Detroit, suffering through bad years with single-digit returns, could not look for indirect aid from San Jose, enjoying larger returns. Rather, Detroit had to find a way—through cutbacks—to reach its mandated goal. Meanwhile, San Jose could not benefit fully from its good times because its success translated not into improvements to the paper but into filling out the corporate bottom line. Thus neither paper benefited from the geographic diversity. One-size-fits-all profit goals also meant, of course, that corporate officers avoided some very tricky balancing acts between the newspapers.

Change Five: You Get What You Pay For, Maybe

Following the advice of Lee Hills when I headed for Wichita in 1975, I wrote some goals for myself and stuck them in a desk drawer for periodic review. They were modest and generalized, about getting along in a new environment and making the newspapers better. They were driven by personal satisfaction and ambition and evaluated according to my own lights. It was a useful thing to do, but Hills's advice was only a first iteration of what, two years later, would become a corporate program of management by objectives (MBO), surfacing and formalizing what had been going on in desk drawers and private thoughts around the company.

Management by objectives had been around in the business world for two decades and had evolved into many different forms, but the common core of the idea was that a company could best meet its goals when they were clearly articulated and each affected manager understood his or her role and stake in reaching those goals. Sometimes the stake was simply "this is how you keep your job." Sometimes the stake was a financial bonus or promotion. Either way, the program involved periodic accountings and some calculation of what percentage of the goals had been met by each participant.

Up until 1977, the Knight Ridder MBO program had been limited to the highest corporate levels, but that year it was spread to about 300 key people: corporate staff members and the publishers and editors of the company's newspapers. It would later be pushed even deeper into the newspapers, including the newsrooms. The company's heritage of autonomy ensured that goals would be arrived at locally. Publishers and editors, in consultation with their corporate superiors, would decide what they wanted to accomplish and what relative weight to put on each goal. In the case of Knight Ridder, there would be money attached, initially up to 10 percent on top of the person's base salary. The program was a way to improve employees' income while aligning their interests with those of the corporation, a juxtaposition that existed comfortably in the first years of the program but would become uncomfortable for many of the company's newspaper editors as the corporation's interests changed over the years.

The same would be true for stock options, a program initiated early in the life of the merged company. The annual grants allowed participants in the program—which included the newspapers' publishers and editors—to purchase a given amount of company stock at less-than-market prices. As long as the stock's value increased over the years, there was money to be made in exercising the ten-year options. If the stock fell below the option price, the options were worthless. That never happened.

The two forms of enhanced compensation worked quite differently for editors over time. The stock options were more or less a windfall, because an individual editor could do little or nothing to affect the company's stock price, upward or downward. Management by objectives money, however, was another matter, because it was based on goals that reflected the employee's direct responsibilities.

With the two compensation enhancements, the natural and unavoidable tension between newspapers' business and journalistic interests became manifest, an important philosophical issue transmuted into a hard-cash issue for people on both sides of the wall of separation. From their benign origins, the programs would precipitate a running battle with a casualty list that often included sound journalistic principle.

The erosion of principles was gradual. At first, editors' MBOs consisted solely of journalistic and personal goals, and the range was as broad as the editors' ingenuity. Some goals might involve content—for instance, to complete four major reporting projects during the year or to carry out a redesign of the newspaper. Some might be related to management, such as setting a goal to improve communication with the staff. Some might even be intensely personal, such as one grossly overweight editor committing to losing a certain number

Sincerely your friend Charles L. Knight

C. L. Knight, about 1920. (Courtesy The John S. and James L. Knight Foundation)

The Ridders, 1952 gathering. Front row, left to right: Bernard H., Jr., Herman H., Bernard J., Daniel H., and Walter T. Back row: Robert B., Joseph E., Bernard H., Sr., Victor F., Joseph B., and Eric. (©The St. Paul Pioneer Press)

John S. Knight at his typewriter in his Akron office, 1965. (Courtesy The John S. and James L. Knight Foundation)

Left to right: Alvah Chapman, Jim Knight, John Knight, Lee Hills. (Courtesy The John S. and James L. Knight Foundation)

Bernard (Bernie)
H. Ridder, Jr.
February 1964.
(©The St. Paul
Pioneer Press)

Tony Ridder, Kansas
Press Association,
April 2002.
(© The Wichita
Eagle & Beacon
Publishing Co.)

Left to right: Jim Knight, Lee Hills, and John S. Knight at NYSE in 1969 when Knight Newspapers went public. (Courtesy The John S. and James L. Knight Foundation)

Jim Batten (seated, with dark glasses) looking over page proofs as editor of *The Charlotte Observer*, August 1974, when Nixon resigned. (© *The Charlotte Observer*)

Larry Jinks. (Courtesy The John S. and James L. Knight Foundation)

The author in the *Eagle* newsroom during the boom times of the 1980s. (© The Wichita Eagle & Beacon Publishing Co.)

Jim Batten in 1991. (Courtesy The John S. and James L. Knight Foundation)

John S. Knight at 85. (Courtesy The John S. and James L. Knight Foundation)

of pounds, or another kicking cigarettes. The goals were a way to address shortcomings and stretch performance, and most of them did not confront editors with a conflict between journalistic principle and income.

THE PUBLISHERS' REVOLT

That did not last, however, and in Knight Ridder what changed it was a revolt by publishers in the face of the early 1980s recession. Up to that point in the program's brief history, editors did not have financial goals, but virtually all of the publishers' goals were based on the fiscal performance of their newspapers and the corporation overall. As the economy tanked, publishers found themselves writing big bonus checks to editors who accomplished their journalistic goals, but getting little themselves because their financial goals were not met. That didn't seem fair to the publishers, and it may not have been. They leaned hard on corporate to require editors to have at least some financial goals, and corporate agreed. But the solution to the dollar inequity would begin a gradual process that, over fifteen years, would change the very nature of the position of editor.

Writing meaningful and effective MBOs in any complex organization is difficult. Some employee goals need to reflect their specific jobs, while others need to reflect the overall mission of the company. It is one thing to set such overall goals for an organization that has one clear ambition: to make money. In public service-oriented newspaper companies, the task is much more delicate because of the tension between journalistic priorities and financial priorities.

Example One. One of my early publishers proposed the following as one of my goals: If you finish the year under the newsroom expense budget by one percent, you get one additional point on your MBO; 2 percent under, you get two points, and so forth, up to ten points, which would have amounted to several thousand extra dollars in my pocket. It also would have meant, however, that money available for news coverage would not be spent, an offensive enough proposition for me personally. But the larger problem, never under-

stood by this publisher because he had never worked in a newsroom
full of savvy reporters and curious editors, was that every decision I
made involving money would have been subject to questions about
personal motivation. Ending his insistence upon the goal required
intervention by the ever-understanding Batten.

Example Two. The production manager of a newspaper is
charged with turning the newsroom's product into printed newspapers, a complex process that involves the newspaper's highest costs:
newsprint and labor. Efficient operation of the mechanical processes
involves good management of both materials and time, because the
newspaper must be printed on a precise schedule if it is to be tossed
on doorsteps by the appointed time. It is natural, therefore, to include in a production manager's MBO goals that measure on-time
press performance and efficient use of materials.

The editor of a newspaper is charged with producing the best,
most complete, most accurate, and up-to-date content. It is natural
to include in the editor's MBO goals that measure those attributes.

"Makeovers," in newspaper parlance, are pages that are changed
after the initial press start. They can be required for a number of
reasons, including late-breaking news, the need to correct an error,
or because of a faulty press plate. Most makeovers are initiated by
the newsroom to update and perfect the newspaper's content. Makeovers cost money. To complete one, a new press plate must be made
and the press stopped to put it on. Stopping the press creates newsprint waste and eats up precious time. Makeovers are economically
inefficient in the short term, but in the long term so are out-of-date
and error-filled newspapers. Thus, a tension arises.

The new production manager in Wichita had a major goal in his
MBO to minimize the number of makeovers, and on this morning
he was angry because the newsroom had initiated ten of them the
previous night, all for valid content reasons.

"You're taking money out of my pocket, food off my table," he
railed.

"Don't ever talk to me about your MBO," I snapped back. "I'm
not interested in that; it has nothing to do with putting out a good

newspaper." (Actually that is not an exact quote; my language was somewhat more colorful.)

This was a no-win situation. The publisher attempted to rectify it by insisting that my MBO henceforth contain a measurement of makeovers, but he did not include in the production manager's MBO any balancing goals involving the quality of the news report. As a result, my ability to make sound, content-only calls on makeovers and my relationship with my sub-editors was potentially compromised, while the production manager was given no balancing incentive to be part of making a better newspaper.

THE EROSION OF NEWSPAPER QUALITY AND MBOS

The "makeover" episode epitomized the way MBOs could and would be used to erode newspaper quality, one small piece at a time, by deflecting editors' financial incentives away from purely journalistic considerations. By the end of my time as an editor, more than half of my goals were related to nonjournalism matters—that is to say, to business matters—and the entire calculation of my bonus was based on a formula involving the *Eagle*'s financial performance and that of the corporation as a whole. This meant that the reward for even the most outstanding journalistic effort was subject to discounting by economic circumstances that often had little to do with the journalism. Conversely, it also meant that if I should decide to edit the newspaper in a way calculated to hold down costs at the expense of quality, I would be even more handsomely rewarded.

Most editors would insist that their MBO incentives never caused them to make a journalistically inappropriate decision. They would be wrong. Short- to mid-term, some of a newspaper's very best public service journalism has no discernible effect on the newspaper's market acceptance; sometimes aggressive journalism actually has a negative effect for a period of time because it offends one group or another. By nature, MBOs are short-term programs—rarely more than a year, often shorter—aimed at measuring short-term market acceptance as reflected on the bottom line. If an editor's personal prosperity is tied to anything other than good journalism, it quickly (if subtly) affects thought processes and decisions. And when no one else in the newspaper building except the publisher and the editor has goals related to good journalism, when in fact many have goals inimical to good journalism, the concept of teamwork becomes only a slogan. You're not playing the same game; you're not even in the same arena.

Newspaper companies that truly regard journalism as the heart and soul of the enterprise can best accomplish their quality goals by ensuring that people in the newsroom spend all of their energy and time on those goals. Such a company would then give all of the supporting parts of the business—the people on the other side of the wall in circulation and advertising and production—clear goals for supporting the journalistic heart and soul.

The fact that no one has yet been able to develop a consistent and auditable measure of newspaper quality does not detract from the need for one. It may be that it's something you cannot define but you can feel when it is present. Certainly when a newspaper or newspaper company is populated by like-minded people bent upon public service journalism, an unspoken consensus definition of quality can arise. But when the people in an organization do not share broad and deep values and goals, and when only things that can be easily tabulated are important, what social scientist Daniel Yankelovich called "the McNamara Fallacy" comes into play. It goes like this:

> The first step is to measure what can be easily measured. This is okay as far as it goes. The second step is to disregard that which can't be measured, or give it an arbitrary quantitative value. This is artificial and misleading. The third step is to presume that what can't be measured easily isn't very important. This is blindness. The fourth step is to say that what can't be easily measured doesn't exist. This is suicide."[1]

Change Six: People and Purpose

In 1985, Alvah Chapman, chairman and CEO, and Jim Batten, president, had worked together for ten years, balancing the delicate tension between Chapman's business background and emphasis and Batten's news background and emphasis. They would continue to do that until 1989, when Chapman would retire.

They managed to make a success of the balancing because they respected each other, brought different personalities to the mix, and shared the conviction that, in Chapman's words, "quality journalism and dedication to high profitability [are] not incompatible. They do go together."

The partnership worked, Chapman said, because, "Jim Batten helped me a lot. . . . His judgment was cool and calm. Sometimes I was too strong and would go too far in some [cost containment] areas, and Jim would be the voice of caution when it was needed." In the Chapman-Batten years through 1989, the compound growth rate of Knight Ridder shares was 23 percent, the company was consistently rated among the best companies to work for, the newspapers won thirty-seven Pulitzers, and the company's contribution to charities in its communities rose each year. "The communities were benefiting. The readers were benefiting. Stockholders were benefiting. Advertisers were benefiting. . . . There's nothing incompatible about having a profitable newspaper and having a good newspaper," Chapman said.

But in 1985, the seeds of important change would be sown. Chapman and Batten restructured the top corporate levels, creating separate divisions for newspapers, business information services, and broadcast, naming a president for each. While it was a sensible move in terms of organizational efficiency, it eliminated the last corporate layer of separation between news and business, vesting in the president and vice president of the newspaper company responsibility for both.

As with any organizational table, how it actually works depends at least as much upon the intentions of the people whose names are on the chart lines as it does on the arrangement of the lines themselves. Chapman and Batten, based on their success at balancing the tensions, assumed (incorrectly it turned out) that the president of the newspaper division would understand the need for that balance and seek its benefits. In furtherance of that, when they appointed Tony Ridder, publisher in San Jose, as the first newspaper division president, they balanced his lack of news experience with veteran editor Larry Jinks, who for a time had worked with Ridder as editor in San Jose. However, Jinks had the title of senior vice president for news *and* operations. He was older than Batten and Ridder and so was not a succession candidate. Ridder, at forty-six years old, clearly was.

With Chapman's retirement in 1989, Ridder, as had been anticipated, moved up to Knight Ridder's presidency, Batten became chairman and CEO, and Jinks left to become publisher in San Jose until he retired. Chapman said that he urged Ridder to seek a strong newsside person to back him up. "Tony needed to get another Jim Batten to back him up. I told Tony that, so I'll tell you that. Tony's in a lot of unnecessary hot water because he didn't have a strong number two person who was clearly his successor and somebody with a news/editorial background. People he picked were nice people, capable people, but they just weren't Jim Batten's quality. . . . He didn't see the need for it. He just didn't. There wasn't any clear person around him to pick and he didn't go outside." Ridder's side of this change of direction and tone is unknown, because he has declined to be interviewed on that subject or any other.

Batten, in his mid-fifties, and Ridder, just reaching fifty, were a long way from retirement when the 1989 succession occurred. They gave promise of being a balanced team of bright, strong-willed leaders for a decade or more, but they would balance each other in the two top positions for less than four years. In October of 1993, the car Batten was driving home from the airport inexplicably veered into a concrete light pole in Coral Gables, critically injuring him. The accident shook everyone in the company, but none more severely than the journalists he so avidly supported.

Imagining KR without Batten was a terrifying but suddenly very real prospect. In the best of circumstances, producing first-class journalism is constantly challenging. In an atmosphere in which first-class journalism is valued only insofar as it does not interfere with ever-increasing profits, it is very nearly impossible. The next five years would see many changes (see Chapter 11) at the top editor levels of Knight Ridder's newspapers as the pain of doing high-level journalism became for them greater than the rewards for trying.

8

Change Seven: Breaching the Wall

"With a bazooka, if necessary." — *Mark H. Willes*

THE MAN STANDING next to me owned a heating and air-conditioning business and was certain he had figured out why our reporter talked with a competitor and not him for one of those aim-to-be-helpful stories about preparing the house for a new heating season. It was, he insisted, because the competitor bought more advertising than he did. As patiently as possible, given that we were standing in a loud crowd of people at a cocktail reception, I explained that the newspaper operated with a high wall between news and advertising, that news decisions did not involve such calculations, and that in fact most newsroom people were deliberately unaware of who bought advertising and who did not. It was, I said, an important and useful separation, and good newspapers were serious about it.

"Oh," he said, sliding a cynical near-sneer into his voice, "I get it. Like the separation of sales and service."

To him, it would have made perfect sense and reflected business practicality if such a story mentioned major advertisers ahead of minor ones, and for the editor to fend off complaints by claiming a separation-of-powers policy. (Yes, ma'am, maybe that's what the salesman said, but this model doesn't come with lifetime filter replacement. Sometimes the people in sales don't understand the service side very well, because we're separate divisions.) Caveat emptor and all that.

The discussion was fifteen years ago, and I was comfortable making the declaration. I would be less so today, not because at least a theoretical wall no longer exists at most newspapers, but because the evidence of its existence and the moral imperatives that are its foundation are blurred by incremental compromises and philosophical rationalizations driven by economic pressures.

Why a Wall?

The notion of strict separation between the business and journalism functions of newspapers is relatively recent in terms of the whole of American newspaper history, and judging by current practice, it may be only a passing phase. Certainly nineteenth-century publishers were unencumbered by such ideas, as the newspapers of that time were widely reviled as corrupt subjects of big money corporations. By the days of the Great Depression, however, people like John S. Knight, Col. Robert McCormick in Chicago, Henry R. Luce in New York, and Nelson Poynter in St. Petersburg were defiantly declaring their independence from pressures of the countinghouse. That they were wealthier than most other people perhaps made such freedom easier to assert, but their matching philosophies found fertile ground in newsrooms. At McCormick's *Chicago Tribune* building, there were even separate sets of elevators for newsroom people and businesspeople. At Knight's *Charlotte Observer*, the advertising director was instructed not to discuss anything of substance with any newsroom employee. The editor's business-side partner, the general manager, spoke only to the editor among newsroom employees.

It is not clear why the idea began to gain credence when it did, but part of the explanation may lie in the fact that in the nineteenth century, advertising provided less than half the total revenue of newspapers. By the twenties, it was up to two-thirds and rising steadily toward its present 80 percent.

At most newspapers, including Knight's, the doctrine of strict separation lasted well into the 1970s. A newspaper or newspaper company either respected the wall between the journalism functions and the business functions or it did not. The wall was either impenetrable, high, and thick, or it didn't exist at all. Its presence, or lack of presence, was determined by the owners, but its viability was never a function of the *form* of ownership: There were public newspaper companies whose leaders respected it and ones who did not; there were private and family owners who valued it and those who did not. If a newspaper was thought of, by its owners, as just another way to make money, the wall was an impediment; the enterprise's financial success could be maximized only if the wall did not exist. Maximizing a newspaper's income is not a difficult process if there are no concerns about public service and intellectual honesty: Write only stories that please advertisers and potential advertisers; allocate newsroom resources to the subjects that surveys tell you people say they want to read; ride the partisan winds in editorial policy; don't rock the boat. Few American newspapers acted that way, which was fortunate for democracy.

Today, however, the wall is increasingly transparent, a relatively recent development that is potentially dangerous to and surely unfortunate for democracy. Instead of doing one or the other, the great majority of American newspapers today try to walk a slack wire across the abyss—tricky stuff akin to trying to be a little bit pregnant. It is not certain how long and in what fashion that balancing act can be sustained, if indeed it can be sustained. Nor is it clear exactly when the balancing act started, but as the twenty-first century opened, most newspapers had at least one foot on the wire, and many of them were several shaky steps along the downslope. There's no safe haven on the other side of the abyss to make the risk worth the danger of a tumble; once out on the wire, the only safe resolution lies in deciding to back away, which, on a slack wire, presents it own set of dangers.

The argument in favor of a high, impenetrable wall incorporates both journalistic and business considerations. A newspaper's credibility is it most vital asset. Its information and editorial opinions cannot be trusted, in the case of news, and persuasive, in the case of opinion, if readers suspect that the judgments behind the information and opinions are influenced by other than journalistic standards. Conflicts of interest between journalistic and business aims, as well as the appearance of conflicts, must therefore be avoided. Likewise, the credibility of a newspaper's advertising lies in the proposition that the space purchased delivers full value for the advertiser's dollar, with no other considerations necessary. If a newspaper provides more to the advertiser than the purchased advertising space itself, the message is clear: Absent additional considerations, the advertising is overpriced and its value is in question. So the wall protects the integrity of both the journalistic content and the advertising content while allowing the people on both sides of the wall to pursue their separate but mutually supportive goals.

The change in newspaper attitudes about the wall is not so blatant as to make a simplistic quid pro quo connection between news and advertising content a routine practice, at least at most newspapers. The change is much more subtle than that, and it is much more insidious because it involves structural changes in the organization of responsibilities of key newsroom people, and it involves their personal compensation.

Editors and other newsroom employees now regularly sit on marketing committees with advertising and circulation managers. They share financial goals through their overlapping MBOs (management by objectives) and other compensation mechanisms. This puts immense direct and very personal pressure on the newsroom people to align their journalistic standards of judgment with the very different business judgments of their non-news peers. Failure on the part of the newspeople to conform their thinking to the rest of the management group can have direct, negative financial consequences for everyone in the room. Entire regular sections of the newspaper as well as special sections are conceived, designed, and executed in that philosophically muddled environment, with ethical and practical results ranging from benign to devastating.

The problem with such structures as interdepartmental marketing committees is that the newspeople are invariably outnumbered by business-side people, and they are also rhetorically outgunned because the business people are dealing in dollars and cents and the newspeople are dealing in a philosophical concept that, too often, business people either do not understand or do not support.

In an ideal—though admittedly fiscally inefficient—world, editors would decide what subjects to write about without regard for whether there was an advertising tie-in opportunity. For example, an editor could decide that the intense public interest in wellness, exercise, and nutrition justified starting a weekly section devoted to that subject. Letting the advertising department know in advance about the launch of such a section would be a logical thing to do, but the coordination would end there, and the section would be driven by news-information considerations. If the advertising department wanted to sell ads for the section, that would be a plus for everyone, including readers, but if the advertising were not forthcoming, the section would still be produced because there were clear informational imperatives involved. That's in an ideal world. In the real world of 2005, most newspapers would not proceed with the section absent advertising support because it could not be cost-justified, even though there was an identifiable reader appetite.

Tying coverage of such matters as health and nutrition to advertising interest may seem a minor compromise of editorial judgment, because while such matters are important, they are peripheral to the most basic Thomas Jefferson/First Amendment kinds of journalism. But insisting upon an advertising tie-in is a step onto the slack wire, and once a newspaper is in that business, it is over the abyss.

Cracks and Gaps

The year 1990 was the worst for newspaper advertising since 1961, and many newspaper owners panicked. The recession of the early nineties was setting in, and major advertisers, themselves wary of the business outlook, were beginning to exploit the technology-driven and often cheaper and arguably more efficient alternatives to newspaper advertising: direct mail, shopping guides disguised as newspapers (called "shoppers"), narrowcasting on radio and TV, and target marketing of all sorts. Many newspapers and newspaper companies, still in denial about the loss of their former hegemony in mass media, first responded by raising their advertising rates. This, of course, did not work, as it had not worked in the recent past. Raising advertising rates means that advertisers, at the minimum, simply reduce the amount of space they purchase for the same budgeted dollars, a doubly perverse impact on both the newspaper's journalism and its readers. Newspapers have an imperative to meet their budgets, of course, so they raise rates, but so do advertisers, so they reduce the space they buy. Less advertising means less newshole, and thus a diminished journalistic product. And, because many people read advertising as avidly as they do news, less advertising makes the entire newspaper less attractive.

Worse, two of newspapers' primary advertising groups, real estate and automotive, recognized that personal and business computing and desktop publishing power now allowed them cheap, if limited, entry into the publishing business themselves. In many cities groups of real estate agents and car dealers banded together or used an entrepreneur to produce their own advertising publications. In effect, those newspapers relying on rate increases created yet another form of competition.

The accumulation of economic pressures put new stress on the wall throughout the early 1990s, creating visible cracks and gaps. On top of the problems with competition from their own advertisers and other media, public newspaper companies felt even more pressure to steadily increase earnings in order to maintain some competitive balance on Wall Street. The go-go technological companies with their millionaire-creating IPOs and outlandishly overvalued stock prices clearly labeled the staid old publishing industry as yesteryear's way of investing.

The scramble to maximize newspaper companies' quarterly returns ratcheted up the pressure on editors to focus more on marketing and, as an inevitable result, less on journalism. Their compensation packages began to reflect that pressure, and their performance evaluations emphasized higher and more intimate levels of coordination with the business side. What publishers and corporate officers saw as necessary and efficient teamwork, some editors saw as unacceptable compromise of their journalistic obligations; in John S. Knight's's words, "sacrificing principle . . . on the altar of the countinghouse."

As most newspapers began to chip away at the wall in one fashion or another, it was perhaps inevitable that some would simply blow it up. Two cases from the 1990s are instructive.

Auto-Mania

Automobile dealers are among the business world's most aggressive competitors, in part because of the broad array of similar products to sell, and in part because they run on narrow, low-single-digit operating margins, certainly far less than the 25 percent to 35 percent common to even the worst-performing newspapers. The recession of the early 1990s and newspapers' subsequent efforts to impose advertising rate increases heightened the tensions that already existed between the two. The auto dealers' ability to use other, even if less effective, modes of advertising gave them the opportunity to flex their considerable economic muscle as the third-largest newspaper advertising buyer (behind department stores and real estate), and they did so.

Newspapers, in their efforts to help readers with their lives, were full of copy about automobiles: safety ratings, reviews of new models, analysis of car-selling techniques, and, of course, tips on how to haggle as well as the car dealers. Many newspapers developed freestanding auto sections, some of them products of the newsroom, some of them done by advertising departments. The newsroom sections tended to be more aggressive in coverage than the advertising-produced sections, of course, and the former also sometimes gave local car dealers indigestion and a reason for taking on the newspapers. The early-nineties period saw dozens of boycotts and threatened boycotts of newspapers by auto dealer associations, and dozens of instances of harried publishers apologizing publicly for what the dealers said were newsroom transgressions.

Three factors eased the tensions: First, the economy began to improve. Second, in 1994, the Federal Trade Commission (FTC) investigated a one-month, $1 million boycott of the *San Jose Mercury News* and declared it an illegal conspiracy to restrain competition among dealers and a chilling of the publication of important consumer information. The *Mercury News'* alleged offense had been a story showing consumers how to analyze factory invoices so they could better bargain with dealers. The next year, the Santa Clara County dealers' association signed a consent agreement not to promote such boycotts. Other auto dealer groups heard the FTC's message and formal, organized boycotts trailed off. The third factor: When dealers boycotted newspaper advertising, car sales dipped, often sharply.

The tension with auto dealers and other major advertisers in times of economic stress led some newspapers to try various routes around the problem. One, *The News & Observer* in Raleigh, North Carolina, transferred its automotive writer from the newsroom over the wall to the classified advertising department in 1991. But Dan Neil was no ordinary auto writer. From the newsroom, he had written provocative, tough-minded, often irreverent stories and new-car reviews, the best of which often were passed around gleefully (and enviously) in other newsrooms. He did not change his style when his boss became the classified advertising manager rather than the editor, and he plied his trade without anyone editing his copy. Finally, however, local auto dealers tired of his aggressive style, and Neil was ordered to run his copy by the classified advertising manager before it was published. He refused and was fired. After several years of freelancing for various publications, he was hired by the *Los Angeles Times* as its auto critic, working out of the newsroom again. And it was a newsroom, as we shall next see, that had been through the Mother of All Wall Breachings.

Where's My Bazooka?

In 1995, the directors of Times-Mirror Corp. were worried about their floundering flagship, the *Los Angeles Times*. From 1960 to 1980, under famed and outspoken publisher Otis Chandler, the newspaper earned prominence for both its business and journalistic performances. After his retirement, however, the enterprise began to drift, and by 1995 the directors, mostly Chandler family members, were desperate for new leadership: The operating margin was at 6.5 percent, down from the mid-twenties; the stock price had skidded from $42 to $18; and circulation was down almost 20 percent. They turned to Mark H. Willes, a General Mills executive whose only newspaper experience was reading them. As CEO and then chairman of the corporation, he also named himself publisher of the *Times*. In 1998, he hired as president of the *Times* Kathryn Downing, an attorney whose publishing experience involved only legal periodicals, not newspapers.

Willes quickly decided that the wall between news and business functions was an anachronistic barrier to financial revival and declared publicly that he would destroy it "with a bazooka, if necessary." Such words from a cereal magnate only a year into the newspaper business horrified and alarmed many journalists at the *Times* and elsewhere, including its editor, Shelby Coffey, who resigned. Predictably, the response did not deter Willes from acting on his conviction by decreeing regular coordination between news and business at many levels. He announced a plan to appoint general managers for each of the newspaper's sections who would coordinate with the section editors; each section would be required to develop a pro forma with readership and profit targets.

The restructuring set up the *Times* to get more than a little bit pregnant and a long way out on the slack wire.

The next step onto the wire was the newspaper corporation agreeing to be a founding partner in development of the Staples Center, a 20,000-seat arena touted as a catalyst to the revitalization of downtown Los Angeles. The agreement had the newspaper paying Staples about $1.6 million over five years in a combination of cash, free advertising, and about $300,000 from later, unspecified joint projects. Similar deals are not uncommon in other cities, despite the fact that a newspaper partnering with a business that its news department covers inevitably raises conflict-of-interest questions about fairness. Some executives argue that a newspaper company has an obligation to be an active participant in community life, and that its journalism responsibilities do not and cannot make it less than a fully participating corporate citizen. However, such deals make life much harder for the newspaper's journalists. They must contend not only with the conflict-of-interest questions but also with assumptions on the part of the partner/news source that its involvement with the business side of the newspaper changes the equation in dealing with the news side. Editors and reporters would much prefer a totally clean-hands situation.

The *Los Angeles Times* involvement with Staples did not stop with the founding membership. As the arena's opening day approached in 1999, people on both the news and business sides were thinking about how to mark the occasion. Editor Michael Parks felt that the opening was an important news event because of the arena's role in the renaissance of the center city. Business-side people saw it as a financial opportunity. Together they developed a plan to devote a 168-page special issue of the *Times'* Sunday magazine to the subject, with the news staff providing the stories and the business managers the financial support. So far, so good.

But unbeknownst to the newspeople, the business side, in one of those "later, unspecified joint projects," had carved out a deal with the Staples Center to share profits on the special issue, thereby helping the *Times* fulfill its founding-partner obligations. The special section was well into production when, to the shock and chagrin of *Los Angeles Times* editors and reporters, *The New York Times* broke the story of the profit-sharing arrangement. The story, and the resoundingly negative reaction to it from journalists and journalism ethicists across the country, made the clear point that the work of the Los Angeles editors and reporters had been compromised—not only on that magazine project, but also on any future coverage of the arena and its various partners.

Three hundred *Los Angeles Times* journalists signed a petition condemning the arrangement, and even the retired but still-revered Otis Chandler weighed in with a letter saying, "Successfully running a newspaper is not like any other business," and calling the Staples deal "unbelievably stupid and unprofessional" and "the most serious single threat to the future during my fifty years of being associated with the *Times*. . . . Respect and credibility for a newspaper is irreplaceable. Sometimes it can never be restored."

Willes and Downing were initially flummoxed, not grasping the seriousness of the ethical breach, but soon they came to accept, if not understand, the seriousness of the offense and apologized publicly. The Chandler family decided it was not capable of managing the company and newspaper without Otis Chandler in the picture. Without the knowledge of Willes, the chairman and CEO, they negotiated a $6.1 billion sale to Chicago's Tribune Company, and Willes, Downing, and many other key players in the event were gone.

David Shaw, media writer for the newspaper and nationally respected for his detailed reporting and analysis on newspaper matters, including those involving the *Los Angeles Times*, spent months reporting on the disaster. The result was a 32,000-word report in the newspaper. For Shaw, the bottom line was that the bazooka shot at the wall created the conditions for the ethical fiasco. "I don't know that the publisher and the advertising department would even have conceived of such an idea were Willes not pushing for new and innovative ways to bring in new revenue," he said in a 2004 interview.

A Coda

By 2003, John Carroll, hired in the wake of the Staples affair as the new editor of the *Los Angeles Times*, had fully rebuilt the wall, and he needed an automobile critic. He personally sought out Dan Neil, who had been through the Raleigh wars of the wall. In 2004, Neil was awarded the first Pulitzer Prize for criticism ever given to an auto critic, one of an impressive five the revitalized *Times* won in that year. How high is the wall now?

"I'm not allowed to talk to anybody in the advertising department. It is forbidden," Neil said.

9

Change Eight: Lie, Cheat, Steal

"Trust everyone, but count your change. He might make a mistake in your favor and give you too much." — Byrd Suiter Merritt

FOR DECADES, the mantra that people in journalism delivered to people who thought they wanted to be in journalism went something like this: You won't get rich and you probably won't be famous, but you can make a difference and have a lot of fun in the process.

For the first half of the twentieth century, the declaration was not received as delimiting, nor as approval of flaccid ambition; it was a statement of reality as the advisers had experienced it. With only a handful of exceptions, journalists toiled in relative anonymity and at the lower end of the economic scale, but there were compensations.

THE REWARDS OF JOURNALISM—CHIEFLY
FOUND IN CONGENIAL EMPLOYMENT—
COMMUNITY SERVICE

That's the title of Chapter X in Chester S. Lord's 1922 book *The Young Man and Journalism*, published as part of a vocational series by

The Macmillan Company. After pointing out that doctors could make more than $50,000 and that presidents of banks, steel companies, and the like had salaries of $100,000 and beyond, Lord, a former managing editor of the *New York Sun*, deflated the aspiring journalist with the information that in New York at the time, copy readers made $2,000 to $4,000 and reporters $1,000 to $7,000, and in smaller cities "not more than half so much." Wrote Lord:

> It surely is a discouraging feature of the calling that, however intellectual or learned a man may be, he rarely achieves more than moderate pecuniary success, as long as he remains an employee. . . . It follows then that our young man must look beyond mere pecuniary gains for the rewards of journalism.
>
> What then are some of the rewards? . . . The important activities of the world pass him in daily review. His mental vision may survey the entire field of human thought, furnishing delightful subjects for consideration, for study, for exposition. In all modesty and without vainglory he may rejoice in the satisfaction of well-directed influence; may find pleasure in the responsibility of influencing public opinion; may take pride in the endeavor to aid in the intellectual and moral uplift of his fellowmen. What greater reward hath man than this?
>
> . . . To take a hand in every political shindy is uproariously good fun; indeed, notwithstanding all of its importance, its responsibilities, its dignities, there is more fun in the newspaper business than in any other occupation known to man."

Given such guidance—and Lord's was typical of the time—it's small wonder that journalism attracted a peculiar sort, people with more on their minds than money and fame, whether it be influence, adventure, pleasure, or even more arcane and imaginative inclinations; at base, people to whom the work meant more than the financial reward. This is not to argue that they were entering a sort of priesthood or that journalism should be deified as more than a very important social tool, but most of the people who chose journalism in the first half of the century did so understanding it was different from other occupations. As with any profession, knaves and fools also got in the door on occasion, and when they did, the mischief they caused often extracted a heavy price on the lives and reputations of people and institutions. But they were a minority, and that was before the age of celebrity journalists.

Certainly in the first part of the century, a few newspaper journalists earned national and worldwide reputations and accompanying high incomes, sometimes for sensational exploits, but mostly for doing their jobs well and for a long time. Yet most journalists toiled in satisfied and underpaid anonymity. Broadcast's early years, however, put voices and images, all of them white and male, to journalists' words and brought them into our homes, changing the equation between journalist and audience, making the transaction between newsgiver and news-receiver seem more immediate and personal. Broadcast journalists were a small, tight group, and while they competed vigorously for shares of what became a national audience, they did so on the basis of credibility, authenticity, and professionalism. In their minds, they were journalists who happened to perform their journalism in public, not media stars who chose news as their backdrop. Edward R. Murrow, Walter Cronkite, Chet Huntley, David Brinkley, Howard K. Smith, and their peers ushered in the era of star journalism, but they did it to stately processional music, not raucous themes. They were men of serious intent and demeanor who understood the stakes that arose when the three nightly newscasts on CBS, ABC, and NBC commanded the attention of a huge majority of Americans. They provided the shared relevance so crucial to a democratic society and were deeply aware of the restraint and responsibility that task demanded.

Never was that more evident than in the hours and days after the assassination of President John F. Kennedy on Friday, November 22, 1963, and the murder of his alleged killer, Lee Harvey Oswald, in the basement of the Dallas City Jail on the following Sunday. The shock of Kennedy's assassination was barely being absorbed when an NBC cameraman caught Jack Ruby's shooting of Oswald, who was in the physical grasp of Dallas police officers. It was an instant that arguably changed journalism forever, for while there had been no live pictures of the Friday assassination, this murder was there for the world to see and speculate about. What was going on? What sort of conspiracy had the nation by the throat? On Saturday, NBC had decided to suspend all other programming and broadcast continually from 7 A.M. Sunday until after the Kennedy funeral on Monday, so its presence in the jail basement just after noon on Saturday was fortuitous. If, at that point in American journalism history, there was still a question about the potential of live television news, the pictures of Ruby firing shots into Oswald's midsection answered it. The events of that November were hardly the first time television had carried a news event live, but it was its first time being present at an event so large and shockingly unpredictable. The on-air murder underlined the importance of immediacy in a way that newspapers could never match, and television news entered a new era.

At the time of the funeral itself on Monday afternoon, 95 percent of Americans were watching. Historian William Manchester observed in *The Death of a President* that such a drama-laden forty-two-hour broadcast "in irresponsible hands could have been dangerous. The possibilities were Orwellian. Brinkley later calculated that 'the shocked and stunned nation was listening to six people at most, us commentators. It would have been so easy to start a phony rumor that would never die, that would be alive fifty years later.'"[1]

But the half-dozen men were cautious and responsible: no reckless speculations by them or other underinformed sources, no hastily arranged panels of experts constructing theories and spinning scenarios on insufficient facts. Neither was there any attempt to immediately put the horrific events into perspective. In what seems, in retrospect, to have been prophetic recognition of changed journalistic circumstances, Brinkley, in a weary, forlorn, and memorable signoff at 12:51 A.M. on the Saturday following the assassination, said:

> There is seldom any time to think anymore, and today there was none. In about four hours we had gone from President Kennedy in Dallas, alive, to back in Washington, dead, and a new president in his place. There is really no more to say except

that what has happened has been too much, too ugly, and too fast.

By today's reckoning, the network performances were as dull and unprogrammatical as the black-and-white tones in which they were rendered. On the day of the funeral, when all three networks were fully committed to uninterrupted coverage, the pictures were of the Capitol rotunda and thousands of mourners shuffling by the flag-draped casket, funereal music in the background. Segments of ten to fifteen minutes passed with no other words or pictures. Ruby's shooting of Oswald, hectic scenes from Parkland Hospital in Dallas, scenes from Kennedy's life, garish logos, and interviews with national and world leaders did not intrude. Technology, or the lack of it, was part of the reason as the networks were not yet capable of whipping around the world instantaneously, but respectful choice was the thrust behind the subdued treatment, and most Americans appreciated it.

Post-Watergate Syndrome

Cataclysmic news events would be the hallmark of the 1960s, and journalism's muscular response to them further evolutionary steps in the profession, not all of them positive. Racial strife; the assassinations of Robert Kennedy, Martin Luther King, Jr., and Malcolm X; the Vietnam War and the Pentagon Papers; Lyndon Johnson's decision not to seek a second term; the lunar landings—all these events left citizens and journalists breathless. But a late-night burglary at Washington's Watergate office and residence complex in 1972 would alter the tone of American journalism more than any of those stunning sixties events.

The sorry eighteen-month story of the Nixon administration's dirty tricks, lying, and cover-ups ended with the president's resignation in the face of impeachment and spawned what has been called the post-Watergate syndrome in journalism. Led by Bob Woodward and Carl Bernstein of *The Washington Post*, the nation's journalists had played a crucial role in the ultimate watchdog effort—bringing down a corrupt United States president.

In the heady aftermath of that unprecedented feat, journalism school enrollments shot upward and newsrooms were superheated with the feverish realization that while everyone cannot bring down a president, a dogcatcher might not be bad for starters. Seeing Richard Nixon as prototype rather than anomaly, journalists began a two-decade-long practice of treating all political figures at any level as potential suspects in the next Whatever-Gate. The journalistic norm became "We catch crooks." Scalps on the belt, particularly government scalps, were the sign of rank and the measure of testosterone at gatherings of the journalistic tribe. The democratic process, which had been superbly served by the Watergate reporting, was enveloped in a flood of self-indulgent and self-serving efforts by journalists-cum-cops to find a bogeyman under every government and institutional bed. There was nothing wrong with looking under the bed, of course; it was in fact an obligation. But in the overheated post-Watergate atmosphere, standards softened. A high percentage of the exposes merely exposed, with no accompanying suggestions about solutions. Like amateur exploratory brain surgery, inexpert and contextless investigative reporting left rather a mess. Not surprisingly, the self-reinforcing emphasis on killer journalism coincided with a decline in consumer appreciation of the effort. As we rushed about chasing crooks large and small, the public's regard for journalists declined almost in proportion to the effort we expended. By 1994, 71 percent of Americans surveyed agreed with the statement, "The news media gets in the way of society solving its problems." It was a particularly stunning indictment, the exact opposite of what we thought we were doing.

Journalism also learned from Watergate that, unlike the era of Chester S. Lord, journalists could indeed become both wealthy and famous, a realization that would turn the occasional knaves or fools who sneaked into the profession into an army of wanna-bes much more sinister and difficult to deal with: serial liars, cheats, and thieves driven by reckless ambition and bereft of the restraint and respect for intellectual honesty that guided most of their predecessors.

In the first thirty-five years of my experience in daily newspapering, I did not encounter any such liars, cheats, and thieves, or at least was not aware of them if they worked around or for me. In the last ten years of my experience, they were everywhere infecting a business, and a society, that seemed to have no useful serum for combating them. The miscreants I was forced to deal with were not on the grand national scale of 2004's Jack Kelley of *USA Today* and 2003's Jayson Blair of *The New York Times*, but only because the stages upon which they committed their transgressions were smaller. Their activities were just as damaging to their employers, their colleagues, the public, and the profession.

My set of dishonest demons ranged from a very talented, experienced, and relentless investigative reporter to a raw college-student summer intern, and the details of their cases, while painful to replay and equally painful to relay, are instructive in several ways. I emphasize that these people are still in the minority, as are Blair and Kelley in their milieu, because the majority of journalists, regardless of their level, talent, and ambition, are people trying to do their best in a profession they chose for old-fashioned and honorable reasons.

Because of that, the tradition of fundamental trust that is absolutely necessary to the operation of time-starved newsrooms can normally be relied upon. And there are safeguards: copy editors and editors who challenge what is presented for print, applying their experience and knowledge to evaluating what is written, testing its internal logic and consistency, asking questions of the reporter such as "Are you sure about . . . ? Have you double-checked . . . ? Did you talk to . . . ?"

Those checks and balances embedded in newsroom editing procedures are not based so much on a lack of trust in reporters as in an abundance of caution and desire for accuracy. When a reporter once asked if my sharply challenging questions about her copy indicated a lack of trust, I replied that there were many good reasons why people need to be certain about things, and told her this story:

When I was about six years old, I went to the drugstore with my mother. She made a small purchase and carefully counted the change put into her hand.

"Why'd you count the change," I asked, "don't you trust him?"

"Trust everyone," she said, "but count your change."

Then, "He might make a mistake in your favor and give you too much."

The point of the story: Getting it right is what matters.

When one of the minority of untrustworthy journalists appears, he or she can game that system of internal trust, at least until caught. Because of the nature of the process, it is usually readers who catch them up, and unfortunately, those readers often are also the subject-victims of the dishonest journalism. When a violation of the system of trust involves outright lying to editors or the fabrication of information or deliberate and obvious plagiarism, it must be one strike and you're out: The offender must be fired. As we shall see, however, that doesn't always happen, and the reasons it doesn't need to be examined, because some of the reasons have more to do with money and fame than with journalism.

Lie . . .

My talented, experienced, and dogged reporter had a hunch that the largest utility in Kansas had misled regulators and the public in order to win approval to build a nuclear plant in the 1980s. If he was right and the numbers justifying the investment in the plant were cooked, either the company would be forced into fiscal peril by the huge cost of the plant or its customers would be faced with crippling bills for the electricity that the company proclaimed would be "too cheap to meter."

The culminating story of his investigation was based on a considerable accumulation of research, a spreadsheet from a consultant on the project, and an interview with the company's chief financial officer in which he was quoted as saying, "We bet the company" on the nuclear plant. In fact, those words were the large, dark headline on the story stripped across the top of the Sunday edition front page. The consultant's document indicated that the company in fact knew the huge risk it was taking before the plant was approved, but ignored it.

On Monday, the CFO, who was a social acquaintance, called me, greatly disturbed by the quote and the headline.

"Are you saying you didn't say that?" I asked.

"Well, I did say it, but it was off the record. I was trying to emphasize to him how vital it was that we build the plant."

I said I'd get back to him.

I told the reporter, who normally tape-recorded all interviews, about the call. He pulled out a transcript of the interview and showed me the quote in a portion of the transcript that was, indeed, off the record. Then he pointed out a later portion of the transcript in which he, cleverly he implied, led the CFO back to that same issue and the CFO repeated the quote, this time clearly not off the record. It was a tricky piece of journalistic business, perhaps, but could be considered within the bounds of tough reporting, particularly since he was dealing with an experienced news source, not a naive citizen who happened to witness a bank robbery.

I called the CFO and told him what I had found. That's not how it happened, he insisted; he only said it once and it was off the record. He feared he would lose his job, because the utility's headquarters was in an understandable uproar over the story.

The next day I told the reporter that the matter was still in dispute and asked to hear the tape itself. "Oh, gosh," he said, "once it was transcribed, I reused the tape for other stuff, like always." Oh.

The company the next day disputed the consultant's figures, saying that the report and spreadsheet we had relied on were preliminary and had been updated when new data became available. The company provided a copy of the revised spreadsheet. But the sheet we had relied on—and printed a portion of in the newspaper—carried a later date than the company's supposed "revised and updated" version, seeming to prove what they knew and when they knew it.

It was getting sticky.

I called the consultant in California, described the particulars of the spreadsheet we had used, and asked if he had a copy in his files. He did. What was the date on it? "That one had no date on it" when he sent it to the reporter, he said, offering to send me a copy. But our copy did have a date, and it was a date that seemed to prove the reporter's point.

Doubly alarmed now, I went to the city desk clerk who had transcribed the interview with the CFO, a bright woman whose discretion I trusted. "No," she said, "I remember the quote and it was only in there once."

A check of the computer system's audit trail showed that the reporter went back into the transcript after the clerk typed it and manufactured the second, on-the-record version of the explosive quote. Later, a forensic expert I hired to analyze the spreadsheet concluded that the date had been added, within 95 percent certainty, by someone using a specific typewriter in the department where the reporter worked.

It was a stunning awakening. I knew that any reporter—or editor—was capable of making an error of fact or interpretation or judgment. It simply was not within my experience or mental grasp that a reporter would fabricate a document, make up a portion of an interview, and try to lie his way through the whole ugly mess.

The reporter was fired, of course, but the CFO's career was over and the company was badly damaged. Yet within four months the reporter had a job on a newspaper in another region of the country. They didn't call for a reference or even to verify his employment. He was not long on that job, however, before another of his investigations was so bloated and off-center that the newsroom staff petitioned management to have him fired, and he was. I heard no more of him until a few years later when a reporter in a Southern state called to ask about him. My former reporter was then a spokesman for the state's governor (again, no reference call to me), and the statehouse reporters felt he was often less than honest with them; in fact, that he lied to them a lot. It was the last I heard of him.

Cheat . . .

For a summer intern, the college student was unusual. He seemed mature, could write better than most at his level, and was energetic and determined. So when the assistant city editor told him, on deadline, that his story needed an additional quote from one of his sources, he leaped to the phone and came back with one that plugged the hole.

The next morning, the source called. It was exactly what she would have said, it represented her position correctly, but she hadn't talked to the reporter the night before, she said. She had not arrived home until very late.

The phone records showed a ten-second call to her number, and when the intern was confronted, he admitted feeling enormous pressure to perform and, in his anxiety, having her say what he "knew" she would have said had he talked to her. His summer ended abruptly, and I do not know whether he continued to pursue a career in journalism.

Steal . . .

The young sports columnist was terrific: sharp, funny, endlessly original, the sort of writer a medium-size newspaper is lucky to get and hopes to keep around for at least a while, but who is clearly headed for the big time. His interview with the new manager of the local Class AA baseball team was a gem. The manager was uproariously funny, using quaint language to weave wonderful stories, and the columnist caught it all. So when the manager called the newspaper the next day, he was almost apologetic. The column made him look so good, so clever, he said, that he probably should not complain, but he thought we should know that he didn't say any of that, though he wished he were that colorful.

It turned out that the column had been lifted from another newspaper. The only substantial change our columnist made was to substitute the local manager's name and team for the original ones. After the columnist was fired, a check of his computer files revealed a cache of literally hundreds of other writers' best work, full columns and bits and pieces of bright writing apparently queued up to be presented as his own. He had routinely collected the items from the various wire services to which he had access. Such collections are much easier to come by these days because of the Internet, where the theft-prone writer can use search engines to gin up words on virtually any subject.

The columnist's plagiarism should have ended the young man's journalism career, but it didn't. The managing editor of a major-market newspaper called months later for a reference; they had been bowled over by the man's apparent talent and potential. I told him the full story. "Heck," he said, "all sports writers steal from each other." If there was ever a time when one could argue that sports was the toy department of journalism and such transgressions could be winked at, that time ended with multimillion-dollar salaries, taxpayer-financed domed stadiums, ten-dollar hot dogs, and criminal records sometimes outnumbering athletic records in the sports pages. Yet many newspapers apparently consider plagiarism a minor offense. The columnist was not hired by the managing editor who called me, but he did stay in journalism and worked for several newspapers.

Early in my career, I hired a reporter right out of college as one of seven staff members on a very small newspaper. This reporter yearned to be a movie critic. After a couple of years doing a good job, he got his chance to review movies for a substantial-size paper, but was fired for plagiarism in an incident that was widely reported in the journalistic media. He was hired by another paper and fired for the same offense of stealing from other reviewers, again with accompanying attention within the profession. Astonishingly, that didn't stop him or the editors who were either willing to take a risk or indifferent about plagiarism. He was hired by a third newspaper that apparently believed in at least three strikes for ethical breeches.

. . . And Trust

The instructive part of those stories is not that they happened. The vocation of journalism, like any other, will always have its bad actors who eventually will trip over their accumulated excesses. As with the *Times'* Blair and *USA Today's* Kelley, however, their malfeasance can go on for years and exact a huge toll on their colleagues, their institutions, and, in the cases of Blair and Kelley, their editors, each of whom was forced to resign from one of the top jobs in journalism.

Because of the First Amendment license to self-define, most journalists are opposed to self-regulation that would involve enforcement of ethical standards, such as with lawyers or doctors. The philosophy—in which I concur—holds that there can and should be no limitations on free expression. Journalism associations often have codes of ethics that serve as useful guidelines and expression of principles for their members but are not enforceable on them. Many newspaper companies and individual newspapers have codes or rules of ethics, written or implied, that they can and do enforce, but the idea that journalists, like realtors or schoolteachers, must meet any sort of qualifying standards other than those set by employers quickly runs afoul of the First Amendment. As an ironic result, journalism, which is absolutely dependent upon accuracy and truth, is particularly vulnerable to infiltration by people with no regard whatsoever for such ideas. It is perhaps remarkable that abuses do not happen more often.

When abuse does occur, when it is clear that a person has violated the tradition—and necessity—of trust, it is essential for the organization's action to be swift and sure. That's why, when the Blair and Kelley transgressions became known, their newspapers reacted not only with dismissals but with long and deep investigations that resulted in detailed public disclosure amounting to multiple pages of newsprint. Such public self-examination and exposure is not simply public relations; it is an obligation for an institution that is beyond the reach and control of everything except public opinion.

And yet, as the anecdotes I've shared reveal, at least some newspapers keep hiring and tolerating people who, in the hierarchy of journalistic crimes, are known felons and capital offenders. The internal investigations by *The New York Times* and *USA Today* each revealed that for years, journalists at both newspapers harbored, and often expressed to editors, concerns about the work of Blair and Kelley, respectively. In many instances, the reporters' news sources complained to higher-ups at the newspapers; signs of potential problems were abundant and routinely ignored or rationalized away, both sets of internal investigators discovered. Four of the people I dealt with for blatant and knowing ethical offenses wound up at other newspapers. Their offenses were not in the nature of accidents or a failure to comprehend, and they did not fall into gray areas; they were deliberate decisions to lie, cheat, and steal.

Given that a newspaper's credibility is its most precious asset, it is difficult to understand why any news organization would risk hiring someone with a record of ethical shortcomings, fail to check references, or hesitate to investigate rigorously the instant that credible questions of unethical behavior arise about a current staffer. *USA Today's* investigative panel of distinguished journalists concluded that Kelley's "star" status provided him with protective coloration from the grumblings of some of his lesser-known or lesser-favored colleagues who knew or suspected his mendacity. Handsome and articulate, he frequently appeared on television news and talk shows and was the newspaper's most-sought-after speaker. That wasn't just self-promotion, though Kelley was good at that; it was also the newspaper's doing as it sought to compete with its more established and respected, even if smaller, competitors such as *The New York Times*, *The Washington Post*, and *The Wall Street Journal*. The investigative panel worried that the newspaper's anxious ambition led its editors to accept Kelley's work without sufficient challenge.

When people inside or outside the organization raised questions about the accuracy of his reporting, they were shrugged off as either jealous competitors or hypersensitive sources. Kelley's (and the newspaper's) overabundance of hubris allowed him to fabricate stories for more than a decade, for he was an integral part of his newspaper's marketing efforts. When Kelley's editor resigned in the glare of the scandal, *USA Today* publisher Craig Moon's choice of language was telling. He did not talk about an opportunity to do better journalism. He said the resignation "opens the door to move the *USA Today* brand forward under new leadership." Was marketing more important than truth in that dark moment for the newspaper?

Bill Kovach, veteran editor, former curator of the Neiman Fellowships at Harvard University, and founding director of the Committee of Concerned Journalists, saw similarities in the Kelley and Blair cases that I felt in the ones I faced: unfettered, incautious ambition.

"One of the common denominators [in the Blair and Kelley cases] was the need to have a star at your organization to help brand your organization and set it apart from competitors. To have a name that people recognized and identified with . . . the be all and end all of their career desires—to be famous. 'I want to be somebody.' And they were not capable, based on their experience and their working techniques, of producing the kind of journalism that would . . . make them better known. So they had to make it up."

Worse, Kovach contended, their editors were subconsciously supporting their deceptions out of a desire to have star reporters. "The pressure on editors in this new competitive atmosphere is such that they're eaten up by management requirements. They go to meetings all the time. Editors spend more time in meetings than they do talking with and working with their reporters. . . . They have to find time to be editors first."[2]

"Who Do I See About . . . ?"

In screenwriter Kurt Luedtke's script *Absence of Malice*, there's a moment in which the Paul Newman character, treated unfairly in a newspaper story, is asked why he did not complain about it.

"Have you ever tried to talk to a newspaper?" he asks ruefully.

It isn't easy. Newspapers receive a constant flow of complaints— about the paper being thrown into the bushes; about too much of this coverage and too little of that; about bias in reporting and bad judgment in picture selection; about being too liberal or too conservative (often on the same day and in reference to the same editorial). Getting to a willing listener who can act on your complaint can be frustrating and time-consuming. In the case of Kelley and *USA Today*, the newspaper's own investigators talked to multiple government sources whose complaints over the years had been so thoroughly rebuffed by the paper's management that they finally gave up. Wrote one source, "Years ago I repeatedly complained about accuracy in Mr. Kelley's reporting. I was met with insult and assured that his longtime standing with *USA Today* and his professional qualifications outweighed any concerns I might have voiced."

Certainly people who complain specifically about a story's accuracy or fairness must receive a close hearing by editors, and newspapers should proactively seek such complaints. Some newspapers do it through one or more mechanisms. "Public editors," people whose job it is to receive complaints about content, can be useful if their presence is broadly publicized and they have the internal clout to do something about the complaints. Another program involves the newspaper sending out "fairness and accuracy" forms for people named in news stories to fill out and return. Newspaper Web sites sometimes have places to register complaints. Teams of editors hold "open house" listening events around the community. But none of those mechanisms will work unless editors, once they have established the validity of a complaint, take vigorous action.

In any human endeavor, as the potential rewards get larger so does the temptation to take advantage of the systems under which the institution operates. That has been seen in brokerage houses, corporate boardrooms, and legislative bodies, as well as in journalism. When "journalist" mutates into "media star," and when book advances, speaking fees, and broadcast royalties far outstrip newspaper salaries, the tradition of trust comes under heavy pressure. The bottom line is that a small number of serial frauds and cheats will always be with us, testing the trust, and it requires a constant interaction between readers/sources and newspaper managers to uncover and deal with them.

Tips for Coping

It may be hard to talk to a newspaper, but it can be done. Newspapers vary in their response and policies, but if you are somehow involved in a story that has inaccuracies, it's your obligation to try to fix it.

First, find out what mechanisms (such as the ones mentioned previously) the newspaper has for dealing with complaints. Use one of them.

Second, don't be in the position of saying, "That's the third time you've made the same error." The first time is clearly the newspaper's problem alone. The second and subsequent times, you share culpability. Newspapers can't correct things they don't know are wrong.

Third, be clear in the nature of your complaint and provide authenticating information if necessary.

Fourth, be relentless and do not be put off by negative responses; go up the ladder. Even small errors need to be corrected. Most newspapers these days are willing to make corrections on matters of substance, but whether it is a matter of substance should be your call, not the newspaper's. If it's important to you, that should make it important to the newspaper.

Fifth, matters of factual accuracy are one thing. Matters of news judgment and interpretation—often seen by the offended as matters of fairness—are another. A common complaint to editors is, "Your reporter must not have been at the same meeting I attended. The important thing that happened actually was . . . " I often ran into that kind of criticism when talking with groups of readers, and at the end of the meetings I would say, "Okay, let's do an exercise. Everyone write on a piece of paper what is the most important/interesting/controversial thing I have said in the last half-hour. If you were reporting on this meeting, what would be your headline?" Though they had all heard the same words, the answers I read back to them would vary wildly. Point made.

Sixth, don't shout and make wild accusations. Newspapers do not want to get things wrong; errors are almost always matters of competence rather than maliciousness. But if you should be unfortunate enough to find you are dealing with one of those "lie, cheat, steal" aberrations, you are obligated to let that be known to the highest-ranking person you can reach, and follow up if nothing is done.

PART THREE: EVENING

10

Doing the Journalism

"In today's world, the communities we serve and the country we serve face very daunting problems that must be solved if we are to continue to realize the promise of America for our children and grandchildren. And I deeply believe that newspapers, well edited, well published, are wonderfully situated to be instruments of helping America find its way, solve its problems, seize its opportunities. And that's an ennobling way to spend one's life." — Jim Batten, spring 1995

PEOPLE INSTINCTIVELY TRUSTED Jim Batten. When he said or wrote something such as the lines above, you knew there was no guile at work, no hidden agenda. It was what he believed to his core. That was the way he led his life and directed his newspaper company—through mutual trust and dedication to principle. He believed in finding the best possible like-minded people and allowing them leeway to do their work. So when, in October 1993, his car veered into the concrete light pole, those people he had enabled to be good journalists were stunned, fearful, and in tears. Even though they were accustomed to seeing life's vagaries reflected in the pages of their newspapers, they were not prepared to accept such a harsh personal dose of reality.

At the time of the accident, newspapers had been in serious trouble for a decade or more, and pressures to improve financial performance were growing. Household penetration—the percentage of households that read a newspaper—was falling steadily. Advertisers were finding more, and they thought better, ways to reach their customers. Technology-driven competitors were edging into what had traditionally been newspapers' core franchise. The "bad guys," whom Batten had declared in 1975 he needed to keep an eye on, were ascendant in the newspaper industry, and they were cutting costs—which inevitably meant cutting the size and quality of newspapers—to satisfy the demand for increasing profits in the drastically changed investing environment.

Batten: That "Special Spark"

Batten's physical peril put at risk, in the eyes of the company's journalists, a fifteen-year record of achievement unparalleled in the profession's history. Under his guidance, Knight Ridder's newspapers had become widely recognized as among the nation's finest, a reputation that was self-sustaining because Knight Ridder was the place bright young people wanted to work. Recruiting staffers, even for its smaller papers, consisted more of selection than persuasion. The company was regularly ranked among the best companies to work for regardless of industry.

Batten and his fellow journalists were not unaware of the volatile and threatening business environment, but they were confident that the company could work its way through the tough times while avoiding the drastic measures they saw being adopted by other newspaper companies. This was more a matter of faith than reality, it would turn out, because the environmental changes were in fact systemic and not cyclical and would require more than a "riding it out" strategy. There was an alternative to draconian cutbacks, but it would be slower and riskier than simply cutting costs. The alternative—finding ways to make even better, smarter newspapers—would be expensive and time-consuming, but such a strategy would not involve the company eating its journalistic seed corn. Knight Ridder's journalists depended upon Batten, as CEO and chairman, to give them the space and time to do that; to maintain a balance in the natural tension between short-term profit and journalistic performance.

Batten was Knight Ridder's solid link back to Jack Knight and Lee Hills. That a person at his organizational level of remove from daily newspapering could exert such a continuing personal influence on the editors and publishers of a $2-billion-a-year, 20,000-employee company of more than thirty far-flung newspapers was testament to his heritage, his personality, and his dedication to substantive journalism. Even with all his CEO/chairman duties, including important civic obligations to the Miami community, he could still find time to flop down on the floor in front of an editor's den fireplace and talk into the night about newspapering, or put together a team of corporate people so they could spend a day traveling to one of the newspapers to learn about and reinforce the innovative things the staff was doing.

His hold on his journalists was earned in their trenches. A native of the Suffolk, Virginia, area, he studied chemistry and biology at Davidson College, twenty miles from Charlotte, North Carolina, intending to go into plant pathology, which was his father's vocation. In his senior year, however, he edited the college newspaper, and through that he came to the attention of Pete McKnight, editor of *The Charlotte Observer* and a Davidson alumnus. McKnight, impressed by Batten's intellect and character, talked him into a temporary summer job at the *Observer* in 1957, a period that put plant pathology out of the young man's mind and printer's ink into his veins. He spent seven years there, his time interrupted by a tour of military duty and a year to earn a master's degree in public affairs from Princeton. In 1965 he moved to Knight Newspapers' Washington bureau as the *Observer*'s correspondent, and within three years Batten was promoted onto the national staff in that bureau.

I was his successor as the *Observer*'s Washington correspondent, the second time in our early careers that we worked closely enough that I could see his skills firsthand. The first was in Charlotte, when I was an assistant city editor and he was a new city desk reporter. The copy he turned in was crisp and clean (that is, once he learned to type, a skill he didn't possess when McKnight hired him), and his reporting was the most thorough on a respected and skilled staff. We would sometimes come into conflict late at night, with a deadline looming, because he always wanted to make one more confirming phone call, recheck one more fact.

In Washington in the 1960s, he focused on the civil rights movement, particularly school desegregation. We collaborated on several stories, including a series about how school desegregation was affecting the lives of families in Cincinnati and Charlotte, cities where contrasting desegregation processes were under way. He took Cincinnati, I had Charlotte. My interviews with parents got me into their minds; his interviews got him into their hearts. I was grateful to be collaborating with him rather than competing against him, for he would outthink, outreport, and outwrite you every time. (We did compete on the tennis court where, at least, I could prevail. He was tall and a bit gangly and couldn't handle balls hit at his feet.) His career moved quickly, to the *Detroit Free Press* city desk, well known as Knight Newspapers' boot camp (so designated by Lee Hills because it was a tough newspaper in a tough town in the midst of a life-or-death struggle with *The Detroit News*), then to Charlotte as executive editor in 1972, and then, with the merger with Ridder Publications, to corporate headquarters in 1975.

At every step, his humanity came through first and most strongly. He cared how you were doing; he was constant, relentless even, in recognizing good work with a note or a phone call, and encouraging in positive ways when the work was not up to his standards. And it was his clear standards articulated with grace and style that allowed him, even as the company's top officer, to inspire the journalists who worked far below him on the organizational chart.

But as Batten lay in a Miami hospital on a ventilator following the 1993 auto accident, his journalists' level of confidence was being tested. Imagining life without Jim Batten, even rendered as a bare possibility, was traumatic for people brought up in the Knight tradition of newspapering and Batten's stewardship of it. Behind him in the company's line of succession for the top-most job of chairman and CEO was Tony Ridder. Without Batten, the company would, for the first time in its history, lack an experienced journalist in the highest seats of power.

In the best of times, Ridder's ascension without a news-side partner would have been a cause for concern on the part of newsroom people. He had the misfortune, however, of taking over the newspaper division and, four years later, the company presidency at the height of wrenching changes in the publishing environment. When he rose to KR president in 1989, he immediately made clear his intention to steadily increase the newspapers' operating returns and set about doing so in ways that elevated the levels of newsroom concern to angst and beyond. He was very good at cutting costs, but he had the additional misfortune, stemming from his background, of not being able to articulate to the journalists a persuasive reason why improvements on the bottom line need not come at the expense of the company's journalistic heritage. Neither did he have anyone to articulate it for him.

Rich Oppel, now editor of the *Austin American-Statesman* and among more than two dozen editors and publishers who would leave KR in a nineties exodus (see Chapter 11), put it this way: "The fortunes of Knight Ridder declined parallel to the decline of Jim Batten's health. As he began to fade and Tony Ridder emerged, you could see where things were going. It wasn't absolutely clear, and I liked Tony and still like him personally—I don't think he is a malign person in any way when it comes to journalism—but I don't think he has the touch, the sensitivity and knowledge of the special spark that is required, that the Lee Hills and Jim Battens had. While Alvah [Chapman] may not have had it himself burning in his breast, he seemed to have an uncanny ability to support people who did."

Keeping alive that "special spark" for good journalism was a heritage that reached back to the days in Akron and Miami, when Jack Knight and Lee Hills responded to difficult economic times by making better, larger, more aggressive newspapers. That heritage flowed forward through the middle years of the century as Knight Newspapers expanded and, in every case, made its newly acquired newspapers better journalistically.

The residual momentum behind that philosophy ignited in the first years after the merger of Knight and Ridder with Batten's arrival at corporate as a vice president for news. In the next eighteen years, Knight-Ridder newspapers would win forty-three Pulitzers and its largest newspapers, *The Miami Herald* and *The Philadelphia Inquirer*, would consistently rank in most versions of the best American newspapers lists. Even some of the smaller newspapers were often cited— such as in 1984, when *Time* magazine named *The Wichita Eagle* and the *Akron Beacon Journal* "among the best of the rest" of newspapers too small to make the magazine's top-ten list.

Great journalism—the kind that helps communities work, that allows people and cities and nations to seize their opportunities, to paraphrase Batten's words at the beginning of this chapter—is always the result of talented people being supported by time and resources and inspiration to do what they know how to do. Gathering prizes awarded by other journalists isn't the objective of meaningful journalism, and much of the very best work never wins that sort of notice, but peer recognition is one measure of good journalism. Although the Knight Ridder Pulitzer streak during 1975–1993 was but a surface reflection of a much deeper and broader run of significant work that the company's newspapers produced, the Pulitzers do offer a readable trail of excellence in the subjective wilderness of trying to define journalistic quality. The stories behind those prizes offer instruction about how such excellence is produced.

Three Mile Island

The trail to an important story or investigative series most often starts with a question. Why is this happening? What can be done about . . . ? Who is responsible for . . . ? What if . . . ? The question can be posed by a reporter, an editor, a citizen, or an official. Or the trail can start with an event (e.g., a major storm, a plane crash) that galvanizes a newspaper staff into action. But a second step is required: the commitment to answer the question or respond to the event. And excellence cannot occur if the first thought is "Can we afford to do this?" because the answer to that question is most likely "No, within our existing budget we cannot afford to do it."

Eugene Roberts never shrank from any of those questions, and in his eighteen years in charge of the newsroom at *The Philadelphia Inquirer*, his reporters, editors, and photographers won an astonishing seventeen Pulitzers as the newspaper grew from a second-place mediocrity in Philadelphia to national prominence.

For Roberts, there was always a way to find the money to do what good journalism required, at least until the corporate accountants started sitting at his shoulder trying to micromanage. One of his operating principles was to think large and early about what could happen, and have a plan for covering it. He'd ask his editors, What's the worst thing that could happen in this city? A nuclear attack? A massive flood? How would we cover it, down to every imaginable detail? He'd ask everything except how would we pay for it; that question was not allowed to affect the plan; that problem would be for later.

So when the nuclear plant at Three Mile Island, near Harrisburg, experienced a near-disastrous failure in the early morning hours of March 28, 1979, the *Inquirer* was not forced to ad lib. Within twenty-four hours, eighty staffers, almost a third of the paper's professional complement, were working exclusively on the story. They would work it around the clock for twelve days, stopping only for catnaps and food on the run. A contingency plan existed to draw more help from the sports staff and the paper's regular city beats should the story expand.

As was Roberts's practice, the attack on the story was two-pronged. One was a team of reporters and editors assigned to provide saturation coverage of daily developments, ranging from the official versions—what officials of plant owner Metropolitan Edison were saying, the reaction of nuclear regulatory agencies, the response of the governor—to the decidedly unofficial: anecdotes of how employees and area residents were dealing with a long-feared crisis, stories about a sudden increase in gun sales, about children's fearful dreams, dozens of stories that not only illuminated events but also helped readers put into perspective both the real and imagined dangers of a nuclear plant running out of control. The other team began immediately focusing on a detailed reconstruction of what went wrong and how it could have been avoided.

The reconstruction team sought answers at all levels and in all sorts of places, including just outside the door of a motel room in which Met Ed officials were cloistered with people from a newly hired national public relations firm to discuss how to deal with the negative impact of the accident without, in fact, talking with the news media. *Inquirer* reporters ran down hundreds of sources, including fifty workers from the plant tracked through license plates in the parking lot and inquiries at the bars where they hung out.

Beginning at noon Friday, April 6, a four-member writing team began pulling together an exhaustive reconstruction that would, when completed twenty-four hours later, occupy nine full pages in the Sunday newspaper. It was a classic of minute detail and big-picture analysis from the points of view of officials, workers, regulators, and citizens. It demonstrated, according to the *Inquirer* narrative that accompanied its entry in the Pulitzer competition:

The lack of any state or federal evacuation plan for the nearly one million people within thirty miles of the nuclear reactor.

The laxity of the federal regulatory apparatus prior to the nuclear disaster and its haplessness and ineptitude during the disaster.

The faulty and too-hasty construction of the reactor itself, and the continued operation of it with inadequate maintenance and repair.

And the lackadaisical and insufficient training of the men and women who operate the reactor and who are relied upon to bring it under control when something goes wrong.

Thankfully, the incident ended much more quietly than it began. The reactor was deactivated and no serious injuries were reported, but there would be months of commercial and political reverberations as Congress and state and federal officials wrestled with the very questions raised by the *Inquirer*, thereby substantiating much of its reporting. For decades, the nuclear industry had operated safely and securely, troubled only by the unrealized fears expressed by antinuclear groups. Three Mile Island was a stark declaration that something awful could in fact happen, and many of its lessons were turned into better evacuation planning, better construction and operational controls, and more complete training. The *Inquirer* staff was awarded the Pulitzer for spot news reporting.

PTL

For televangelists Jim and Tammy Faye Bakker, it was always about not having enough money. Just a few more dollars, they would tell their nationwide audience, and the Lord's work will surely get done. For more than ten years, from a modest start in Charlotte, North Carolina, their seemingly heartfelt prayers and pleas duped more than 116,000 Americans into sending them more than $158 million. After all, there was evangelical work to be done in places like South Korea and China, overwhelming sin to combat in the United States, and their multimillion-dollar Heritage USA living and recreational development in South Carolina would provide a Christian environment where their supporters could choose to live out their lives in security and peace. If only the Bakkers could raise enough money.

For reporter Charles Shepard of *The Charlotte Observer* and his editor, Rich Oppel, the accumulation of that much money raised questions of accountability, and with the Bakkers' PTL (Praise the Lord) ministry, there was no public accounting. They were only one of a boom in television evangelists during the 1970s and 1980s, but they were the most flamboyant and aggressive of them, and for the people at the *Observer* they were local news as they steadily built over the years an enormous, dedicated, and open-pursed following.

Along the way, questions arose. In 1979, the *Observer* reported that money raised for a South Korean evangelist never got there. In 1983, the *Observer* reported that the Bakkers, while pleading poverty on the air, had bought and decorated a Florida condominium. In 1984, the Bakkers announced that they had given everything they owned to PTL (and urged others to do the same), but the *Observer* reported that they still owned an expensive home, a Mercedes, and a Rolls-Royce in California. Also that year, Shepard learned of, but did not then report, accusations by a church secretary of coerced sex with Bakker in 1980 and alleged payoffs to keep her quiet. Each of these stories and reporters' inquiries about other matters brought stonewalling from the ministry and called down on the newspaper the wrath of PTL and its supporters. Angry letters and phone calls excoriated the paper for daring to challenge the Lord's good shepherds.

In 1986, PTL launched an all-out offensive against the *Observer* and Knight Ridder. In a national media campaign it called "Enough Is Enough," PTL, in the words of Oppel, "sought to bury the *Observer* under an avalanche of subscriptions stops, advertising withdrawals, telephone calls and letters, including dozens directed to Knight Ridder."

The deluge of mail from across the nation was mostly negative and often apocalyptic, as this one from Oklahoma:

> You will have boils, tumors, scurvy, and itch, for none of which there will be a remedy. You will have madness, blindness, fear, and panic will come over you. You will watch as your loved ones are taken by dope, booze, or maybe prostitution. You will eat the flesh of your sons and daughters in the days of siege ahead. This not something I thought up. It is the Word of God.

PTL also hired private detectives to keep twenty-four-hour watch on Oppel and Publisher Rolfe Neill, hoping to find some way to discredit them. On the air across the nation, the Bakkers tried to turn the subscriber and advertising boycott against all of Knight Ridder's newspapers, which quite naturally drew the attention of KR corporate, including Chairman Alvah Chapman.

In May, an evangelist who knew both Chapman and Bakker arranged for a meeting in Miami, which PTL characterized as a demonstration that KR corporate was concerned about the *Observer*'s credibility. But when Bakker learned that Oppel and Neill would attend, at Chapman's insistence, he backed out. Neither Chapman nor any other KR corporate officer normally would become involved in a newspaper's battles unless invited, but the heat from the PTL national campaign was directed at more than the *Observer*. The day after the meeting fell through, Chapman called to quiz Oppel about whether the editor had any doubts about the stories and whether there was anything that he wished he had done differently. Oppel's response was that he was comfortable with the content of the PTL coverage; that was the end of corporate involvement.

After another year of dogged reporting, Shepard submitted a series of written questions to Bakker and PTL detailing what he felt he knew, including the information about the payoff to the church secretary and the over-subscription of the ministry's "Lifetime Partnerships" that promised various perks, including annual stays at Heritage USA. On March 19, 1987, Bakker resigned from PTL, again claiming a lack of money. "I am not able to muster the resources to combat a new wave of attacks that I have learned is about to be launched against us by *The Charlotte Observer*, which has attacked us incessantly for the past twelve years," Bakker said.

The resignation broke loose a logjam that enabled the *Observer* to report over the next six weeks that the payments to the church secretary, with PTL money, totaled $265,000 and were laundered through a PTL contractor; that the Bakkers and other PTL officials, unknown to the PTL board, had paid themselves millions of dollars in bonuses; that viewers had sent in $49 million to help build a hotel at Heritage USA that was budgeted for $29 million and was, in 1987, still unfinished; that one of Bakker's personal assistants received $610,000 in fifteen months, while his secretary was paid $160,000 a year.

In 1989, Bakker and three of his lieutenants were convicted in federal court of swindling 116,000 PTL followers out of $158 million. Bakker received a sentence of forty-five years in prison, his assistants ten years. The jury took only ten hours to unravel the complicated case, and Judge Robert Potter said at the sentencing, "Those of us who do have a religion are sick to death of being saps for money-grubbing preachers." Bakker was released in 1994.

The Pulitzer committee awarded *The Charlotte Observer* the Gold Medal for Public Service for its investigation of Bakker and PTL.

Kentucky Basketball

Kentucky Wildcat basketball in the 1980s was "the one thing that unifies all classes of people and all regions of the state," in the words of John S. Carroll, then editor of the *Lexington Herald-Leader*. So when reporters Jeffrey Marx and Michael York uncovered widespread payoffs to Kentucky players by school boosters, they and their newspaper were seen as betrayers of a great tradition.

Their series of stories emerged from the most basic kind of journalism—source cultivation. They won the confidence of dozens of former Wildcat players by spending time with them—on the basketball court, at discos, in church. Interviewing the thirty-three players took them to eleven states. Twenty-six of the players admitted that they broke NCAA rules and named the boosters and others who participated in the violations. Some of the players opened up once they learned that the stories would deal with endemic abuse and not just one or two cases, believing this might help end the pattern of abuse. The *Herald-Leader* went to court against the university and the state government in order to get records under the state's freedom of information laws.

All of this did not sit well with Wildcat fans. The reporters were threatened even before the series of articles was published, and players they had talked to were pressured to change their stories. Once the stories naming names appeared, the hostility increased. The newspaper plant was cleared by a bomb scare, a shot was fired into the pressroom, the woman answering the newsroom phones was reduced to tears by the verbal assaults, a subscriber chased a carrier with an axe handle, subscription cancellations flooded in, the reporters and their editor Carroll were threatened with violence. There was even a "Trash the Herald" rally of supporters, and anti–*Herald-Leader* T-shirts, caps, and bumper stickers enriched entrepreneurs across the state.

The 1985 expose was hardly the first in Kentucky's basketball history, which already included two point-shaving scandals and many recruiting misadventures, but it was the first to be documented by one newspaper's aggressive and unpopular reporting and resulted in a Pulitzer Prize for investigative reporting.

A KR corporate cultural footnote to the uproar: Some time later, Northwestern University honored its Pulitzer Prize–winning alumni with a dinner attended by Marx. Batten was also there as an honored guest and they shared a ride back to the hotel when Batten said, "Let's have a beer." Marx, then twenty-three years old, had been planning to meet a college buddy for a few beers in the lobby bar but this was, after all, the CEO of his company. When Marx introduced Batten, his friend asked, "Oh, do you work with Jeffrey at the paper?" Batten, Marx recalls, made a noncommittal response, they chatted over their beer, and Batten excused himself. When Marx and his friend later tried to pay their tab the waitress said that she had been told "by the other gentleman" to leave the tab open and he would pay it. It was Batten's way of saying, "I like you guys and I appreciate what you're doing," Marx said, "just an unexpected nicety."

Hurricane Andrew

Sometimes major news stories hurl themselves at a newspaper, as Hurricane Andrew did in August 1992. Killer storms, earthquakes, and floods test not only a newspaper's journalistic reflexes but also the personal courage and resolve of its staffers as they struggle to cover the story even while their own homes and families are in peril. For *The Miami Herald* and KR corporate headquarters itself, Hurricane Andrew would present the toughest possible test as it wreaked billions of dollars in damage in a brief twenty-four hours of climatological mayhem.

It was, as the *Herald*'s day-before-landfall headline read, "The Big One" for a tropical city accustomed to annual hurricanes, but not one of Andrew's size and power. As the storm bore down on Miami from the Caribbean, the *Herald* produced a special edition, in Spanish and English, with no advertising and distributed free, offering not only news of the storm but also information about shelters and relief agencies and suggestions for preparing homes and businesses. Less than ten hours after the eye passed over the city's southern suburbs, a second special edition of some 110,000 copies was available in shelters, hotels, and the distribution boxes that had not disappeared in the storm's wrath.

Even after sixty newsroom staffers' homes were destroyed and scores more heavily damaged, the reporters, editors, artists, and photographers told the story and began an extraordinary effort to help the community recover. In the first two weeks after the storm hit, the newspaper produced more than 200 full pages and another 200 partial pages in editions aimed at helping citizens cope with the area's worst-ever natural disaster. Despite the fact that the *Herald*'s distribution area sustained heavy damage and three warehouses were destroyed, production and circulation people managed to deliver newspapers to 65 percent of subscribers in Dade County.

Those editions' content did much more than chronicle the devastation. Up to three of the open pages daily were devoted to free exchanges of personal messages—people looking for family members, relatives, friends—and listings of ways to get help and repair materials. In the first three weeks, 40,000 copies a day were distributed free in the hardest-hit areas just south of the city, where, because of lack of electricity and telephone service, the newspaper was the area's only link with the outside world. The papers included a special Help tabloid aimed at those citizens. The newspaper also organized a kids-to-kids program that raised more than $70,000 for children who had lost clothes and school supplies, and it printed daily updates on the condition of roads, water supply, and electric and telephone service. Hard questions were addressed quickly, such as the enormous number of homes and businesses that, in the storm's wake, showed clear signs of building code violations and sloppy housing inspections. The misconduct was detailed in a sixteen-page report called "What Went Wrong."

The extraordinary effort to help a devastated community find a way back fulfilled the Pulitzer criteria for the Gold Medal: "A distinguished example of meritorious public service by a newspaper through the use of its journalistic resources."

Margins of Excellence

The level of professionalism, inspiration, and plain hard work reflected in those stories, and the hundreds like them produced during Knight Ridder's "Pulitzer Years," cannot be reached without a budgetary margin for excellence. Investigating complex situations, developing webs of contacts, and searching through voluminous public records require time, money, and unwavering support from the highest levels. Standing up to institutions, readers, government officials, and advertisers unhappy with aggressive reporting requires a commitment to more than the bottom line. When there is no margin for excellence, editors are faced with doleful choices: attend to the newspaper's basic reportorial duties and forgo the more complex and substantive investigative stories, or cut back on basic coverage in favor of a minimum level of investigative reporting. Doing both well is not a possibility when all but the most basic resources are sucked onto the bottom line.

The selection of the annual Pulitzer winners is often controversial and sometimes marred by whiffs of professional politics. But even given that, a strong argument can be marshaled that the relentless drive to increase Knight Ridder's annual operating returns, despite a period of stagnant circulation and advertising growth, has diminished the ability of its newspapers to produce the kind of journalism upon which it was founded.

Again, the readable trail of Pulitzers is helpful.

It begins in 1980, when Batten was promoted to senior vice president for news, extending his reach and influence to all of the company's newspapers. Larry Jinks, former editor of *The Miami Herald* and the *San Jose Mercury News*, soon joined Batten as vice president of news for the company's largest papers. The thirteen years from 1980 through 1993 would see KR newspapers produce thirty-eight Pulitzers, including three Gold Medals for Public Service, the most prestigious of the Pulitzers. Jinks would leave the corporate staff to become publisher in San Jose in 1989 and Batten's auto accident was in 1993. In nine years from 1994 through 2003, the newspapers produced nine Pulitzers.

During 1980–1993, the company's operating return hovered in the low teens. In the late years of the 1994–2003 period, it rose to more than 20 percent.

The following list provides details of Pulitzers and profits for KR newspapers. (Awards are given for work in the previous year, so prizes for 2004 represent work during 2003. Profit margins are for the fiscal year preceding the award year.)

(Note: Columbia University in New York City maintains the archives of the Pulitzer Prize recipients. Winning entries for the years 1917 through 1995 are on microfilm at the Lehman Reference Library there. Winning entries for 1987 to the present are available in print. A summary of all the prizes since 1917 and winning entries from 1995 to the present are also available online at www.pulitzer.org//archive/archive.html.)

Pulitzers and Profits

1980   The Miami Herald, for feature writing, "Zepp's Last Stand."

The Philadelphia Inquirer, for local general or spot news, for coverage of the Three Mile Island nuclear accident.

KR operating return: 9.0 percent.

1981   The Charlotte Observer, Gold Medal for Public Service for exposing the health risks of textile workers from brown lung disease.

Detroit Free Press, for feature photography of conditions at Jackson State Prison.

The Miami Herald, for international reporting on Central America.

KR operating return: 8.5 percent.

1982   No Pulitzers. Operating return 8.1 percent. Batten becomes KR president.

1983   The Miami Herald, for editorial writing exposing the illegal detention of Haitian immigrants.

The News-Sentinel (Fort Wayne, Indiana), for local general or spot news coverage of a massive flood that crippled the community.

KR operating return: 7.8 percent.

1984   No Pulitzers.

KR operating return: 14.9 percent.

1985   The Macon Telegraph & News, for specialized reporting on the conflict between athletics and academics at the University of Georgia and Georgia Tech.

Philadelphia Daily News, for editorial writing on a variety of subjects.

The Philadelphia Inquirer, for feature photography from Angola and El Salvador.

The Philadelphia Inquirer, for investigative reporting on the excessive and abusive use of K9 dogs by city police, which resulted in the removal of twelve officers.

KR operating return: 15.7 percent.

1986 *Lexington Herald-Leader*, for investigative reporting that brought reforms related to booster payoffs to University of Kentucky basketball players.

The Miami Herald, for spot news photography on a volcano eruption in Colombia.

The Miami Herald, for general news reporting on the police beat by Edna Buchanan.

The Philadelphia Inquirer, for national reporting on scandalous Internal Revenue Service human and computer failings that led to reforms and an IRS apology to U.S. taxpayers.

The Philadelphia Inquirer, for feature photography illuminating the plight of the city's homeless.

St. Paul Pioneer Press, awarded prize in feature writing for a five-part series showing the growing pressures on farm families.

San Jose Mercury News, for international reporting that traced massive transfers of money out of the Philippines by Ferdinand Marcos.

KR operating return: 13.3 percent.

1987 *Akron Beacon Journal*, for general news reporting on an attempted takeover of The Goodyear Tire & Rubber Company by a foreign corporation.

The Miami Herald, for national reporting for its coverage of the Iran-Contra scandal.

The Philadelphia Inquirer, for investigative reporting of Pennsylvania prisons that led to the freeing of an improperly confined man.

KR operating return: 14.3 percent.

1988   *The Charlotte Observer*, Gold Medal for Public Service for exposing abuses by Jim Bakker and others in the PTL televangelist operation, which resulted in prison terms for four people convicted of fraud.

The Charlotte Observer, for editorial cartooning.

The Miami Herald, for feature photography illustrating the connection between the city's substandard housing and drug abuse.

The Miami Herald, for commentary by Dave Barry, humor columnist.

The Philadelphia Inquirer, for national reporting exposing the Pentagon's secret "black budget."

St. Paul Pioneer Press, for feature writing about AIDS in the heartland.

KR operating return: 15.0 percent.

1989   *Detroit Free Press*, for feature photography about life in a Detroit high school.

The Philadelphia Inquirer, for national reporting detailing special interest influence on, and profit from, the Tax Reform Act of 1986.

The Philadelphia Inquirer, for feature writing on "Being Black in South Africa."

KR operating return: 13.0 percent.

1990   *The Philadelphia Inquirer*, Gold Medal for Public Service, for exposing widespread problems in the nation's blood supply, leading to reforms in Red Cross procedures.

San Jose Mercury News, for general reporting on the killer Bay Area earthquake of October 17, 1989.

Detroit Free Press, for feature photography coverage of political unrest in Eastern Europe and China.

KR operating return: 14.1 percent.

1991   *The Miami Herald*, for spot news coverage of a series of murders linked to a Miami cult.

KR operating return: 12.9 percent.

1992 Lexington Herald-Leader, for editorial writing about the problem of battered women in Kentucky.

Philadelphia Daily News, for editorial cartooning.

KR operating return: 13.1 percent.

1993 The Miami Herald, Gold Medal for Public Service, for coverage of Hurricane Andrew and for the role the newspaper played in the community's recovery.

The Miami Herald, for commentary about Haitian- and Cuban-Americans.

KR operating return: 14.7 percent.

1994 Akron Beacon Journal, Gold Medal for Public Service, for addressing the problem of race relations in Akron through news stories and by helping the community organize a broad set of conversations on the issue.

KR operating return: 14.4 percent.

1995 No Pulitzers. Batten dies, Ridder becomes chairman and CEO.

KR operating return: 15.9 percent.

1996 The Miami Herald, for editorial cartooning.

KR operating return: 14.2 percent.

1997 The Philadelphia Inquirer, for explanatory journalism in a series about dying with dignity.

KR operating return: 15.3 percent.

1998 Grand Forks Herald, Gold Medal for Public Service, for coverage of the flood of 1997 and for aiding in the community's recovery.

KR operating return: 18.8 percent.

1999 The Miami Herald, for investigative reporting about massive fraud in a mayoral election whose results were ultimately overturned.

KR operating return: 15.3 percent.

2000 Lexington Herald-Leader, for editorial cartooning.

St. Paul Pioneer Press, for beat reporting on academic fraud involving the University of Minnesota basketball program.

KR operating return: 20.5 percent.

2001 *The Miami Herald*, for news reporting on the Elián Gonzales raid by federal government agents.

KR operating return: 20.0 percent.

2002 No Pulitzers.

KR operating return: 15.9 percent.

2003 No Pulitzers.

KR operating return: 21.3 percent.

2004 *The Miami Herald*, for column writing.

KR operating return: 19.3 percent.

This summary cannot be read to imply that if a company's newspapers do Pulitzer-level journalism it cannot make money, and in fact, Knight Ridder's operating margins rose slightly during the years it won the most Pulitzers. Nor, conversely, can it be read to imply that if a company makes money it cannot do such work. Rather, the summary reflects the expressed priorities of the company's leadership during those years of change, the level of its journalists' skills, and the culture of the company itself.

High-level journalism requires for its support that margin of excellence beyond bare-bones resources. When training and travel expenses are slashed; when a staff's institutional memory, traditions, and most experienced members are dissipated through mandated, across-the-board buyouts and layoffs; when perceived financial vulnerabilities make publishers timid, that "special spark" goes out.

"An Incredible and Spectacular Honor"

In November 1994, Knight Ridder's editors were shocked and dismayed when they saw Batten at the opening night of their annual meeting in Miami. Following the October 1993 auto crash, they had been kept informed of his slow but steady recovery from those critical injuries. But the relief of that news had been short-lived. Persistent headaches had led to the diagnosis of a brain tumor of a particularly aggressive kind, and by mid-1994, his contributions to the company—and to the balance between journalism and business—were limited. He had talked by phone with many of them over the months, but they were totally unprepared to see the awful toll that the cancer and chemotherapy had taken on their friend and leader, who was obviously in desperate shape. In breaks during the next three days of meetings, which he could not attend, they struggled to find words and deeds that could somehow express their feelings. They decided to create, out of their pockets and hearts, the Foundation for the Batten Medal, and by the end of the third day the editors had personally pledged $50,000 as a start. Then they had a tricky piece of business to do: making it known to him without being maudlin.

They arranged to have him and his wife, Jean, attend the closing luncheon session. After spending the morning in treatment at the cancer ward, Batten met for the last time with his editors.

Mike Jacobs, editor of the *Grand Forks Herald*, spoke for the editors, winding up a presentation delicately balanced between humor and honor, with no words of dying:

> Each of us may credit chance or fate or beneficent providence, but each of us knows what an extraordinary privilege it is to call Jim Batten colleague, leader, friend. So, Jim, I'm here without gimmick or guile, as bare as a blue crab at low tide. It's right this way, because it's not possible to say "We love you" with slapstick.
>
> And love you we do, and we want to give you something to prove it. We're going to strike a medal and create a prize and name them after you. . . .
>
> . . . It's our way of putting your principles in front of our colleagues so that they can have the experience we have had; so that your vision, your example, and your leadership will draw out from them more than they know is there, more than they dare hope; so it will be a beacon calling forth excellence in our company and in our country.

Batten's response, after a long and tearful standing ovation by the seventy editors, began:

Thank you all very much. In case there's any question in your mind, this is clearly the most amazing day in my life. . . .

". . . . [K]now how enormously grateful I am to every single one of you for what you have done for me, for Jean, indirectly for our children, and we are going to win this battle. . . . When I look at the flood of support that is mine and when I go down to the clinic, which is where I have been the last two days, damn it, instead of with you all . . . I see so many people who do not have the kind of support, concern, love that I do, and it has occurred to me, powerfully, that when I think about the special advantages that are mine . . . to lose this battle, which I do not intend to do, would be humiliating and it would look bad on my record, so I do not intend for that to happen. . . .

The journalism that this company stands for, and has stood for, for years, is something that I am immensely proud of and I know all of you are immensely proud of, and you are now in the process of redefining and reshaping how to be even more valuable to our communities and our country at a time when there is a need for that redefinition, so you all have done me an incredible and spectacular honor and please know from my heart how deeply touched I am.

The endowment would grow to $100,000 within weeks. No corporate contributions were allowed, nor gifts from publishers or other officers. The Batten Medal annually recognizes, with a $5,000 award, a body of work by individual reporters, columnists, editorial writers, photographers, and graphic artists that reflects Batten's passion and humanity. Editors at any level are not eligible.

A Coda

In the spring of 1995, Martin Merzer, a senior writer for *The Miami Herald*, drew what could only be described as the short straw. Surgery and other treatments had not headed off Batten's tumor, and it was increasingly clear, despite his determination, that he would not recover. Merzer was assigned to prepare his obituary, including interviewing him.

"It should have been the most painful day in my life," Merzer recalled in 2004, "but he made it not so. He knew the purpose of the visit, of course, and after that part was done, he turned it around and wanted to talk about my family and how the people at the *Herald* were doing. I didn't know him that well, I was just another employee, but he made it special."

His interview with Batten produced the quotation at the beginning of this chapter, and Merzer's obituary, printed on June 25, 1995, ended as follows:

Deeply engaged in battle against the tumor, Batten chose not to dwell on medical details. Instead, he spoke about what he had learned.

This is what Jim Batten said:

"All of this is a reminder that whether you're sick or not, you must appreciate the precious nature of time. That you dare not shrug off the beauty of time with family, time with friends.

"That you must focus on what's important in your life."

11

Saying Good-Bye

"You could say those editors were from a different era and the breed died out. You also could say they were systematically exterminated." — Jim Naughton, former KR editor

"It took me about four seconds to decompress. I quit newspapers faster than I ever imagined I could." — Walker Lundy, former KR editor

"I just couldn't do this cutting anymore and live with myself." — David Lawrence, Jr., former KR editor and publisher

THE DAY Executive Editor Jim Naughton resigned from *The Philadelphia Inquirer* after eighteen years at the paper, he wore a rented dinosaur costume to the newsroom meeting where the staff would be told of his departure. It was "partly to make a wry statement on the extinction of traditionalists like me, but mostly so I would be able to hide the emotions I was feeling about giving up the best job in journalism," Naughton said years later in an interview.

Only a newcomer to the *Inquirer* staff—and there were few of those following several years of hiring freezes—would have been shocked to see the executive editor thus decked out because the bittersweet gesture was pure Jim Naughton. The event, if not the gesture, was also another break in the ever-thinning chromosonal chain stretching back more than ninety years to C. L. Knight's acquisition of the *Akron Beacon Journal*. It was 1995, and newspaper modernity had caught up with the intense, thoughtful Naughton and run him over.

At fifty-seven years of age, he had lost neither his ardent love for reporting news nor the fey sense of humor that made him one of the most notable characters in a newsroom well known for eccentrics. (for instance, celebrating the forty-seventh birthday of editor Gene Roberts, fondly called "The Frog," by putting forty-seven bullfrogs in his executive bathroom.) But Naughton had lost his bearings in a journalism world that was, he felt, changing in the wrong ways for the wrong reasons. "The suits" had taken over, in his view, and accountants trumped editors and marketing trumped news; pressure for profit trumped all. The view of Naughton from the corporate offices was that of an obstructionist unwilling to adjust to changed circumstances and new economic realities. As the executive editor of one of the company's largest newspapers, he was in the way, but simply firing him was not Knight Ridder's style, at his age was legally risky, and because of his status and reputation, could create huge problems at a newspaper and in a company where morale was already in a tailspin.

As would become a corporate pattern over the next few years, the path to resolving the dilemma began with conversations about Naughton's future. The job of chief of the Washington bureau had opened (Naughton had been a Washington reporter for eight years earlier in his career) and his editor, Maxwell King, asked if Naughton were interested. He wasn't, and his answer led to a trip to Miami corporate headquarters, supposedly to talk over the Washington possibility but actually, in Naughton's words, "to find out whether Knight Ridder and I had the same values and where I stood in corporate's view."

> Obviously Max had forewarned the two people I was to see in Miami—Clark Hoyt, then vice president for news, and Mary Jean Connors, then vice president for human resources—that the conversations would be more about how I was perceived at corporate than about the job in Washington. Clark and Mary

Jean both gave me the identical, presumably rehearsed, line: Change was necessary in Philadelphia and I was perceived as an opponent of change. "What change did corporate want?" I asked Clark. "That's not for corporate to say," he replied (adhering to the idea of local autonomy), "just change." I asked . . . what caused them to perceive of me as an opponent of change given that Philadelphia had undergone constant and major change in my eighteen years there. Both of them, ludicrously, said the same thing: *Why you won't even let them carpet the* Inquirer *newsroom.* I'm sure I laughed.

It was true that for years I had . . . used the no-carpet mantra as a way of fending off the kinds of so-called reforms—isolationist cubicles and mandates to leave nothing on the desktop overnight—that had not merely made so many newsrooms antiseptic but had diminished natural collaboration, the ability to radiate information across the staff. The conversations with two people I had always considered allies were unsettling. I got on the downtown people mover and rode the circuit three or four times, digesting the discussions, and left Miami aware that my best hope for the kind of work I wanted to be part of was to stay in my Philadelphia job, helping good people pursue good stories.

Though it did not immediately dawn on him, that was not among Naughton's options. Within a few weeks, King and Naughton had another conversation that resulted in Naughton saying he would be open to a favorable buyout from "the best job in journalism" and King arranging it.

"You could say," Naughton reflected years later, "those editors were from a different era and the breed died out. You also could say they were systematically exterminated."

His words could have been uttered twenty-five years earlier by any number of editors and publishers of Ridder Publications, Inc. Following the 1975 merger, Knight's leadership moved vigorously to replace the people who had been running those newspapers. A company's leadership is entitled, after all, to staff its newspapers with like-minded people whose styles and aspirations match the leaders'. The moves were necessary, in the Knight leadership's view, to match the newspapers' journalistic performance to the new company's standards. The people in many key Ridder positions were, the Knight people felt, dinosaurs.

By 1995, the company's leadership and, more important, its fundamental culture had changed once more with the ascension of Tony Ridder to the position of president after his term as newspaper division president. Naughton was among the first of more than two dozen publishers and highly placed editors who would leave the company during the next seven years. Few of them were of normal retirement age and most were company veterans of the 1970s and 1980s and Batten protégés. Was it a purge, or a self-purge by unhappy journalists whose world was changing in ways they could not abide, or simply natural attrition in a mature company?

Yes. All of those. Many of them had become, in one sense, dinosaurs because they were unable or unwilling to cope with a vastly changed corporate culture and newspaper environment. The new leadership of the company needed people who would meet the new standards, and there is a narrative thread running through the accumulated stories of the editors and publishers who left. All of them were, at some level, beaten down: discouraged by cutbacks, frustrated by seeing their primary jobs morph from tellers of news to keepers of accounting ledgers, apprehensive about the course of an organization that seemed to them to be abandoning its heritage and losing the core values that made it different from most other newspaper companies.

A Philadelphia Story

In many ways, *The Philadelphia Inquirer* was at the center of the maelstrom. Its top newsroom job was filled by four different people in the six years from 1997 to 2003. King, who had held the job since 1991, resigned in 1997. Within six years of Naughton's arranged departure, all of the upper-level editors who had worked with Gene Roberts in building the *Inquirer* had departed, none at normal retirement age. Many of its best reporters had left for *The New York Times* and *The Washington Post*.

This foment was not the first upheaval for the *Inquirer*'s newsroom. Months after Knight Newspapers went public in 1969, it bought the *Inquirer* and the afternoon tabloid *Philadelphia Daily News* from Walter Annenberg. Jack Knight, alone among the company's directors, voted against the purchase, arguing that the newspaper was of such poor quality, its union contracts so restrictive, its physical plant so outdated that it would never make the money required to give it journalistic independence. The *Inquirer* at the time was a poor second to *The Philadelphia Bulletin* in the city, and its news staff was laden with marginally qualified reporters, editors, and photographers. John McMullan, former editor of *The Miami Herald*, was dispatched to straighten out the mess. Blunt, determined, highly combative, and a superb editor, he quickly swept out ten of eleven newsroom department heads and parted with seventy reporters and editors, then began rebuilding. In 1972, he handed off the job to Roberts, newly arrived from *The New York Times*, where he had been national editor. It took another twelve years before the *Inquirer* and *Daily News* had driven the rival *Bulletin* to the wall, corralling the city's newspaper market for Knight Ridder.

It was Akron and Miami and Charlotte repeated—the Knight newspaper overwhelming the competition with the most fundamental of tactics: making a clearly better newspaper and selling it aggressively. But being alone in the field in Philadelphia after the *Bulletin* surrendered in 1982 was not the panacea it had become in those other cities. As Jack Knight had worried, the cost of overtaking and passing the *Bulletin* (Roberts more than doubled the 250-person newsroom staff), the need for expensive new presses and other facilities, the pressures from labor contracts and occasional strikes, and the resources needed to convert former *Bulletin* readers resulted in Philadelphia not reaching the earnings levels anticipated by Wall Street. Those realities depressed Knight Ridder's overall earnings and drew a big red bull's-eye on the *Inquirer*'s chest. A monopoly metropolitan operation that, in the accountants' and analysts' minds, should be a prime moneymaker was generating huge amounts of money but making lower percentage returns than most of the company's other papers.

Between 1972 and 1985, Roberts was left virtually alone to operate his Philadelphia empire. He was a resource wizard, knowing every nook and cranny of his $30 million to $35 million annual newsroom budget. He was both daring and adept at back-door and indirect funding and could easily outwit the occasional visiting corporate auditors about exactly where the money had gone. An example: He could not get corporate budgetary authority for a national bureau, which he badly wanted, so he established a bureau in Pittsburgh, on the western edge of the *Inquirer*'s natural coverage area, and instructed the reporter to "cover everything West of the river." He meant it literally, and the reporter roamed the rest of the American continent turning out major stories while Roberts ginned up his travel money from hidden corners of the budget.

Only Roberts and an assistant knew the budget numbers, insulating even his executive editors and managing editors from having to make news judgments based on dollars or become embroiled in fights with corporate. "It made our shop a happier one," Naughton said, "that the fights were in private."

Ridder was deeply interested in every budget nuance, however, especially at the financially underperforming *Inquirer*. From his new position as president of the newspaper division, Ridder lasered in on the *Inquirer* for the same reason Willie Sutton robbed banks—that's where the money could be found—and, while Wall Street cheered him on, journalism-watching publications and members of the newsroom staff were aghast. Said one stock analyst familiar with Knight Ridder operations, "Tony gets a bad rap sometimes. Knight Ridder [had] margins and profit ratios that were significantly lower than the industry's. You were in a very go-go bull market and there was tremendous pressure on management to do better, or get out of the way and somebody would do it for them. The company's independence was at stake. [T]here was no reason for the Philadelphia newspapers to have sub-ten percent margins. Tony *had* to [get them up] for the survivability of the company. . . . [Knight Ridder] can be bought and sold and dismembered tomorrow. Tony had to focus on getting margins to a respectable level." In the journalism community, however, he found himself dubbed Darth Ridder, a play on the *Star Wars* villain Darth Vader.

In the seventies and eighties, Roberts had told corporate, "Here's what I need," received most of that, and created the rest through budgetary alchemy, but now Ridder insisted on knowing all the numbers and making them dance to his tune. In the newspaper business, that sort of detailed control over budget is tantamount to control over strategic coverage decisions. Roberts-Ridder was not a pairing likely to last in close proximity, and it did not. Reflecting on the newsroom concerns about ceding news authority to the bookkeepers, Naughton tells a story about walking into a room at a Knight Ridder corporate gathering and overhearing a vice president talking about how "we have to get control of the *Inquirer* newsroom." The remark could have been interpreted in several ways—for instance, as a comment on costs only—but for a veteran newsman who valued independence above all, it meant only one thing: The suits were taking over.

In 1986, when Ridder became president of the newspaper division, the heat was turned up high under The Frog; but unlike the proverbial frog on the slow-warming stove, Roberts knew it and felt it. Roberts was the only editor still reporting directly to corporate, and that was about to change with the appointment of Sam McKeel, the longtime general manager, as publisher. Told by Batten and Larry Jinks of the change, Roberts said he would quit. Anxious to keep his star editor, Batten worked out an agreement that if Roberts would stay at least two more years, he would have a very favorable buyout package. That worked for more than two years, but by 1990, fifty-eight years old and at the height of his powers, Roberts walked away.

"It was," Roberts said in a 2004 interview, "constant cost pressures and a general sense of panic in the building" that finally caused him to invoke the buyout. "At some point in the late 1980s, Tony got a computer faster than anything we had at the *Inquirer*. Tony would figure out by five or so on Friday whether we had met the week's budget. . . . If we were off budget at all—I mean a few bucks or a few thousand—you could bet there would be a call, and just pandemonium would ensue . . . because nobody wants to be in the position of the boss knowing things that you don't know. We must have spent a small fortune doing manually . . . what Tony could do with that computer, so that nobody would get caught by surprise [by the telephone call]. . . . You could tell at some point that Knight was gonna be governed by quarterly profits, and to make sure that they made quarterly profits they started probing around even monthly and weekly profits."

It was time to say good-bye.

It was not only a matter of oversight and autonomy, however; it was also a matter of strategic vision for the newspaper. Roberts and everyone in the *Inquirer* newsroom wanted it to be not only Philadelphia's newspaper but also a national leader that competed with *The Washington Post*, *The New York Times*, and the *Los Angeles Times* for both stories and prestige, despite far smaller newsroom budgets. The business side of the *Inquirer* was under pressure from advertisers to reach deeper into the affluent and expanding suburbs and pay less attention to the city itself, which, like many other cities, was increasingly hollowed out and poorer. There was not enough money to do both well. The strategic ambivalence would plague the paper for more than a decade.

Maxwell King, an *Inquirer* veteran, succeeded Roberts. King had been hired by John McMullan in 1972, and during the period from 1987 to 1990 had cross-trained on the business side in preparation for an assignment as a publisher somewhere within Knight Ridder. He had risen to senior vice president for circulation and distribution of the Philadelphia operation when Roberts left. His unexpected return to the newsroom as Roberts's successor gave him arguably the toughest newspaper job in the country because of his predecessor's reputation, not to mention the seventeen Pulitzers that Roberts had overseen. But King did have a rapport with Ridder that others lacked, and he remained for seven years, leaving for the presidency of the Heinz Endowments. King was not upset with Ridder personally, there was no blow-up; but, finally, he told *American Journalism Review* in 2001, spending more time with budgets and less with good stories is "a brutal process. . . . It consumes your time. If you're a top editor, you're diverting all your time to those issues. I felt there might possibly be another world out there and, by God, there is."[1]

King's successor was Robert Rosenthal, whom King called "one of the smartest, most committed, most aggressive editors in the country" with "the right instinct about what the story is and about [how to motivate] people" in the newsroom.[2] Like King, Rosenthal was a protégé of Roberts and would be the last of that clan to head the *Inquirer*. When he left in 2001, after less than four years as editor, it was because of a disagreement with Publisher Robert Hall, and again the subject was how rapidly the paper should expand its coverage into the financially promising suburbs and how much of those resources to take away from the core newspaper. Adding staff to make the foray into the suburbs was not an option; in fact, there had been two rounds of news staff buyouts in previous years. Rosenthal felt the newspaper's heart and its aspirations for journalistic stature would be cored out to meet corporate bottom-line demands.

Rosenthal's successor, in November 2001, was Walker Lundy from KR's *St. Paul Pioneer Press*, not a Roberts clan member but a KR veteran reporter and editor with ties to the Batten era. Lundy felt that the newspaper's future did lie in the suburbs, painful as that might be for many staffers, and his get-acquainted conversations with news-room people left him with the feeling that what the demoralized staff needed, above all, was a plan, almost any plan, that gave them some measure of confidence about the future. "They had seen more than a hundred of their brothers and sisters walk out the door with buyouts, a lot of them to *The New York Times* and *The Washington Post* and so forth. . . . The 535 full-time employees that were left, they saw that there were more than 600 a few months ago, so I saw it as my job to get the ship righted. . . . They had said, 'Even if we don't agree with the plan, get us a plan and allow us to stick with it,'" Lundy said. That plan was a suburban offensive.

Lundy also heard from many of the employees the sentiment—fear, actually—that if things stayed tough, KR would pull the plug on his plan. "No, no," he said. But in the spring of 2003, the fiscal hammer came down. Publisher Hall announced at an operating commit-tee meeting that the Philadelphia newspapers were mandated by corporate to reach 25 percent operating return in two years. They were then at about 18 percent; advertising was flat because of the weak economy, and some twenty suburban newspapers were shred-ding the *Inquirer*'s still-growing suburban base. The only way to reach the number was more cost cutting, as many as 200 positions, including about fifty in the newsroom.

The papers, Hall said, needed a new economic model, something dramatically different, but he did not suggest what it might be. Lundy's assessment was that it was simply a matter of trying to cost-cut the way to prosperity.

"I went home and told my wife I didn't think I wanted to do that," he said. They had previously looked into the possibility of early retirement, and their financial adviser had run the numbers and they were comfortable with the prospects. Given the new mandate, Lundy calculated, why not pull the plug on thirty-nine years in the business. "It took me about four seconds to decompress," he said in 2004. "I quit newspapers faster than I ever imagined I could." He had been the paper's editor for only twenty months and was fifty-eight years old.

A Columbia Story

Gil Thelen moved inland from the Knight Ridder newspaper in Myrtle Beach to the editorship of *The State* in South Carolina's capital city of Columbia in 1990. It was by way of a rescue mission, as the newspaper's close and historic ties to the South Carolina political establishment that existed under its former ownership were proving to be an embarrassment for its new owners, Knight Ridder, which had acquired paper in 1986 from the Morris family. The immediate precipitating event for Thelen's promotion was a fiscal and sexual scandal involving the president of the University of South Carolina that *The State*'s cross-border rival, *The Charlotte Observer*, had uncovered and exploited in *The State*'s backyard. *The State* had not only been slow to respond, but also had supported the president well beyond the point of reasonableness.

Publisher Frank McComas, who had taken over in Columbia in 1988, told Thelen to "cover the story straight up," and supported him when the predictable heat came down on the paper. "Frank was stalwart," Thelen said, about that and other discomforts that arose as Thelen went about transforming the newspaper. It wouldn't be easy for either of the top executives, as South Carolina's always Byzantine political atmosphere became emotionally charged over such issues as a legislative scandal in which one-third of the legislators were indicted, a bitter lawsuit that opened The Citadel military school to women, and a struggle about the flying of the Confederate flag over the state capitol. As the people running the state's largest newspaper, they were caught between the need to cover those events in Knight Ridder's usual aggressive style and the baggage of the newspaper's cozy former ties with the state's establishment. Thelen was comforted by the steady support of McComas and Knight Ridder corporate during the storms that arose around *The State*'s journalism. The corporate support was sternly tested, and passed the test, when The Citadel's extensive network of military old boys petitioned fellow graduate Alvah Chapman, then chairman and CEO of Knight Ridder, to please do something about that upstart editor.

But Thelen's support network didn't last. In 1994, the ailing Batten persuaded McComas to move to corporate as a vice president for operations, an extension of their mutual trust and friendship when they had been together in Charlotte, McComas as a circulation manager and Batten as editor. McComas's newsroom experience was limited to a few months of cross-training in Charlotte, but Batten believed that he had an understanding of newspaper purposefulness, and the Columbia experience had proven that judgment correct. McComas was replaced in early 1995 as publisher of *The State* by Fred Mott, a forty-eight-year-old CPA with sixteen years of business-side experience in Knight Ridder corporate finance and at newspapers in Tallahassee, Florida, and Gary, Indiana, but no newsroom experience.

Mott and Thelen simply did not speak the same language, and after less than three years, their conflicting core values had shredded the relationship. The differences were of both style and substance. Thelen's management style was collaborative—top-down managers would condemn it as soft—and his personal style extroverted. Mott's management style was line-of-command and his personal style introverted. But it was on matters of journalistic substance that the potential partnership foundered. One event Thelen recalls, still with a tinge of bitterness, was Mott's reaction to a story about a lesbian commitment ceremony that aroused some of the city's conservatives. Mott, who did not write a column for the newspaper, was moved by the uproar to write one without consulting with Thelen. The column said the newspaper had erred in running the story. Thelen said he was "deeply troubled" that Mott refused to discuss with him either the column or its potential effects both inside and outside the newsroom. Later, they disagreed sharply on the philosophy behind the newspaper's establishing zoned editions for neighborhood news. Mott felt strongly that the editions would be financially successful—that is, attract more advertising—if they followed demographic patterns in what was still a highly segregated city. Thelen felt such a design would drive a wedge between blacks in the city and whites in the affluent suburbs; that the sections should be used to narrow the racial divide rather than widen it. It was a classic clash of marketing values versus news and civic values and was the precursor of the final break.

That came, again, via Knight Ridder's management audit, the time set aside to consult about future plans and aspirations. Thelen's ambition was to be the editor of *The State* or some other Knight Ridder newspaper until retirement. The line was drawn cleanly in the sand when, Thelen recalls, Mott told him during the review, "You won't be editor of this or any other Knight Ridder newspaper a year from now unless you *resolve* the conflict between marketing and news."

"What had always separated Knight Ridder from other companies every day," Thelen said in recalling the moment, "from the top throughout the company, was *balancing* that tension, not surrendering either way." He said he told Mott, "If you're asking me to not worry about that [balancing], I can't be your editor any longer." He went home and told his wife, "I think I just resigned."

The next day, Thelen found that the familiar lifeline to corporate wasn't there. "I found out that there was no longer the [organizational chart] dotted line to the vice presidents from the editors, and realized for the first time that my only boss was the publisher." Thelen's corporate contacts, Marty Claus and Clark Hoyt, tried unsuccessfully to patch the wounds, but Mott was doing quite well the job he had been sent to do—maximize profits—and Thelen was seen as standing in the way of that. Mott's job description did not include keeping an experienced, talented editor happy, so Thelen was through. A temporary corporate position was arranged for him, consulting with other newspapers on newsroom organization "until another editor's slot turns up." None did. He was offered a chance to train to be a publisher but ruefully, and it turns out, unpropheticaly, told Knight Ridder, "I don't think I'd make a very good publisher." In 1998, Thelen was hired as editor of *The Tampa Tribune*, owned by Media General, Inc. The man who hired him there was Reid Ashe, a Batten protégé who had just left *The Wichita Eagle* and Knight Ridder and was publisher in Tampa. In a move pregnant with irony, two years after Ashe was promoted to chief operating officer of Media General, Thelen became his Tampa publisher. Still more irony: Mott in 2002 was named president and general manager of PNI, the operating company of *The Philadelphia Inquirer* and *Daily News*.

A Miami Story

When David Lawrence, Jr. took over as publisher of *The Miami Herald* in 1989, he was in many ways the classic product of Knight Newspapers' journalistic and operating philosophy. Lawrence had worked as a reporter and editor for eight years when Knight hired him as managing editor of the *Philadelphia Daily News* in 1971. Following the merger with Ridder and Batten's move to corporate, Lawrence became editor of *The Charlotte Observer* and later was named executive editor, then publisher, of the *Detroit Free Press*. He was a journalist trained to be a publisher. While he was publisher in Miami, the newspaper won five Pulitzers and expanded its reputation as one of the nation's best.

But by 1995, Lawrence was feeling increasingly uneasy, he said in a 2004 letter. Economic "pressures occurred on every CEO's watch. Such pressures have been unavoidable at newspapers for many years . . . but until the mid-nineties, the company was, I believe, quite successful in achieving a balance between business and news. That balancing act was clear in the decisions over the years to pair a CEO with someone of different emphasis, [for example], Lee Hills, Jim Batten, and so forth. Only in recent years have the two most visible people in the company been businesspeople—and not journalists. . . . The business ethos became the paramount driver from the mid-nineties on. The balance is gone."

Lawrence was chafing under what he viewed as unwise and destructive pressures to cut back in order to meet ever-higher short-term operating return goals. "You decide to cut off so-called 'out-state' circulation. You bring fewer resources to bear on production and advertising and marketing and circulation. You [corporate] don't tell your publishers and editors to take certain steps; you just tell them how much they have to cut. And if you are semi-constantly cutting, which is the story with Knight Ridder most of these past ten years, then you operate a newspaper with a permanently unsettled staff . . . and that is clearly unhealthy."

What he called "this drumbeat over the years" finally became too much for him in the spring of 1998. "I was being asked to get to 25 percent [operating return] over three years, and that would have meant cutting 185 positions. I just couldn't do this cutting any more and live with myself." In July, after a conversation with ninety-two-year-old Lee Hills in which, Lawrence said, Hills commented, "Jack Knight would be turning over in his grave" to hear what was going on, Lawrence decided to resign. That conversation "gave me enough gumption to do what I had to do," he said later. Lawrence wrote a letter resigning as of the end of the year. "Did I love newspapers?" he wrote later. "Maybe too much. In thirty-five years at seven newspapers I never missed a day of work. I love newspapers, but they finally changed more than I was willing to change." He was fifty-six when he became president of The Early Childhood Initiative Foundation in Miami, making a new career out of a passion for early childhood development and school readiness.

His editor at the *Herald*, Doug Clifton, would not be far behind. Clifton, fifty-six, just shy of thirty years with the company, had been, like Lawrence, feeling what he called "an accretion of annoyances that sometimes bordered on the pathological" from the struggles over news space, people, travel money, and expense reductions since 1995. "David was a known quantity and supported the editorial efforts, and besides, he was a damn good editor," Clifton said. The corporate selection of Lawrence's successor as publisher, Alberto Ibarguen, "changed the equation," Clifton said. Ibarguen was from the business side and, said Clifton, "It was clear that he did not have any of those editorial sensibilities that David brought to the job, and that ultimately I think he was going to move in conformity with the financial dictates," which would include the profit mandate.

The frustrated Clifton had been privately considering options, including consulting with a financial planner to see if he could afford to retire at fifty-eight, perhaps teach a little, and take a break from the accumulated pressures of daily newspapering. Then came a call from Advance Publications, the Newhouse family's mega-publishing conglomerate, about the editorship of *The Plain Dealer* in Cleveland. His exploration gave him a glimpse of a very different world: an "under-achieving but well-resourced newspaper in an organization that had no incredible pressures to produce profits by the quarter. Not that they were indifferent to making money, but I sensed a completely different atmosphere." Small wonder. Advance is a private company, a publishing giant with twenty-five daily newspapers around the country, Condé' Nast publications (*Vanity Fair*, *Glamour*), and the American City Business Journals, and it is among the top-ten publishing companies. Its owning family members answer only to themselves. When he looked more closely at *The Plain Dealer*, he saw a newspaper where "they didn't do budgets, with a bigger editorial expense [than the *Herald*], a bigger newshole, more people. [laughing] What the hell? . . . It made it easier to take the call." Clifton departed in May 1999, leaving on the wall of *The Miami Herald* five Pulitzer Prize certificates that he and his publisher partner Lawrence had been instrumental in winning. The temptation to retire early was gone, his journalistic fires were reignited.

This Miami story would have an ugly, acrimonious, and public epilogue. In August 1998, when efforts to change Lawrence's mind about resigning were obviously failing, Ridder and McComas arranged a meeting with *Herald* executives to try to calm things. It was a time of multilayered turmoil on Biscayne Bay. The *Herald* executives were facing the 25 percent mandate and Lawrence's resignation while watching Knight Ridder headquarters on the building's sixth floor moving out to San Jose, Ridder's old and comfortable stomping ground. Some corporate people were losing jobs, others were facing moves to the West Coast, and the city was losing the prestige of a Fortune 500 headquarters and the civic contributions in talent and resources such a headquarters makes to a city.

Ridder had announced the headquarters relocation at 4 P.M. on April 28, as shareholders headed home after the 1998 annual meeting at which the decision was not mentioned. The move was necessary, he said, so that KR could have its "senior officials in the middle of Internet activity so that we can make the best decisions about the future of the company." He denied that his twenty-two years in San Jose entered into the decision, but many observers saw the move as the prevailing *ritter* taking the spoils back to his homeland after a long campaign. The relocation would cost $20 million. Lone among board members, Chapman, the former CEO and chairman, opposed the move. "The symbolism is unfortunate," he said.

Amid all that tension, the *Herald* people were stunned to hear Ridder say in the meeting with *Herald* executives that he had not been aware of the 25 percent mandate and did not approve of it. The *Herald* people were incredulous, given that it had been imposed by McComas, the person Ridder relied upon to direct the Miami operation, and given Ridder's well-known attention to financial detail. Lawrence, Clifton, and others concluded that they were being lied to for reasons totally unclear to them. At the meeting, Ridder dropped the three-year goal and set a two-year goal of reaching 22 percent, which represented little practical respite for the *Herald* because in 1998 the operation had been at 18 percent. After the meeting, according to Lawrence, McComas said that he "had taken a bullet" for Ridder. (McComas declined to comment on that or any other Knight Ridder matters.)

Details of the meeting and indications of the bitterness underlying it surfaced very publicly in December 2001 in a *Fortune* magazine story entitled "Tony Ridder Just Can't Win." The thrust of the story was that cost cutting was alienating the company's journalists yet still not satisfying Wall Street analysts, a lose-lose situation. Ridder was horrified about both the negative framing of the magazine story and the specific implication contained in it that he had lied about the Miami cuts. *Fortune*'s story quoted Lawrence as saying, "It [Ridder's denial of knowledge] was a very, very painful moment. Knight Ridder had always been a company where nobody ever lied to you. This was really a big lie." In a sharp letter to the magazine, in an exchange of e-mails and letters with Lawrence, and on the company Web site, Ridder said that in fact he had learned of the mandate imposed by McComas shortly after it had been given, and before Lawrence's resignation letter, and had challenged it. He should have made that clear at the meeting, he said; he had not been trying to duck responsibility for the goal.

That explanation, including Ridder's release of a memo from McComas to KR executives backing Ridder's version, was almost three years too late for Lawrence and Clifton, however. McComas retired in 2001.

A San Jose Story

Jay Harris, chairman and publisher of *The Mercury News* in San Jose, California, one of KR's fiscally top-performing and journalistically finest newspapers for more than two decades, knew what he had to do that Saturday morning when the knot in his stomach woke him up at 3 A.M. It was March 17, 2001.

The day previous, Friday, had been consumed in a grueling budget meeting with a group of Knight Ridder executives headed by Steve Rossi, recently appointed by Ridder to head the company's newspaper division. That appointment not only positioned Rossi as the direct boss of the company's newspapers but also as No. 2 to Ridder and heir apparent in an eventual corporate succession, though Ridder was only sixty-two and Rossi fifty-three. Rossi brought to the table a B.A. in economics from Ursinus College, an M.B.A. from The Wharton School, more than a decade of corporate work with AmeriGas Industrial Gasses and IU International Corp., a worldwide conglomerate, and nine years as a KR executive in various business-side positions. He had never worked as a journalist or in a newsroom.

In grooming and then promoting Rossi, Ridder passed over several people with long histories of news involvement with the company, thereby, intentionally or not, declaring an official end to the succession tradition of balancing the tensions between the business side and the news side. David Lawrence in Miami, Frank McComas in corporate, and Harris himself had been seen by many people inside the company as potential successors or at least long-term balance wheels for Ridder's lack of news background.

Among Rossi's first tasks as president of the newspaper company was to boost *Mercury News* returns, despite the fact that it had maintained operating margins in the 22–29 percent range for more than a decade. It was necessary, Rossi told the group, to maintain that level of margins even in the face of drastic reductions in revenue caused by the Silicon Valley recession, "in order to be in step with the goal to move KR's overall margins up." The newspaper's long-time financial success had been tied closely to classified advertising, particularly employment advertising, during the boom years of the Silicon Valley. That success had enabled the paper to make serious circulation and advertising inroads into the San Francisco market and dominate its area of California. It was consistently ranked among the nation's ten best newspapers. But as the new century opened, its advertising base was being eroded as Silicon Valley entered a new and downward cycle. There was no place to turn for additional revenue, so Harris and his fellow *Mercury News* executives fully understood that drastic cuts, including layoffs and reduction of space devoted to news, were the only alternative if the margin goals were enforced by corporate.

After the KR executives departed the Friday meeting, Harris and his people, charged with devising a plan by noon Monday to meet the goal, were glum. They agreed to think things over and join in a conference call on Sunday. Meanwhile, Rossi put together an e-mail memo to Harris, copied to Ridder and other KR executives, with his suggestions, styled as "feedback on yesterday's discussion." It was stunning in the scope of its intrusion upon news judgments, in which he had no experience. Rossi wrote:

> I would recommend rethinking the newspaper from the outside
> in, that is, from the viewpoint of what will win the market,

rather than what can be cut. I would recommend taking a hard look at the recent reader research. If the *Mercury News* market is similar to our other markets, the research will indicate that our readers want more local news. The *Mercury News* front pages are consistently local and compelling, while the inside of the A section is very heavily weighted toward foreign news. This may be something to reconsider. Readers want tighter editing, and they want relevance. They want to know why a story is important to them, and they want to see clear utility. Readers want a consistent format, anchoring, and design. I commented to you and [executive editor David Yarnold] that the *Mercury News* is particularly complex in this regard. There are numerous small sections which float in and out on various days of the week. Finally, you have a unique opportunity to rethink all of the above in conjunction with the upcoming 50-inch web conversion. I would recommend getting your readers and business community leaders involved to create a feeling of buy-in and to generate some hype around this event.

The "web conversion," a major trend in newspapers at that time, involved adopting a narrower width roll of newsprint. The change resulted in cost savings but at the price of less space for news.

The memo went on to deal with cuts in the Sunday magazine and geographically variable pricing for single-copy sales, depending upon what the competition was charging. It added: ". . . the *Mercury News* historical financials show that in the past two economic downturns in 1985 and 1991, there was considerable cost containment to mitigate the revenue slippage, so we are not talking about a reversal of management tradition at the newspaper."

The memo ended with a statement that was seen by *Mercury News* journalists as both gratuitous and totally tone-deaf: "We need the *Mercury News* management team to take a leadership role in sorting through the complex options for the newspaper and devise a plan which you will recommend and believe you can succeed with. *I felt a sense of entitlement rather than ownership in some of yesterday's discussions with the group.* [emphasis added]."

If the journalists in that meeting had exuded a "sense of entitlement," it reflected their understanding of the historic role of newspapers juxtaposed against the imperative of making a number, as Harris would write later. "What troubled me—something that had never happened before in all my years in the company—was that little or no attention was paid to the consequences of achieving 'the number.' There was virtually no discussion of the damage that would be done to the quality and aspirations of the *Mercury News* as a journalistic endeavor or its ability to fulfill its responsibilities to the community. As importantly, scant attention was paid to the damage that would be done to our ability to compete and grow the business." Prior to the meeting, Harris had written a budget overview that argued, ". . . while we *could* achieve the near-term savings being sought, those savings would be more than offset by a long-term diminution of the vitality and potential profitability of Knight Ridder's Bay Area franchise."

Harris knew whereof he spoke, even if it was in a language Rossi and Ridder would not understand. He was one of those hybrid newspaper executives, a journalist with a broad grasp of the total business. His journalism career began in 1970 at the Wilmington (Delaware) *News Journal* as a reporter. He served for seven years on the faculty of Northwestern's prestigious Medill School of Journalism and was hired by KR in 1985. As executive editor of the embattled *Philadelphia Daily News*, he had to do his share of cost cutting and, as a KR vice president for operations for four years, he required others to trim back in tough times. He admired the way that his *Mercury News* predecessor as publisher, Larry Jinks, had guided the paper through the recession of 1991. But this time, there was no more flesh to give; only, he felt, muscle and even bone.

He talked with his wife, Christine, after that wakeful Saturday morning and made his decision. On Monday, he began a memo to Rossi, with a copy to Ridder, this way:

Steve asked to review my thoughts on how to proceed at the *Mercury News* in light of the current economic downturn. I will share them in this memo.

I also use this letter to submit my resignation as chairman and publisher of the *Mercury News*.

I do so with deep regret.

But I resign in the hope that doing so will cause you to closely examine the wisdom of the parameters for 2001 profit Steve gave the *Mercury News* senior executive team at our meeting Friday. Meeting the goal will necessitate deep and ill-advised staff and expense reductions at the *Mercury News*.

The profit targets Steve laid out on Friday cannot be achieved short of layoffs. I recommend, therefore, that a lower target be established given the mutual desire to avoid layoffs.

Given the substantial number of our readers, and residents of our community, who were born in other nations, the equally significant number employed by global businesses, and the many readers for whom such news is a priority, I would recommend that the weighting is proper and should not be changed. . . .

. . . More important than anything else, I recommend that you take greater time and the appropriate care with the . . . decisions ahead. Particularly important are those decisions that will affect the quality and reputation of the newspaper.

Before taking his letter to KR headquarters in downtown San Jose, Harris arranged for a farewell e-mail message to his staff to be sent while he was at the corporate office handing in his resignation—there would be no turning back. The letter to his staff, one "I never thought I'd be writing to you," outlined his memo to Rossi and Ridder and said he was looking forward to a period of "reflection and rejuvenation." It ended: "It has been my great privilege to be a part of this great newspaper for the last seven years. In the years ahead I will always be rooting for you. Keep the faith. Strive for excellence. Fight for the right. And, above all, hang in there. You, what you are doing, and what you believe in are worth the effort."

Harris's resignation as head of *The Mercury News* was one of more than two dozen departures of KR publishers, editors, and key sub-editors following Batten's death, most for reasons related to cutbacks and other economic pressures. The affected communities, in addition to Philadelphia, Columbia, Miami, and San Jose, were Lexington, Kentucky; St. Paul; Kansas City; Akron; Bradenton, Florida; Detroit; Long Beach; Boulder; Macon, Georgia; Wichita; and the Washington bureau.

If those changes for closely connected reasons constituted dark clouds rumbling over the company landscape, Harris's very public protest and resignation was a thunderclap and lightning bolt directly overhead for not only Knight Ridder but all of journalism. Coverage of the split overflowed the expected journalism publications into general news magazines and the news networks.

By an accident of timing, the annual meeting of the American Society of Newspaper Editors (ASNE) came only three weeks after the San Jose storm broke. Luncheon and dinner speakers for the convention are lined up months in advance and often include such people as the sitting U.S. president, the chief justice of the United States Supreme Court, congressmen, and foreign dignitaries. By another accident of timing, the ASNE president for the year was Rich Oppel, the editor of the *Austin American-Statesman* who had left Knight Ridder in 1995. The executive director of ASNE was Scott Bosley, a thirty-four-year veteran of KR positions in Detroit, Gary (Indiana), and Washington. They had a speaker cancellation, so when Harris's resignation became known, they decided it would be a good idea to have him address the convention's closing luncheon. He delivered to the nation's editors a classic exposition of the role of journalism in American democracy and the importance of properly balancing the eternal, natural tension between a newspaper's business interests and its public responsibility. He told the editors:

It was the conviction that newspapers *are* a public trust that brought me to Knight Ridder in 1985.

I understood then and understand even better today that a good newspaper and a good business go hand in hand. Indeed, without a good business, it would be impossible for a newspaper to do good journalism over the long haul.

But at some point one comes to ask what is meant by a good

business. What is good enough in terms of profitability and sustained year-to-year profit improvement? And how do you balance maintaining a strong business with your responsibilities as the steward of a public trust? Maybe that is the most important question, because our business—if you approach it as a public trust as well as a business—is different from most businesses. . . .

. . . The press is protected in the First Amendment. . . . It is the only business so protected because the framers saw a free press as essential to the maintenance and health of our democracy.

My arguments today are not First Amendment arguments, though. The First Amendment protects nearly all forms of speech and press activity. My argument today applies in particular to newspapers, newspaper companies, and the leaders of such companies who believe their newspapers have a special responsibility to our society.

My argument today is that freedom, a resource so essential to our national democracy that it is protected by our Constitution, should not be managed primarily according to the demands of the market or the dictates of a handful of large shareholders.

In managing a newspaper or a newspaper company in the public interest you are faced with these questions. When the interests of readers and shareholders are at odds, which takes priority? When the interests of a community and shareholders are at odds, which takes priority? When the interests of the nation in an informed citizenry and the demands of shareholders for ever-increasing profits are at odds, which takes priority? . . .

12

Wichita ... Saying Good-Bye

"En masse, shareholders represented by institutional investors and mutual funds have no conscience. They do not care whether the people of rural Kansas are informed. They do not care whether [The Wichita Eagle] publish(es) newspapers or shoe catalogues or make(s) widgets." — Davis Merritt, in a 1996 column

"How lucky I am to have something that makes saying good-bye so hard." — From the movie Annie

OVER THE YEARS in Wichita, starting in 1975, Libby and I gradually changed and added to the rambling, one-story prairie-stone house we stumbled upon that year. By 1990, two of the vacated kids' bedrooms had become offices for each of us, the third a guest room and occasional makeshift dorm for visiting grandkids. We also added a terrace on the south side and a deck on the north side to take advantage of Kansas's persnickety weather, the south terrace providing a sun-struck winter shelter from the chilly north winds, the north deck a haven from summer's torrid south winds.

It has never occurred to us to move from the private, tree-sheltered place we found almost by accident weeks after the disastrous tour in Duke Tully's Cadillac (see Chapter 4) had convinced us that Wichita was a flat, treeless, refinery-and-grain-elevator Midwestern moonscape. That tour had been demoralizing for us, but Wichita was going to happen in our lives, and so we former residents of lush

North Carolina and even-greener northern Virginia told a real estate agent, "Find some trees and if there's a house under them, we'll take it." She did and we did, and it has been home to this day.

On the personal side, the fifteen years from 1975 to 1990 were crammed with helping teenagers survive that uncertain passage, enjoying high school and college graduations, weddings, and grandchild births. On the professional side, *The Wichita Eagle* became well established as a strong medium-size newspaper that emphasized aggressive coverage of a community that it cared about. It was not immune from the pressures imposed by the waves of change affecting the industry, but Knight Ridder under Jim Batten's leadership provided an atmosphere that encouraged publishers and editors to think creatively about ways to deal with the economic and sociological pressures without compromising on public service journalism. It seemed to be working. The *Eagle* was making an operating return in the high teens—meaning profits on the order of $12 million to $15 million each year—and circulation was at least holding its own most years. My staff had filled the walls of a large conference room with the symbols of our journalistic effort: state, regional, and national recognitions of our efforts to tell the Wichita and Kansas story and make that story a better one.

It should have been a time of satisfaction. The *Eagle*'s publisher was Reid Ashe, former editor of the Jackson, Tennessee, newspaper. Impressed by Ashe's energy and background, Batten had lured him to Miami as part of the Viewtron experiment. When Viewtron folded, Ashe came to Wichita as general manager and eventual replacement as publisher for the genial Norm Christiansen. I was on a roll, with two consecutive publishers who valued the core mission of journalism.

But on this day in mid-August 1990, more changes, and more personal ones, were hanging in the air like the late-afternoon storm clouds that threatened to interrupt our leisurely dinner on the north deck. After the dishes were cleared and we were well into a wonderful Frog's Leap Merlot, my mind plucked once more at a loose thread in the fabric of my professional life. We were doing journalism, at least by the conventional reckoning of our peers, at a high level. We had "comforted the afflicted and afflicted the comfortable," had been aggressive and thorough in writing about the city and the state's challenges, had been the faithful watchdog on government and institutions. And yet fifteen years of that had not seemed to make much real difference. The same public problems continued to cycle with frustrating regularity: crime, the economy, citizen apathy and disengagement; the litany of a democratic society's seemingly incurable maladies. Simply telling the news of those maladies, no matter how aggressively we did it, wasn't changing anything, and the democratic process itself seemed stuck in a cycle of irresolution.

More immediately, the state was beginning yet another political season, a gubernatorial campaign certain to be in the contrived style of all recent elections: a series of photo ops and pseudo-debates in which the news media would perform its ritualistic role of water-carrier. Between the political handlers and the traditional news media, the "campaign" would be about what the candidates wanted it to be about. Citizens would have no role except as spectators.

The nation had been through just such an ordeal two years before, with a presidential campaign featuring images of George Bush in a flag factory, Michael Dukakis wearing an outsize military helmet in an armored vehicle and looking distressingly like a bobble-head doll, and a skulking Willie Horton threatening the women and children. Only 50.1 percent of Americans had bothered to cast a vote.

The week after that election, disheartened by the turnout and disgusted by the spectacle, I had written in an op-ed page column:

> The Constitution requires that we do it again in four years whether we need it or want it, and that's not a pretty thought as we stand in the shambles of the 1988 presidential race and contemplate the threat of another one sometime soon.
>
> The dreary thought has nothing to do with who won or lost the presidency. Rather, it has to do with the nature of the campaign, the performance of the journalists and candidates in it, and what those say about the future of the election process. . . .
>
> The campaign just concluded showed at its frustrating worst

the mutual bond of expediency that has formed over the years between campaigns and the media. . . . Together they have learned that feeding the lowest common denominator appetite among voters is safer, cheaper, and less demanding than running the risk, for the campaigns, and the expense, for the media, of providing in-depth information.

The hard truth that journalists and their organizations face is that the campaign people aren't going to change simply because it would be right to do so. The campaigns have learned that they can produce results without risk. So changing the contract is up to the media.

I suggested, among other things, that the news media needed to take the alleged risk of boring readers by writing about issues in depth, and to stop participating in superficial horse-race polling.

The 1988 column and the emotions behind it came flooding back that night in 1990, and I told Libby that "this may cost me my job," but that some things were going to change in the *Eagle's* approach to election coverage.

The next week I wrote:

In the interest of disclosure as the 1990 gubernatorial campaign begins, I announce that the *Eagle* has a strong bias. The bias is that we believe the voters are entitled to have the candidates talk about the issues in depth.

I outlined a general coverage philosophy, the thrust of which was to insist that the candidates address the issues that truly affected citizens, whether or not it was their own strategy to do so. We would be aggressive—insistent—about that.

If our insistence . . . winds up seeming to cost one or the other votes, so be it. I am perfectly comfortable defending the notion that you as a voter have the right to know what the candidates intend to do once in office, and if the candidates won't say what they intend go do, letting you know that very plainly. . . . What the eventual winner intends to do with the great gift that voters will bestow is a straightforward question that deserves a clear answer.

Other journalists had been thinking along similar lines since the 1988 campaign, and in an remarkable coincidence, just as I finished editing that piece, I answered a phone call from Glenn Guzzo, then an assistant to Jennie Buckner, Knight Ridder's vice president for news. Knight Ridder, he said, was shopping around for a newspaper willing to try new approaches to election coverage to see if the alarming trends in voter turnout and issueless campaigns could be affected. KR would provide extra budget for the effort and for research to test its efficacy. You've come to the right place, I said.

Details of what followed are well documented in public journalism literature. Our coverage totally reversed the circuitry of the campaign, making the power flow from citizens to the candidates and back, rather than the other way around. We found out through polling what citizens were most concerned about and insisted that the candidates address those issues as well as the ones on their own agendas. Post-election research showed that the turnout in the areas where we circulated was higher than in other areas of the state, and voter cognizance of the issues was much higher.

That experiment would be replicated and expanded upon in several cities during the 1992 national election season, and those experiences led to further changes in election coverage around the country in later years.

But that night on the deck was only the beginning of an adventure that would, in a backdoor and not wholly unwelcomed way, "cost me my job."

Public Journalism

The election experiment led to some intriguing insights about journalism and its role in democracy: Given appropriate information, people would engage at a higher level; journalism need not be a passive, detached observer in order to fulfill its obligations about objectivity and fairness; newspapers were in a unique position, among all media, to support the democracy that supported them.

Those thoughts, extended beyond election campaigns, led to other changes in the way the *Eagle* applied itself to its public service mission, and those experiments resulted in contacts with other journalists and institutions similarly concerned about the role of journalism in a democracy. Chief among the new contacts were The Kettering Foundation in Dayton, Ohio, and Jay Rosen, journalism professor at New York University. At Kettering's urging, Rosen and I wrote a manifesto of sorts, a paper beginning to outline our shared thoughts about journalism and democracy.[1] In order to write about the concept and the changes it implied for journalism, we needed to give the accumulated ideas a name. We settled upon "public journalism," because it embodied the dual ideas of journalism as accepting its role in, and obligations to, public life, and because newspapers adopting it would be public, that is to say open, about their intentions. In 1993, the John S. and James L. Knight Foundation approved a three-year grant for Rosen to establish The Project on Public Life and the Press. The Pew Charitable Trusts would later provide a multiyear grant to found the Pew Center for Civic Journalism.

By 1993, a burgeoning movement—and a loud argument—was under way within journalism. The idea that journalists can and should do their work in ways calculated to help people re-engage in public life had instant appeal for many of them and instantly repelled many others. For more than ten years, debate within the profession would rage, spawning hundreds of seminars and panel discussions and learned and not-so-learned articles and more than a dozen books.

One of the books would be mine, called *Public Journalism and Public Life: Why Telling the News Is Not Enough*. In 1993, infused with new energy about my profession and ready for a break from thirty-seven years of daily journalism, I asked for and received from the *Eagle* and Knight Ridder a year's leave of absence to think about the ideas, try to expand them, and write a book. The timing of the request for a leave also stemmed from very pragmatic considerations. During budget discussions in late summer 1993, it became clear that I would not be able to create a key newsroom management position that was sorely needed if I was to pursue the public journalism idea to its fullest and still produce the newspaper I wanted to see. Opportunity and travail coincided. Taking my salary out of the newsroom budget for 1994 would more than make room for the new salary, so I proposed the leave.

After the book was published and I returned to the *Eagle* in 1995, my world was totally changed. Jim Batten, who had been the rock behind KR's support for public journalism as well as a great friend, was dying. Tony Ridder's corporate power, with its bottom-line emphasis, was being consolidated through the corporate advancement of a group of nonjournalists. Creeping corporatism was at its height, with every important news decision having a marketing subtext. The raging debate within the profession about the ideas of public journalism seemed to me far more broadly crucial to the future than did tomorrow's newspaper or next year's operating return.

But there was tomorrow's newspaper for the editor to worry about, and it wasn't nearly as much fun anymore, certainly not in the way promised by old Chester S. Lord back in 1922. The job had become one of dealing with constant financial pressures, the cutting back of newshole, staff reductions and hiring freezes, declining newsroom morale, all pointing to an uncertain future and a sure lack of psychic reward.

From Collegiality to Confrontation

KR's vice president for news during this troubled time was Clark Hoyt, a long-time friend from years together in the Washington bureau in the early 1970s, where he had been co-winner of a Pulitzer Prize for national reporting, and his four years as my managing editor in Wichita from 1981 to 1985. He had returned to Washington as bureau chief after his Wichita stint, and in 1993 he went to corporate in a three-way shift of key people that ultimately resulted in Rich Oppel, winner of two Pulitzers in Charlotte, leaving the company for the editorship of the *Austin American-Statesman.*

Hoyt and I had been able to help each other at crucial times in our careers. When I hired him as managing editor, his life had hit a major bump. In 1980, he had been in charge of the *Detroit Free Press*'s coverage of the Republican national convention. This was no small deal within Knight Ridder, for when a city hosts a national political convention, the newspaper is in a glaring spotlight. The conventions are a major circulation and advertising opportunity, but even more important for the newsroom staff, it is a two-week period in which the nation's political journalists and some of its most important political figures are reading the newspaper daily as it competes with the country's all-star political reporters. It can be a make-or-break time for people involved in the coverage effort.

This was widely understood within the *Free Press*, including its labor unions. More than a year of Hoyt's careful and imaginative planning for that event went down the tubes with an ugly sucking sound when the unions walked out the week the convention opened. The *Free Press* and it bitter rival, *The Detroit News*, were forced to produce highly truncated combined editions, which meant scrapping huge chunks of Hoyt's elaborate coverage plan. He was devastated, and his next career step was unclear. When my managing editor spot opened and I heard he was available, I leaped at the opportunity. A dozen years later, he would reciprocate by helping arrange my 1994 leave of absence.

Post-leave, however, everything was different. In the late summer of 1995, yet another round of painful budget discussions approached and, without my knowing it, a line of demarcation.

In my first fifteen years in Wichita, the budget process was a more-or-less collegial negotiation between corporate and the newspaper's publisher and editor. Normally at issue was whether we could manage to pay for the new things we wanted to do, the staff expansions and content improvement we wanted to make. Corporate would assemble the proposals from all the newspapers and project what bottom line that would produce. In the 1980s, that operating return number fluctuated between 7.8 percent and 15.0, averaging 12.2. After Batten's death, the average through 2003 was 17.8 percent, with several years over 20 percent.

At individual budget meetings up until 1990, there could be lively give-and-take about revenue projections ("You sure you can't get more out of that?") and costs ("What if you only did part of that this year and the rest the next?"). It was an assessment of realistic possibilities between two sides sharing a philosophy about newspapers. We rarely got everything we wanted for the newsroom, and sometimes considerably less, but the prevailing atmosphere was one of trust: that each side was doing its best for a common goal.

That began to change in the 1990s, in part because of the weakening economics of newspapers and in part because of Ridder's 1989 promotion to president. Within two years, the dynamics of budgeting reversed, becoming top-down as corporate set operating return targets for each newspaper without consultation with the publishers, leaving the newspapers to find a way to conform. In 1993, a grim-voiced Ridder told a conference call of editors and publishers that the days of accommodation were over, the bar was being raised. Full fiscal performance based on steadily rising operating returns at each newspaper would be mandatory, and people who did not perform would not be around for very long. It was a blunt-instrument blow delivered without regard for anything except the bottom line. The days of budget negotiations were over and the days of budget confrontations had arrived.

We prepared a budget draft for 1996 with an operating return a few tenths of a percent less than the previous year's 20.9, and holding it to that small a decline would be a stretch. In prior years we had tightened expenses everywhere we could imagine, with corporate's ambiguous admonition always in the background: You need to cut everything you can—oh, but without doing real damage to the newspaper. We had years ago passed the point where damage to the newspaper began, but corporate was in denial about that. Do more, we were told, but always gratuitously added was, "Don't do anything you don't think is right."

The toughest problem for the 1996 budget was soaring costs. Newsprint was spiraling out of sight. It 1992, we paid an average of $420 per ton for it, about $7.2 million a year. In 1996, the cost was projected at $790 per ton, an astonishing increase of 88 percent, and we were looking at a newsprint bill of $13.5 million at our then-existing circulation. Newsprint has always been, like gasoline, a commodity subject to the tricky nuances of supply and demand. In the eighties and early nineties, newspapers cut back on newshole and advertising fell off, so the supply was ample and newsprint mills did not invest in new capacity. This led, as always, to what the newsprint mills sought: shorter supply and higher bid prices. But in a special irony for journalists, the 1993–1996 price increases were also fueled by the emergence of a free press in the former Soviet Union and parts of Asia, a massive and wholly unforeseen new demand factor that allowed the mills to hold out for almost any price they wished.

Other costs were on fast up escalators, too. The cost of travel, by airplane and car, soared, so we rooted against the old home team, hoping that the state's college and professional teams would be just mediocre enough not to make playoffs and bowl games, coverage of which added expense without, in a middle-size market, selling very many more newspapers. Employee benefits, particularly health care costs, were steadily rising. Litigation costs, including the cost of filing lawsuits for access to public records, as well as the cost of defending against libel claims, were near the outrageous level, making newsrooms overly cautious about offending anyone and super reluctant to aggressively pursue, through legal action, legitimate claims on information.

In prior years, we had eliminated virtually all off-site training and stopped attending conferences and meetings of professional associations; we no longer followed local and state sports teams on the road and had reduced internships drastically; we took a pass on pursuing freedom-of-information claims beyond the first, cheapest steps; we cut back sharply on syndicated opinion columns for the editorial pages; we held vacancies open for months, or eliminated them altogether.

There was no fat left; we had cut through muscle and maybe chipped some bone in preparing the 1996 budget, but we would discover it would get worse.

"No Matter What It Takes"

The session in the paneled, windowless, clubby board room at Knight Ridder's Miami's headquarters was tense. On my side of the table sat publisher Ashe and Dan Moehle, chief financial officer for the *Eagle*. On the other side, Hoyt and Frank McComas, the former publisher of *The (Columbia) State*, whom Batten had persuaded to move to corporate. McComas shocked us by announcing that we would have to make a 22.5 percent return, meaning we would have to identify $1.2 million more in either cost or revenue on a total budget of about $64 million. A "down" year would not be acceptable under any circumstances.

It struck me as an arbitrary number, as it was so far off our best and most honest projections, and I said so.

That's the number, he said.

Where did it come from?

We looked at what the company needs to make and that's what your contribution must be.

"Are you telling me, Frank, that we have to make that number, no matter what it takes?"

"That's right."

Ashe talked about some possibilities, some revenue-enhancement long shots, but none that could approach 22.5 percent. Meanwhile, I was ruminating that even one-half of one percentage point of relief, about $320,000, could add a crucial 5 percent to the newsroom budget for the year and surely would not do great damage to a $2.8 billion corporation. But there would be no relief, from either the tough numbers we had projected or the even more drastic ones McComas was mandating.

I asked again, "I just want to make sure of what you're saying. We have to make that number *no matter what it takes?*"

"Yes," McComas said. Hoyt was silent throughout the session.

Afterward, standing in the broiling Miami sun for the first time since Batten's funeral a few months before, I was fuming. Hoyt's silence during the meeting seemed to be a clear signal that the dotted-line connection between the editor and his corporate vice president was now a one-way path downward.

To Hoyt, standing with me, I said, "This company has become no different from Gannett or any other. There's just no difference. Journalism just doesn't matter anymore." He demurred, insisting that nothing had changed about that commitment and spoke of my "disaffection," warning that it could lead to problems.

"You know, Tony is no great fan of yours," he said.

"Nor I of him," I intemperately shot back.

Ashe, Moehle, and I returned to Wichita to try to improve the profit picture, an unlikely prospect and a debilitating exercise. One way to avoid cutting costs, and thus quality, is to raise revenue. Increasing subscription prices had proved to be counterproductive: Doing so usually turned regular subscribers into occasional single-copy buyers. The same applied to higher advertising rates: It turned half-page advertisers into quarter-page advertisers. We had discussed several ideas that could only be classified as experiments: a "tailored" newspaper offering individual subscribers more of some things they would request—sports, for instance, or national news—in place of other content, and weekly "value added" sections along the same lines. Corporate, however, required a positive pro forma for any such departures—a clear profit the first time out, which effectively barred true experimentation.

Further cuts in staffing or newshole or coverage would make the paper perilously less attractive for all readers, including our core Wichita-area readers. The only way, we concluded, that we could get within hailing distance of the 22.5 percent was by slashing circulation outside the immediate Wichita area.

While a newspaper deliberately cutting circulation seems self-defeating, if not absolutely suicidal, the short-term economics can be there. In a place with great distances between small towns, such as Kansas, hauling a morning newspaper 250 miles and selling it for fifty cents is a money-losing proposition. Additionally, advertisers, most of whom are local merchants, made it clear each time we raised their rates that they were not particularly interested in paying to reach people a hundred miles or more away who might be only occasional customers of theirs. Yet outstate circulation has important benefits that can make subsidizing it worthwhile for both the newspaper and its city. In the part of Kansas we covered, roughly the southern half at that time, Wichita was a business and political force, at least in part because of the wide circulation of the *Eagle*. Editorial reach and influence in a largely rural state can mean a great deal in its legislature, and Wichita's educational, cultural, and business institutions were direct beneficiaries of the connection the newspaper made with people in rural areas.

And, more personally for a journalist, cutting circulation to make an arbitrary profit number is like donating your liver to a lifelong drunk—a gesture without a real future for either party.

The first slash was 10,000 copies, almost a tenth of our daily circulation. We simply told people west of an arbitrary line that as of January 29, 1996, they could no longer buy our newspaper. It was not an easy decision to explain to the hundreds of angry and anguished Western Kansans who called and sent genuinely heartbreaking letters and petitions. Nonetheless, I attempted to explain our decision in a New Year's Day column headlined "No market for social conscience," which said in part:

> I have spent much of the past few days talking to many of the 10,000 *Eagle* readers who, as of Jan. 29, will no longer be able to buy our newspaper.
>
> Some are outraged; some are deeply saddened; some express frustration at being cut off from information they value. Many have been loyal readers for decades; many have family and business connections in Wichita. Others simply care about what is going on in the state and nation. . . . Some like the comics or editorial pages or the sports section. The reasons they take *The Eagle* and their responses at being cut off are varied.
>
> But what all these about-to-be-canceled readers share is that they live too far from Wichita. . . .

I explained about the cost equation and the skyrocketing price of newsprint:

> No business can sell its primary product at a loss and stay in business.
>
> Of course, to many readers a newspaper isn't simply another product, like a bar of soap. It's a lifeline to some, a habit. A

necessity. A connection to community, a teacher, a familiar friend.

So the people we are cutting off are unhappy, and so am I.

If you and I owned *The Eagle*, we might make a different decision. We might conclude that continuing to circulate in those distant areas, even at a loss, was important to us as a matter of conscience, and important to the affected people, to Wichita, to the state, and to the moral imperative of keeping people informed in a democracy. We could choose to accept less profit.

But you and I do not own *The Eagle*. It is part of Knight-Ridder, Inc., a publicly held company that is owned by shareholders all across the nation.

En masse, shareholders represented by institutional investors and mutual funds have no conscience. They do not care whether the people of rural Kansas are informed. They do not care whether The Eagle & Beacon Publishing Co. and Knight-Ridder publish newspapers or shoe catalogues or make widgets. They care only that the company, any company, and its subsidiaries maintain a level of profit, and that the levels rise each year. . . .

. . . Who is a fault? Those of us at *The Eagle* who make decisions are free to make any decision—except the decision to make less profit. The people who run Knight-Ridder are in a similar position. They could decide to make less profit, but would quickly be dismissed by the faceless and nameless institutional shareholders in favor of someone who would grow the profit at any cost. . . .

All of this, I wrote, ". . . raises the personal question, after four decades of effort, 'Why bother?'" So I explained my personal stand as well:

. . . [T]he answer I keep coming back to is this:

I made up my mind forty-three years ago that journalism was a worthwhile calling; that we have a useful role to play in democracy and the direction of society. . . . There is important work to be done in the area that we do serve, and if we do it well, as we intend to, good things will happen.

So I will tend to the things that I can affect and push into the background (to a place of real but muted hurt) those things I cannot.

This does not help the 10,000 people who want our newspaper and cannot get it. But it will help the people who can.

We Didn't Mean *That*!

As so often happens to the issuers of ultimatums, the corporate people were aghast at what theirs had wrought. "We didn't mean for you to do *that*!" was the reaction, but in fact, the $1 million that the cutback in unprofitable circulation sent to the bottom line was our only way to get close to the profit mandate, short of virtually dismantling the news operation. Nor did my public explanation of the reason win applause in Miami, where Hoyt was "appalled," he said.

Corporate may have been shocked, but people there were pleased when the *Eagle* hit the budget target for the year. In a final irony to that brutal budget cycle, newsprint prices dropped sharply late in 1996, but corporate mandated a budget adjustment to recognize it, so we could not use that good fortune to avoid further late-year cuts.

Early in 1996, McComas paid one of his periodic visits to Ashe's office. The conversation began to echo those taking place at several other newspapers. McComas knew that Ashe, who was born and raised in Charlotte, hoped to succeed Rolfe Neill, then nearing retirement as publisher of *The Charlotte Observer*. "Reid, you're not going to get the Charlotte job," McComas told him bluntly. In fact, he said, "Tony doesn't like you very much" and you don't have much of a future with Knight Ridder. McComas didn't say what might happen if Ashe did not leave, but Ashe got the message. By mid-year, he had been hired as publisher of *The Tampa Tribune*, owned by Media General, Inc., operator of fourteen network-affiliated television stations and twenty-one daily and a hundred weekly newspapers. It was only the first step in an intriguing series of moves involving a pair of Batten protégés. Ashe hired Gil Thelen, the former Columbia *State* editor, to head his Tampa newsroom. In 2001, Ashe was promoted to president and chief operating officer of Media General. In 2003, he appointed Thelen, the man who once feared he wouldn't make a very good publisher, to that very position at the *Tribune*. When Neill retired, the Charlotte publishing job went to Peter B. Ridder, Tony Ridder's younger brother.

Before Ashe left Wichita, he and I began the periodic, and often foreboding, corporate management audit, with its questions of "What do you want to be doing down the road?" and the urging to be honest and imaginative about it. My naively too-honest response was, "In my ideal world, I would like to bring in someone strong to run the daily newspaper and spend more of my time working on and promoting public journalism." As the next step in the process, Hoyt called one evening to talk about it. I repeated that desire.

"That isn't going to happen," he said.

"Well, I guess then I'll just go on doing it the way I have been," I said.

"That can't happen, either."

Silence on my part.

"Why don't you come to Miami in the morning and let's talk about it," he said.

"What's the point, if the decision has been made?"

"Come on down. We need to talk."

Fortunately, Libby was out of town, so I didn't have to explain immediately that my four decades with the company appeared to be over. I was sixty years old, five years away from normal retirement and two from a reasonably comfortable early retirement. I was just as weary of rattling corporate cages as corporate was intolerant of having them rattled. An unknown new publisher was on the way, to be selected by a management team whose values I no longer shared. Did I want to start around that 1975 track one more time? Such overnight thoughts led me to catch a plane the next morning.

We did not waste time talking about the whys of the matter. My old friend had a plan. Starting January 1, 1997, I would be senior editor at the *Eagle* for two years and work on public journalism projects with KR's newspapers and editors. The title senior editor was everything that such honorifics traditionally imply ("He's old and has no authority"), but that was all right with me. I had two years to do work I thought was important, then could go into early retirement on an upbeat and with my values intact. It was a generous and practical resolution. Backed by a substantial amount of money to help budget-tight newspapers move beyond routine coverage, I was able to do public journalism work with two dozen KR newspapers and communities, a dozen universities, and with journalists in Sweden, Chile, Argentina, Colombia, Jamaica, Puerto Rico, and Jordan.

By January 1, 1999, all I needed was to borrow Jim Naughton's dinosaur suit and move along to the next phase of my life.

13

What Now?

"Citizens will decide, in the long run, what sort of democracy—and what sort of journalism—we have. Maximizing newspaper profits cannot make better democracy. Maximizing citizens can." — Davis Merritt, 2004

HOWELL RAINES, the executive editor of *The New York Times* dismissed in the wake of the Jayson Blair scandal, wrote afterward, "It [the *Times*] is the indispensable newsletter of the United States' political, diplomatic, governmental, academic, and professional communities and the main link between those communities and their counterparts around the world."[1]

Raines is certainly capable of hyperbole and some will dismiss those words as typical hubris of a *Times*man. People at a number of other newspapers, such as *The Washington Post*, *The Wall Street Journal*, and the *Los Angeles Times*, might argue that *The New York Times* is not the sole legitimate claimant on that role. But whether sufficiently broad or not, his words describe what should be one of any newspaper's goals within its own community and reach.

He continued, "And yet a harsh reality of our era is that if the

Times ever ceased to exist, it would not be reinvented by any media company now in operation in this country or the world."

In other words, once lost, the commitment to journalism first that drives the *Times*, and many other newspapers, would not be found or rekindled in today's corporate circumstances. The connective role that Raines sees the *Times* playing on a global scale is reproduced hundreds of times over in communities all across the nation, scale being the only difference. If those commitments are allowed to expire because of corporate focus on profits, those connective roles also would be lost, perhaps forever.

This is our central dilemma. If what Philip Meyer calls the "harvesting" of the nation's newspapers continues at its present pace, frittering away and watering down the accumulation of decades of journalistic skills and standards, the wake-up call for newspaper journalism and for democracy may come too late. Can the newspaper industry find a way to migrate its unique journalism genetic code to new technologies before that gene pool is dissipated?

In his book, *The Vanishing Newspaper*, Meyer says of harvesting:

> There is a textbook solution for a mature industry that is unable to defend against a substitute technology. Harvard professor Michael E. Porter calls it "harvesting market position."[2]
>
> A stagnant industry's market position is harvested by raising prices and lowering quality, trusting that customers will continue to be attracted by the brand name rather than the substance for which the brand once stood. Eventually, of course, they will wake up. But, as the harvest metaphor implies, this is a nonrenewable, take-the-money-and-run strategy. Once harvested, the market position is gone. . . .
>
> . . . [C]utbacks in (newspaper) content quality will, in time, erode public trust, weaken societal influence, and eventually destabilize circulation and advertising. So why would anyone want to cut quality? If management's policy is to deliberately harvest a company's market position, it makes sense. And pressure from owners and investors might even lead managers to do it without

thinking very much about it because reducing quality has a quick effect on revenue that is instantly visible while the costs of lost quality are distant and uncertain.[3]

Too many of America's newspaper companies are in harvesting mode. While few, if any, would admit to such a policy, the trail to the edge of the abyss is littered with the evidence:

› *Smaller newspapers.* Fewer and smaller advertisements are a part of it, but only a part. Newsholes are tighter; there's simply less to read. (Thirty years ago, Jim Knight would pick up the day's *Miami Herald* and, palms up, heft it up and down, feeling its bulk and, smiling impishly, say, "Now *that's* a great newspaper.") Even the width of the sheet itself has shrunk from a standard of fifteen inches wide to 12.5 inches, resulting in a 7 percent to 9 percent savings in newsprint, but also a loss in news content and the width of advertisements. Meanwhile, prices for readers and advertisers have constantly risen.

› *Smaller, less effective news staffs.* In 2002, newsroom employment nationwide was 4 percent less than in 1990. The loss was not merely in numbers, however; the most dangerous loss was qualitative. Faced with what they felt was a financial crisis in the first years of the twenty-first century, many newspapers, including the largest and best, launched buyout programs that appealed to the most experienced and highly paid journalists, who were then replaced, if at all, with less experienced, lower-salaried people.

But even that does not tell the entire story of the shrinkage of newsroom resources. During the decade of the nineties, with full implementation of pagination technology that did away with composing rooms and their hefty payrolls and high full-time-equivalent counts, the entire process of preparing the newspaper for printing shifted to the newsroom. This meant a smaller percentage of the people in smaller newsrooms doing the actual work of reporting and editing, because the computerized pagination process, efficient as it was, did not absorb all of the time and work formerly done by composing rooms. Newsroom people composing pages on computer terminals meant fewer reporters and copy editors doing the basic work of journalism. Thus, the 4 percent absolute drop in newsroom numbers was actually much more severe.

▸ *Astonishingly higher profits.* Merrill Lynch analyst Lauren Rich Fine estimated that newspaper operating margins almost doubled between 1991 and 2002, from 14 percent to 27 percent. Advertising revenues rose 60 percent during that period, and overall profits jumped 207 percent.

▸ *Journalists feeling the strain.* A 2004 study by The Pew Research Center for the People & the Press showed that 66 percent of journalists at national news organizations felt that bottom-line pressures were hurting news coverage, compared with only 41 percent in 1995 and 49 percent in 1999. Among local journalists, the percentages were slightly lower (57 percent in 2004, 33 percent in 1995, and 46 percent in 1999), but the pattern of rising concern was repeated.

Whether the newspaper companies busily harvesting their market positions are driven by conscious policy or are simply oblivious to the implications of cutbacks for journalism and for democracy, the outlook is ominous. Is that outlook short-term, mid-term, or long-term? No one can say with certainty, but given the pace of change in this century, the step over the edge of the abyss likely will come sooner rather than later.

A lot of smart people have spent a lot of time worrying about the future of newspapers, if not about newspaper journalism itself. No one has a magic bullet or even knows for certain what the target should be should a magic bullet be discovered. Here is an accumulation of ideas about what's going wrong and what going right might look like.

Migrating to the Internet Faster

The mid- to long-term future of newspaper journalism does not depend upon dead trees, but upon bits and bytes, which are in infinite supply. The scramble is on by newspaper companies and their competitors to be the portal of choice for Internet users, who within a generation will be the vast majority of people.

Creating such a gateway is one thing; figuring out how to attract money through it is quite another. Newspapers can't afford to give away their expensively gathered news content, yet Internet users have generally been reluctant to pay for newspaper content online. Likewise, there is the dilemma of persuading major advertisers to move online while also staying in the print edition.

In late 2004, newspapers with online editions were increasingly requiring would-be users to register before getting access, and in the process, they've stirred up opposition from both individuals and privacy watchdogs. The initial reason for requiring registration is to gather information about the users in order to show advertisers the potential audience. The information required varies, depending on the site, from simple demographics, such as age and location, to much more extensive data, including income and personal preferences. Eventually, the registration requirement could be a way to charge for access. And that's where resistance gets very high among most potential users.

If that conundrum can be resolved, it could eventually be possible for newspapers to support their reporting resources solely online. The timing and pace of that migration is, however, critically important. As we have seen, the cutbacks in newspaper staffs, the erosion of training budgets, and the reduction of newshole are steadily thinning the pool of reportorial resources. If the practice of harvesting outpaces the development of business practices that allow newspapers to make enough profit online to sustain high-level journalism, newspaper companies could nevertheless face the cruel irony of being ready in every way to take advantage of the technology except for the most crucial aspect: enough trained, experienced, dedicated, and talented journalists.

A few companies are experimenting with the concept of "convergence," which has the potential to speed up the migration of newspaper journalism to other platforms. Convergence involves training journalists—from the university level up—to operate across technological divides. Historically, newspaper journalists have been trained in quite a different manner from those in broadcast, and the emergence of online news created a third category of skill requirements. Convergence addresses the problem of the distinct audiences that exist for broadcast, print, and online news. While there is overlap within those audiences, at the instant consumers pick up a newspaper or turn on a TV or log onto the Internet, the expectation is different for each. The newspaper reader expects depth, detail, context, and portability; the television news seeker is prepared to passively receive information; the Internet user wants immediacy and searchability to find more information. News organizations of the future will need the skill and resources to meet each of those distinct appetites.

Convergence is clearly a work in progress, and the only way to speed up the needed migration is through trial-and-error, with many experiments going on at the same time, a process ensuring that many—and expensive—false turns will be taken. There is no evidence that most newspaper companies have tolerance for such risks in the prevailing environment of short-term bottom-line pressure.

Going Private

While much of the impetus to cut back on the level of newspaper journalism comes from the industry's heavy proportion of publicly traded companies, getting out of the Wall Street pressure cooker by going private is no guarantee of better journalism. Publicly held companies do not have a corner on greed; privately held companies can be equally as enamored of dancing numbers as public ones. And climbing out of the Wall Street pressure cooker can mean tumbling into the fire.

Trying to take a company private puts it into play, making it subject not only to an unfriendly takeover but also to possible breakup, with the most profitable newspapers bringing a premium and the least profitable being subject to a fire sale. The new owners of the parts may be even more ardent harvesters than the former owners.

If a way could be found to avoid the dangers of takeover, a company converted from public to private could set its own standards of what level of financial success would be appropriate. But its problems would not end once it is in the calmer waters of private ownership.

Among the reasons newspaper companies go public is the ability it gives them to raise money for expansion and improvements. A private company would have the same needs and might merely be trading the tyranny of Wall Street for the tyranny of private lenders.

Undertaking Corporate Reform

What if one could restructure newspaper corporations with the aim of maximizing incentives toward public service journalism rather than solely toward profit? What might such a corporation look like?

Academics Gilbert Cranberg, Randall Bezanson, and John Soloski recommended such reforms in their 2001 study *Taking Stock: Journalism and the Publicly Traded Newspaper Company*.[4] As ways to "alter the direction of change, though not the fact of it," they suggested the following reforms:

> Boards of directors should have more than one member who is a retired or active journalist of high repute and who does not work for the company. At least one of such members would be on the compensation committee or the committee responsible for setting compensation policy . . . including compensation of executive management and compensation guidelines for editorial staff of the newspapers.
>
> The board of directors should consist primarily of outsider members.
>
> Except for directors who are employees of the company, directors should not receive compensation in the form of stock options or other incentives tied to the stock market performance.
>
> Bonus and other incentive compensation for executive management of the parent company . . . should be based in significant part on the circulation and journalistic quality of the newspapers.
>
> At least half of the incentive compensation for publishers . . . should be based on criteria strictly related to circulation and journalistic quality.

Editorial management and news personnel of the newspapers should not receive any incentive compensation based on financial performance. Their incentives should be based strictly on circulation and journalistic quality, and should consist only of bonuses and not include stock options.

Newspapers should report to the public such matters as total revenues and expenses and operating margins, circulation, and the names and compensations of board members and the publisher and the three highest-paid employees of the newspaper.

The company's standards of journalistic quality should be established in advance after consultation with an external group of journalists and others who are knowledgeable about journalism.

The last suggestion raises the persistent dilemma of how to measure quality. Knight Ridder is experimenting with one measurement, an attempt to quantify quality based on what it calls "seven tenets of good journalism" that are incorporated into all management MBOs. They are:

1. *Watchdog.* Does the paper do a good job of guarding the public trust?

2. *Trust.* Is it trustworthy and credible?

3. *People Like Me.* When I read the paper, can I identify with at least enough of the people who are written about that I feel it's a paper for me?

4. *First and Only.* Am I seeing things first in my paper? Is the content unique?

5. *Utility.* Does the newspaper help me live my life, with everything from gardening tips to movie time clocks to investment advice?

6. *Easy to Use.* Can I find what I want simply and quickly?

7. *Storytelling.* Is the writing compelling? Do the articles draw me in and keep me engaged?

Few would argue with those goals in the abstract, but the evaluations of the tenets are based on surveys of readers. If one conceives of readers as *customers* in a *market*, and the newspaper as a *product* (all of those italicized words, unfortunately, dominate current newspaper thinking and conversation), then making people feel good about it would be a reasonable goal, and a survey of those customers would be a valid way of measuring their satisfaction, just as you might do with coat hangers. However, respondents who are satisfied at the moment of the survey may be good customers but not necessarily well-informed or challenged citizens. Likewise, readers who are unhappy with the newspaper for some perceived offense at the moment of being asked about it may negatively influence the outcome.

More important, a newspaper that does not occasionally distress one or another segment of its readership probably isn't asking all the right questions and looking in all the right places as part of its public service responsibilities. Given the quite natural ambitions of MBO-enhanced newspaper employees to succeed, the survey method of evaluating performance on the seven tenets urges the newspaper to take on the cultural, moral, and values patina of its audience. That is not a bad thing as a business practice, but what does it mean for journalistic practice? Could a newspaper driven by reader approval have supported civil rights in the South in the forties, opposed the Vietnam War in the early sixties, or taken on the likes of PTL's Jim Bakker or the University of Kentucky basketball establishment? Can such a newspaper stick with its journalistic compass in today's bitterly partisan political environment of "red states" and "blue states"?

Even with those caveats, however, the KR experiment is worth watching because the seven tenets are part of the management by objectives (MBO) plan for people in all departments, not just the newsroom. So advertising and circulation directors have a direct and tangible stake in newsroom performance, too, which can be a good thing for journalism. Over time, it would be useful to analyze whether the tenets produce better journalism as well as pleased customers, and whether non-newsroom employees' stake in newsroom performance creates internal pressure on newsrooms for better journalism or simply pressure for better survey results.

Talking Differently to the Street

Hodding Carter III is president and chief executive officer of the John S. and James L. Knight Foundation, which has within its mission the improvement of American journalism through many mechanisms, including endowed chairs at journalism schools. Carter is also, by genetics and training, a newspaperman inflamed by the idea of journalism as a public trust. And he's angry about what is happening to newspaper journalism. In a speech at Kent State University in April 2001, he argued that newspaper companies need not march to Wall Street's drumbeat of ever-increasing profits.

It is a fallacy, said Carter, that newspaper companies "must accept the market's logic and demands," and he went on to say:

Actually you don't [have to accept it], as long as you're not emphasizing profit growth as a masculinity surrogate, a macho game of "my profit growth is bigger than yours." *The Washington Post* goes to the market. *The New York Times* goes to the market. Neither comes close to the profit margins the market allegedly demands. Neither will as long as current management endures. Both these great newspapers prosper and lead.

What it takes is a little guts. A little cohesion among media managers and all would echo [*Washington Post* CEO] Don Graham's remarks to Wall Street analysts not long ago. You want profits, he told them. We want profits. But we know what matters. Our journalism is not the focus of your interests, but it is the focus of mine, and it is better than ever. It's going to stay that way.

Let me put a proposition to you. Today, GM averages around a 5 percent to 6 percent profit. Suppose GM went to 20 to 25 percent. Would you buy its cars? Would you believe the product was as good at a 25 percent return as a product at 5 percent? And yet the newspaper industry has doubled what used to be the acceptable profit margin, well past what we routinely called "obscene profits" in the oil industry in days gone by, and thinks it can't live below 25 percent.

Of course, the way Wall Street sees it is determinative for

some. Terry Smith of *The News Hour with Jim Lehrer* did a segment on the issue of newspaper profits. Well, he asked the bright analyst, what margin does Wall Street expect from a publicly held newspaper company? If they average in the twenties, is that enough? No, she replied, it's never enough, of course. This is Wall Street we're talking about.

Precisely. And what we should be talking about is journalism in the public interest.

That, Carter said, would require newspapers to stop being "knowing participants in our own debasement." He continued:

> . . . [J]ournalism has withdrawn, or is withdrawing, from deep, wide coverage of its communities in favor of features, flash, blood and gore, sports and business news. All of these are necessary ingredients of any complete news package. But a problem [that is] highlighted by massive packages that win Pulitzer prizes is that they stand in such contrast to the week-in and week-out coverage of public events and public affairs by most of the same publications that concentrate their resources upon the blockbusters.
>
> Business and economic news are vital, but too much of this newly expanded coverage is aimed at a tightly segmented and predominantly elite audience. As far as much of the rest of the audience out there is concerned, this coverage could be about Pluto. And while I love sports, to cut the newshole and expand space available to sports represents priorities gone berserk.
>
> . . . [A]fter all of the market research, after all the redesigns, after all the dummying down, newspapers continue to lose readers and even worse, readers' respect. That is what really kills us. . . . We don't have the public's respect, at least in part, I suspect, because they know our institution doesn't really respect them. We speak of "markets." They think of themselves as individuals, as citizens.

In *The Vanishing Newspaper*, Meyer, who used the harvesting metaphor, argues that newspapers can justify expenditures on quality through the use of "the influence model," a concept developed by Hal Jurgensmeyer at Knight Ridder in 1978. Newspapers, Jurgensmeyer said, were not in the news business or even the information business, but in the influence business.

Wrote Meyer: "A newspaper, in the Jurgensmeyer model, produces two kinds of influence: societal influence, which is not for sale, and commercial influence, or influence on the consumer's decision to buy, which is for sale. . . . A news medium's societal influence can enhance its commercial influence. If the model works, an influential newspaper will have readers who trust it and therefore be worth more to advertisers."[5]

How does a newspaper acquire societal influence? In a word, expensively—which unfortunately adds to, rather than helps resolve, our central dilemma of migrating newspaper journalism to the new technology in time to save it. According to Meyer:

> The appeal of the influence model is that it provides a business rationale for social responsibility. The way to achieve societal influence is to obtain public trust by becoming a reliable and high-quality information provider, which frequently involves investments of resources in news production and editorial output. The resulting higher quality earns more public trust in the newspaper and not only larger readership and circulation, but influence with which advertisers will want their names associated. . . .
>
> . . . Over the long term, social responsibility in the democratic system supports, rather than impedes, the fulfillment of a newspaper's business objectives, through the channels of obtaining public trust and achieving societal influence, which then feeds back into further fulfillment of the public mission, thereby creating a virtuous cycle.

It is difficult to rebuild that "virtuous cycle" when short-term financial goals require cutbacks in the newsroom resources that are essential to creating and maintaining societal influence.

In fact, the change in marketing strategies by newspapers, driven by advertisers, reverses the flow of the influence cycle. The new cycle starts with advertisers telling newspapers whom they want to reach (e.g., "single, middle-class men between age 26 and 43") and the newspapers, through their marketing committees in which editors participate, seeking to gain some sort of influence with that group by producing content allegedly interesting to them. In an environment of limited space and resources, that content drives out content that might appeal to a broader spectrum of the population and have more societal than commercial usefulness.

Few readers will tell researchers that what they really, really want from their newspaper is more coverage of the state legislature, or the city government, or the problem of chronic unemployment. But, if asked, they will tell researchers that they want their lives to get better and their communities to be healthy. It is difficult to understand how more stories about the latest reality TV fantasy can accomplish the latter.

Will Wall Street buy the influence model? Or be swayed by Carter's doggedness and call to higher values? In *Taking Stock*, Cranberg and his coauthors interviewed the leading newspaper stock analysts. Their conclusion:

> The stock analysts we encountered are bright, hardworking, well-informed about the newspaper business, and respected by newspaper company executives. They are also mindful that newspapers aren't an ordinary business, that they have a public service role in their communities. That said, the bottom line is that it's the bottom line that counts. We were told repeatedly by the analysts that they evaluate newspaper companies strictly as businesses, that the companies are judged without reference to the First Amendment, that no slack is cut because newspapers play an informing role in society.

In other words, there is no problem with quality journalism as long as it translates immediately to the bottom line; but if it doesn't, priority certainly goes to the bottom line. This is an understandable view on the part of market analysts because, after all, they exist to advise people how to make the most money possible, not on how to create a better society or solve the problem of world hunger.

The analysts are not the problem. It's their clients: us. Finally, Americans will get the kind of journalism they demand. If they want journalism that produces large and ever-increasing profits, there is a qualitative price to be paid for that. If they want journalism that, over the long haul, serves the public, there is a quantitative price to be paid for that.

How Big Is Big Enough?

Consolidation of news and entertainment outlets into the hands of fewer and fewer mammoth companies is the rolling media story of the last twenty years and a common cause of hand-wringing and calls for reform or limitations. But there is no end in sight to the consolidations. Conventional wisdom holds that this is not a good thing. Certainly when so many elements of the media mix—broadcast, newspapers, book publishing, TV and movie production, and Internet access and site development—are in the hands of only a few fully integrated giants, the potential dangers are not only easily imagined but in fact are manifest in such phenomena as the politicalization of news by Rupert Murdoch's Fox networks.

Yet size can be a defense against economic pressures. A major media company headed by people who recognized the value of newspaper journalism could, if it chose, subsidize that part of its operation to protect it from the negative forces of Wall Street. The major television networks did that for decades, until *60 Minutes* invented a new form of television journalism, the news magazine. That show's huge advertising success demonstrated—unfortunately, as it turned out— that television journalism could make money on its own. It was downhill from there, as the networks and their megacorporation owners tried to turn every news segment into a profit center. Keeping score that way quickly drove news-show content toward the entertainment side of the spectrum.

Subsidizing news operations has not, so far, been the nature of the media giants who, after all, are creatures of the Wall Street syndrome that threatens newspaper journalism. But if a Murdoch can decide to use the news parts of his empire to promote a specific sort of politics, a person in a similar situation could use them for more public-spirited purposes.

Such a helpful decision need not be wholly a product of altruism. If journalism winds up in the hands of only a few major corporations, their economic self-interest might require that they provide quality journalism as a competitive weapon, at least for as long as there is competition among them.

We can all earnestly hope for that, at least.

Nonprofit Alternatives

At the other end of the spectrum from megamedia corporate giants, foundations and other nonprofit entities might have a role to play in pulling journalism back from the edge of the abyss.

Many are playing indirect roles now, notable among them The Pew Charitable Trusts, which has supported public journalism initiatives for a decade; the Knight Foundation, which endows chairs in journalism schools; The Poynter Institute, which trains journalists in all disciplines; the American Press Institute, which for a half-century has educated both domestic and foreign journalists; Harvard University's Neiman Foundation of Journalism and Dayton's Kettering Foundation, which conduct seminars and help find funding for research and writing.

But what if a foundation bought a newspaper and operated it as a public trust? The newspaper would have to make some level of profit, or else it would cannibalize the foundation; but one has to work terribly hard to not make some level of profit with an established newspaper. Profits in the modest range—by today's standards—of 15 percent to 20 percent would at least match the foundations' normal investment income. A foundation acquiring a for-profit newspaper would be in a legal and regulatory thicket, to be sure. But partial models for such an operation already exist.

The best-known is the *St. Petersburg Times*, the majority stock in which is held by The Poynter Institute, a journalism school founded by former *Times* owner Nelson Poynter. (Chapter 3 recounts the story about his men's room conversation with Jack Knight about going public and risking independence.) Poynter established the Modern Media Institute in 1958 as a nonprofit educational institution and, upon his death in 1978, it inherited control of the newspaper. For Poynter, it was all about independence for a local newspaper and its staffers. A newspaper, he said in a 1977 interview, must make a profit and must have no other source of income than from its readers and advertisers if it is to remain independent. Even "a benign foundation" would be a threat, he said. Given that concern and the entanglements of tax laws, he decided that a school with the purpose of improving journalistic practice would be an appropriate owner.

A few other nonprofit situations exist, all delicately maneuvering through the legal thicket in both their structure and operations. *The Christian Science Monitor* is owned and operated by the First Church of Christ, Scientist. *The (Manchester) Union Leader* in New Hampshire is affiliated with the Loeb family's communications school. H. Brandt (Brandy) Ayers, owner of Alabama's *Anniston Star*, is establishing an institute at the University of Alabama to buy or inherit ownership of that well-respected small-town newspaper.

The existing models involve owners giving away their newspapers to a foundation or educational institution, a circumstance that requires not only great generosity but also great tax accountants and lawyers. Even more complex would be the steps required to allow a foundation to directly purchase and operate a for-profit newspaper, but a growing body of academic and professional sentiment suggests that it would be good public policy to allow that to happen. Even with existing legal and regulatory hurdles out of the way, foundation ownership of newspapers raises substantial new questions about independence, for both the newspaper and the foundation. Would it bring both under inappropriate scrutiny by the Internal Revenue Service or other government entities? Could the newspaper operate independently from the owning foundation and its values? Even if it could do so, would public perceptions of influence damage its credibility? And those questions are aside from the primary one: Newspapers cost a great deal of money; even with assured long-term returns, how and at what risk could the capital be found?

The Final Coda

Can newspaper journalism survive the eventual passing of newspapers themselves? Will the substance provided by newspaper journalism, even with all its faults, be present in the new forms of communication just over the horizon?

If newspaper companies continue to sublimate their obligations to public service and democracy to ever-increasing profit considerations, the answer is most certainly "no." And if serious journalism continues to be replaced by news-as-entertainment, the answer is almost certainly "no."

For newspapers driven by the bottom line, people are seen as customers to be wooed rather than citizens to be helped, and the nation is seen as an audience to be accumulated and tallied rather than a democracy to be cherished and sustained.

The great irony is that in America no one, no authority, can dictate what newspapers ought to do. This is a freedom that stems from, and is essential to, democracy. The democracy that sustains journalism is itself sustained by responsible, public-oriented journalism. Newspaper companies that fail to understand that connection and fail to act as if it matters will not only destroy themselves but democracy itself.

Democracy, finally, is us: the people who pay attention to public affairs and those who don't; the people who invest in newspaper companies and those who don't; the people who want news and opinion that confirm their biases and those who want news and opinion that challenge their inclinations.

Citizens will decide, in the long run, what sort of democracy—and what sort of journalism—we have. Maximizing newspaper profits cannot make better democracy. Maximizing citizens can.

Chapter 1

1. Daniel Yankelovich, *Coming to Public Judgment: Making Democracy Work in a Complex World* (Syracuse, NY: Syracuse University Press, 1991), p. 6.
2. Maxwell McCombs and Davis Merritt, *The Two W's of Journalism: The Why and What of Public Affairs Reporting* (Mahwah, NJ: Lawrence Erlbaum Associates, 2004), pp. 41–42.
3. John S. Knight, *1969 Annual Report*, Knight Newspapers, Inc., pp. 4–5.

Chapter 2

1. Charles Whited, *Knight: A Publisher in the Tumultuous Century* (New York: E. P. Dutton, 1988), p. 302.
2. William Swanson, "The Paper Lions," Corporate Reports, *American City Business Journals* (June 1974), p. 20.
3. Swanson, "The Paper Lions," p. 20.
4. Whited, *Knight: A Publisher in the Tumultuous Century*, p. 302.
5. Swanson, p. 21.
6. Whited, p. 304.
7. Daniel H. Neuharth, interview with John S. Knight in October 1978, as printed in "John Shively Knight 1894–1981," *Akron Beacon Journal* (June 1981), p. 9.
8. Ibid, p. 9.
9. Nixon Smiley, *Knights of the Fourth Estate* (Miami: E. A. Seeman Publishing Co., 1974), p. 194.
10. Ibid, p. 193.

Chapter 3

1. Jack Claiborne, *The Charlotte Observer: Its Time and Place* (Chapel Hill, NC: University of North Carolina Press, 1986).
2. Charles Whited, *Knight: A Publisher in the Tumultuous Century* (New York: E. P. Dutton, 1988), pp. 255–256.
3. Geneva Overholser, "State of the American Newspaper," *American Journalism Review* (December 1998), www.ajr.org/Article .ASP?id = 3290.
4. Whited, *Knight: A Publisher in the Tumultuous Century*, p. 282.
5. "Knight-Ridder Will Become Largest All-Newspaper Firm," *Editor & Publisher* (November 16, 1974), p. 12.

Chapter 6

1. Robert D. Putnam, *Bowling Alone* (New York: Simon & Schuster, 2000), pp. 256–257.
2. Joe Cappo, *The Future of Advertising* (New York: McGraw-Hill, 2003), p. 66.
3. Gilbert Cranberg, Randall Bezanson, and John Soloski, *Taking Stock: Journalism and the Publicly Traded Newspaper Company* (Ames, IA: Iowa State University Press, 2001), p. 61.
4. "Two Brothers, Two Worlds," *Columbia Journalism Review*, May-June 2001.
5. Cranberg et al, *Taking Stock*, p. 59.

Chapter 7

1. Daniel Yankelovich, "The New Odds," presentation to Sales Executive Club of New York, October 15, 1971.

Chapter 9

1. William Manchester, *The Death of a President* (New York: Harper & Row, 1967), p. 530.
2. Bill Kovach is quoted in "Catch a Falling Star," at www.haaretz .com (May 13, 2004).

Chapter 11

1. Valarie Basheda, "Bailing Out," *American Journalism Review* (October 2001), www.ajr.org/Article.ASP?id = 88/.
2. Kathryn S. Wenner, "Not So Rosey in Philly," *American Journalism Review* (December 2001), www.ajr.org/Article.ASP?id = 2422.

Chapter 12

1. Jay Rosen and Davis Merritt, *Public Journalism: Theory and Practice* (Dayton OH: The Kettering Foundation, 1994).

Chapter 13

1. Howell Raines, "My Times," *Atlantic Monthly* (May 2004), p. 49.
2. Michael E. Porter, *Competitive Strategy: Creating and Sustaining Superior Performance* (New York: Free Press, 1998), p. 311.
3. Philip Meyer, *The Vanishing Newspaper: Saving Journalism in the Information Age* (Columbia, MO: University of Missouri Press, 2004), pp. 10–20.
4. Gilbert Cranberg, Randall Bezanson, and John Soloski, *Taking Stock: Journalism and the Publicly Traded Newspaper Company* (Ames, IA: Iowa State University Press, 2001), p. 61.
5. Meyer, pp. 8–20.

INDEX

ABOUT THE AUTHOR

Davis (Buzz) Merritt was a reporter, Washington correspondent, and editor for Knight Newspapers and Knight Ridder for forty-two years. For twenty-three of those years, he was editor and senior editor of *The Wichita Eagle*, the largest daily newspaper in Kansas.

Born in Roanoke Rapids, North Carolina, he began his newspaper career in high school as sports editor of the *Hickory (N.C.) Daily Record*. He attended the University of North Carolina as a Morehead Scholar and graduated with a degree in journalism in 1958. Over the next eleven years, he was a sports writer, government reporter, assistant city editor, city editor, copy desk chief, and national editor for *The Charlotte Observer*. In 1969, he became the *Observer*'s Washington correspondent, and in 1970 he was named editor of *The Boca Raton (Fla.) News*, which, like the *Observer*, was owned by Knight Newspapers. In 1972, he returned to the Knight Newspapers Washington bureau as news editor. He became editor of the *Eagle* in 1975.

In 1994, Merritt took a year's leave of absence from the *Eagle* to write a book about public journalism. The book, *Public Journalism and Public Life: Why Telling the News Is Not Enough*, was published in 1995, with a second edition in 1998. The book received a citation for media criticism as part of the 1995 Bart Richards Award from Penn State University. With Maxwell McCombs, he is coauthor of *The Two W's of Journalism: The Why and What of Public Affairs Reporting*, published in 2004.

Merritt retired from Knight Ridder on January 1, 1999 and has been an adjunct professor of journalism at the University of Kansas and Wichita State University, a writer and columnist, and a public journalism consultant since that time.

He and his wife, Libby, have been together since 1953 and live in Wichita. They have two sons and a daughter and six grandchildren.